DATE DUE

DEMCO 38-296

Work and Pay
in the United States and Japan

Work and Pay
in the United States and Japan

CLAIR BROWN

YOSHIFUMI NAKATA

MICHAEL REICH

LLOYD ULMAN

New York   Oxford

OXFORD UNIVERSITY PRESS

1997

Oxford University Press

Oxford   New York
Athens   Auckland   Bangkok   Bogota   Bombay   Buenos Aires
Calcutta   Cape Town   Dar es Salaam   Delhi   Florence   Hong Kong
Istanbul   Karachi   Kuala Lumpur   Madras   Madrid   Melbourne
Mexico City   Nairobi   Paris   Singapore   Taipei   Tokyo   Toronto   Warsaw

and associated companies in
Berlin   Ibadan

Library of Congress Cataloging in Publication Data
Work and pay in the United States and Japan
/ by Clair Brown . . . [et al.].
      p.   cm.
    Includes bibliographical references and index.
    ISBN 0-19-511521-X
    1. Industrial management—Japan.   2. Industrial management—United
States.   3. Labor—Japan.   4. Labor—United States.   5. Industrial
relations—Japan.   6. Industrial relations—United States.
7. Employees—Training of—Japan.   8. Employees—Training of—United
States.   9. Wage payment systems—Japan.   10. Wage payment systems—
United States.   11. Labor productivity—Japan.   12. Labor
productivity—United States.   13. Japan—Economic conditions—1945–
14. United States—Economic conditions—1945–   15. Comparative
management.   I. Brown, Clair, 1946– .
HD70.J3W667   1997
331.2′0952—dc21   96-39268

9 8 7 6 5 4 3 2 1

Printed in the United States of America
on acid-free paper

Preface

The research for this project began in 1989 when Clair Brown, Michael Reich, and David Stern joined forces at the University of California, Berkeley, to study the changes in employment systems that were occurring on the shop floor in large companies in the United States, largely in response to the highly regarded and efficient Japanese production system. After spending three years in field work in American companies, we were approached by Yoshi Nakata and his colleagues at Doshisha University, who had been engaged in studying the employment system in large Japanese companies and asked us to join them in undertaking comparative field work together. This provided the American authors, who did not know Japanese, with the unique opportunity to conduct field work and data collection in Japan. In this way, the research project expanded to become a more interesting comparative analysis.

After our first trip to Japan, we realized that a firm's employment system in either country could not be studied in isolation from national economic institutions since the two are inexorably intertwined. Once again we expanded the scope of the project by persuading our Berkeley colleague Lloyd Ulman to analyze Japanese wage-setting institutions in a comparative context.

We owe a special debt of gratitude to David Stern. His ideas and knowledge of the importance of work-based learning taught us at the start to examine how firm-based training operates in both the United States and Japan. David was an energetic organizer of many of our site visits and an insightful partner in the surveys, the field work, and the development of our conceptual framework. He was coauthor of field notes and several articles, and we have drawn particularly on his contributions in Chapter 3. Although David's departure for a post at Organization for Economic Cooperation and Development and then his appointment as director of the National Center for Research on Vocational Education precluded his participation in the latter stages of the project, we want to acknowledge his important intellectual contribution to the present work.

A research project of this scope requires considerable resources and many collaborators. The Institute of Industrial Relations (IIR) at the University of California, Berkeley, provided both financial and staff resources in addition to the intellectual environment that allowed us to pursue this project. On the Japanese side, the Center for American Studies at Doshisha University played a similar role. We are also grateful for the financial support of the U.S. Department of Labor, the Pacific Rim Foundation of the University of California, the Gakujyutu Syourei Kenkyuu Fund of Doshisha University, the Kansai International Institute of Industrial Relations, the National Center for the Workplace funded by the U.S. Department of Labor, the National Center for Research in Vocational Education funded by the U.S. Department of Education, the Japan Society for the Promotion of Science, the Japan Foundation, the Alfred P. Sloan Foundation, the Japan–United States Friendship Fund, Nihon Keizai Kenkyuu Syourei Zaidan (Japan Economic Research Promotion Foundation), and the Berkeley Programs for Study Abroad. The American project was headed by Clair Brown and the Japanese project was headed by Masao Takenaka.

We are indebted to our Japanese colleagues with whom we conducted field work and who deepened our understanding of Japanese practices. They included Mitsuo Ishida, Kazoo Kagawa, Hiroyuki Fujimura, Koshi Endo, Hirokazu Tanaka, and Megumi Nakamura.

An invaluable part of our research team was a group of highly talented and hardworking students. Theodore Gilman and John Jay Tate performed expert service as translators on two trips. We would like to acknowledge the contributions made by graduate student researchers Chris Ahmadjian, Helen Cagampang, Kaku Furuya, Mark Glickman, Adriana Kugler, Rhiannon Patterson, Krishna Pendakur, Steven Raphael, Judith Ruha, Ken-Ichi Shinoraha, Dennis Toseland, and Vincent Valvano and undergraduate interns Ashok Ramani and Michelle Vesecky.

Our project was fortunate to have an excellent and dedicated support staff. In particular, we are indebted to Diane Leite, who oversees the staff and fiscal operations at IIR; Frozan Wahaj, who oversaw the drafting and preparation of the manuscript; Myra Armstrong, Judy Greenspan, and Amrei Kieschke, who were in charge of making arrangements for our many field work trips in the United States and Japan; Elaine Meckenstock, who administered the grants; Terry Huwe and Janice Kimball, who provided reference and information services; and Glen Ozawa, who provided computer support.

We also have benefited from the insights and comments of Norman Bowers,

Takeshi Chujyo, Robert Cole, Ronald Dore, Robert Flanagan, Knut Gerlach, Tadashi Hanami, Susan Houseman, Kazuo Koike, Kazutoshi Koshiro, David Levine, James Lincoln, Carl Mosk, Hikari Nohara, Paul Ryan, Yasuo Sakakibara, Harley Shaiken, Shoichi Shinohara, David Soskice, Masao Takenaka, Charles Weathers, and the anonymous reviewers.

Our acknowledgments would be incomplete without mentioning the numerous officials at companies, unions, and government agencies and the workers in companies in both countries who generously provided their time to answer our detailed and lengthy questions and who patiently responded to our follow-up visits and questions. Their hospitality in allowing us to observe their production and employment systems, conduct extensive interviews, and distribute questionnaires provided the basis for this research.

The proceeds from this book will be contributed to the Lloyd Ulman Graduate Student Fellowship at IIR. In recognition of the importance of educating the next generation about labor economics and industrial relations, we dedicate this book to our students.

Berkeley, California	C. B.
Kyoto, Japan	Y. N.
January 1997	M. R.
	L. U.

Contents

Work and Pay
in the United States and Japan

1

Comparing Employment Systems

Since the early 1970s, Japan has led the United States and most other industrial countries in economic growth and industrial competitiveness. Not surprisingly, many U.S. observers and competitors came to regard Japanese policies and practices as best practice and worthy of emulation. Indeed, many Japanese management practices have been imported and adopted by U.S. businesses.

In the first half of the 1990s, however, these two economies experienced a reversal in fortunes and performance. As economic prosperity and growth in Japan gave way to lengthy recession and stagnation, some of the country's most distinctive labor policies were criticized and regarded in some circles as structural impediments to recovery. The reversal was so sharp that sentiment in favor of importing certain management practices from the United States gained support in Japan.

Are the management policies that once were credited widely with contributing to Japan's exceptional record of growth and prosperity now inhibiting Japanese economic performance? Can individual policy instruments be detached from their indigenous business and social contexts in one country and imported like the latest gadget by their trading partners? More generally, what lessons might each country reasonably draw from the employment systems and national economic policies of the other?

Recent experience invites a fresh look at the past. This book analyzes how large Japanese and U.S. companies manage their employment systems and how these systems are interrelated with labor market institutions and national economic performance. First, we analyze how the Japanese and U.S. employment systems work within their distinct institutional environments. Many scholars have identified the Japanese practice of employment security for workers and the associated emphasis on the company's human resource system as primary contributors to the high level of Japanese economic performance. At the same time, U.S. practices permitting employer flexibility in hiring and firing labor and employee flexibility in changing jobs have been identified as primary contributors to the high level of U.S. job growth. We discuss these arguments, draw conclusions concerning the different strengths and weaknesses of the two systems, and develop instructive lessons that each country's experience implies for policy changes in the other. In contrast to previous studies, this book emphasizes how the component parts of the employment system in each country are integrated and consistent.

Second, since company practices must be consistent with national economic conditions, we analyze the interactions between Japanese and U.S. employment systems and their respective national economic and industrial relations structures. We show how the relative costs and benefits of alternate employment security and compensation systems vary with the stability and strength of the national economy, and we detail the important role of Japan's national wage-setting system in achieving full employment with low inflation.

Comparing Japan and the United States

At the outset, we note the well-known fact that Japan has realized considerably higher growth than the United States. Between 1979 and 1990, real gross domestic product (GDP) grew at an annual rate of 4.1 percent in Japan but only 2.6 percent in the United States. The relative difference is even higher if we look at GDP growth per worker. In Japan, GDP per employed worker increased 2.9 percent annually from 1979 to 1990; the annual increase for the same period was 1 percent in the United States (OECD, 1992a). Since 1970, growth in output per hour in manufacturing has been similar in the United States and Germany while it has grown more rapidly in Japan, especially since the late 1970s (Figure 1.1). Even during Japan's 1990s recession, productivity growth continued in manufacturing.

The relatively impressive performance of Japan is the product of many factors. First, rapid growth was due to the final phase of a "catch-up" process that began shortly after the end of World War II. Through actively importing Western technologies, Japan transformed itself into a mature, high-technology economy. This transformation has been presided over by an interventionist regime that has succeeded in mobilizing and directing capital resources, as reflected in the relatively high rates of savings and investment in Japan. Over the period 1960–1993, Japanese savings as a percentage of GDP averaged 33.9 percent annually; the comparable figure was 18.7 percent in the United States. Over the same period, gross fixed capital formation as a percentage of GDP averaged 31.3 percent annually in Japan

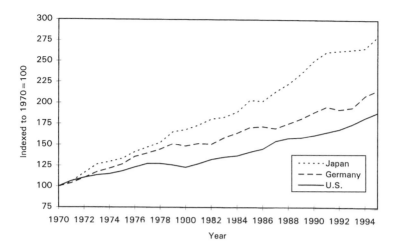

FIGURE 1.1. Output per Hour in Manufacturing, 1970–1995

Source: U.S. Department of Labor (1996). The years 1970–1976 are estimated for the United States.

and 18.4 percent in the United States. These high rates of savings and investment contributed to increased output per worker by increasing the ratio of capital to labor.

The distinctive human resource systems of Japanese firms also provided an important source of increased efficiency and growth. Japanese firms tailored Western production processes to be consistent with labor market institutions, such as lifetime employment security and steep seniority wage structures, that were exogenously imposed by labor demands during the 1950s. The introduction of lifetime employment and seniority wages for union workers led to the development of career ladders and of skill accumulation, achieved primarily through structured on-the-job training. The process of adapting imported technology to the idiosyncrasies of the Japanese labor market produced innovations in the production process and human resource systems such as continual training, the flexible assignment of labor, work teams, and just-in-time inventory systems.

A third source of growth consists in Japan's distinctive national wage-setting institutions. Company practices that provide employees with employment security and wages that increase with age both require and reinforce full employment and growth. We detail how the national wage-setting system of Shunto plays an important role in achieving full employment with low inflation and high growth. Moreover, Japanese wage-determining institutions and practices, at both the company and national levels, have contributed to the high savings rates by restraining wage growth relative to productivity growth.

In this book, we seek to explain the linkages between these differences in performance and the differences in firms' employment practices. Our research reveals three remarkable and apparently paradoxical contrasts between Japan and the United States:

1. In Japanese firms, high degrees of employment security have been conducive to high levels of employee efficiency and growth in production rather than having served as a disincentive to effort and efficiency.
2. In Japan, high rates of economic growth went hand in hand with high levels of income equality—a double contrast with U.S. performance.
3. During the 1970s and 1980s, Japan enjoyed higher levels of employment and lower rates of inflation than the United States or any other major industrialized economy.

In achieving these superior economic outcomes, Japan has incurred some significant social costs. While overall unemployment rates in Japan have been outstandingly low, heavy costs have been borne by women and young graduates, whose cyclical patterns of employment have buffered the fixed costs imposed by the employment security extended to "regular" male employees. Costs have also been borne by regular male employees in several ways: less freedom of career choice within a firm or across firms, longer working hours, and lower ages of compulsory retirement than are available to their less secure but more mobile and autonomous American counterparts.

We also find that the efficiency and viability of the Japanese management practices and wage-setting institutions that contribute to the economy's record of growth, employment, and stability themselves are functions of the variables they help to determine. For example, at higher levels of growth and demand, costs incurred by Japanese employers under no-layoff guarantees are lower than during periods of sluggish growth. Success at the macro and micro levels reinforce each other and provide buffers against small disturbances of the system. As slow growth becomes prolonged, however, unions become impatient with slow real wage growth, which could potentially impair the ability of Japanese institutions to restrain labor costs. And, as companies are saddled with aging work forces and payroll costs increase accordingly, management becomes more dissatisfied with seniority as a determinant of wages, while workers grow impatient with declining opportunities for promotion. Large disturbances could thereby turn a virtuous circle into a vicious one.

Nonetheless, the security and pay practices of Japanese firms have survived slower growth in the 1980s and stagnation in the 1990s. In contrast, the U.S. system of externally provided income security and labor market mobility has become substantially weaker. While real wage growth slowed in Japan in response to an economic slowdown, real wages stagnated and wage dispersion increased in the United States, even after economic and productivity growth improved in the 1990s. The stagnation of real wages and rise in inequality in the United States have been interpreted as symptomatic of a deficit in skill levels and in training of the work force, areas in which the Japanese economy has excelled. Later, we shall discuss how U.S. firms have accommodated elements of Japanese employment practices to the preferences of U.S. management and workers for greater freedom of choice and mobility. First, we discuss our data sources and then provide a framework for analyzing employment systems.

The Data

Our data comprise two types. Firm-based data were collected through field work at major companies in the United States and Japan; national-level data are based upon a variety of micro and aggregate data sets and surveys from the two countries. We cite sources for the national data as they are used. Here we describe briefly the firm-based data collection.

Field work to collect data for this book took place from 1987 through 1995. We chose a sample of establishments in three major industries—automobile, electronics (including consumer electronics as well as semiconductors), and telecommunications—that included Japanese-owned businesses operating in the United States as well as Japanese- and American-owned businesses operating in Japan as well as the United States. This sampling strategy was designed to detect the separate influences of country of ownership and country of operation.

To the extent possible, Japanese and U.S. firms were paired within three important industries. The automobile industry was of interest because Japan overtook the United States in this industry during the 1970s and the U.S. companies had become more competitive by the late 1980s. Since the automobile industry had already been extensively studied by others (e.g., Womack et al., 1991), much comparative information on productivity and costs was already available, and our findings from the other two industries could be benchmarked to the automobile industry. The electronics industry was of interest because Japan and the United States had competitive edges in different sectors and because the industry is both changing and growing rapidly. In addition, the automobile and electronics industries represent Japan's two most important export industries. The telecommunications industry was of interest because it is considered a leading sector for economic development and a rapidly growing industry that was present in all industrial countries.

Six representative companies are discussed specifically (using pseudonyms) in this study: one U.S. automobile company (Together Manufacturing) and one Japanese (Agile Auto); one telecommunications company in the United States (CommEx) and one in Japan (CommSun); and one U.S. electronics company (Hi-Tech) and one Japanese (Star Electronics). We did case studies at over two dozen other business units of companies in Japan and the United States over seven years. In the electronics industry, we visited and collected data from a dozen other plants in four other companies producing consumer electronics and semiconductors. In autos, we studied a half-dozen other plants in three other companies. We also visited and collected data from companies in other industries, including insurance, health care, and education. The companies span a large range of sizes, age, union environments, and geographic settings. When applicable, we refer to the data that we collected at these other firms.

The level of data collection varied by site. Many companies were visited several times. At each company, we interviewed corporate managers, plant managers, supervisors, workers, and union representatives (if unionized). We always toured the facility and observed work, team meetings, on-the-job training, and classes or formal training. At each company, we collected data from several plants or sites. At seven sites, we distributed written questionnaires to a sample of employees in key work groups. In Japan, we conducted interviews through an interpreter or in English and the questionnaires were translated into Japanese.

We also consulted with leading Japanese academic experts and government officials and have drawn from each country's published data sources. We also conducted interviews with leading representatives of Japanese union federations and management industry associations.

Conceptualizing Employment Systems

A firm's human resource (HR) system fulfills the firm's labor requirements by recruiting and hiring workers, allocating or assigning jobs, and motivating workers. Motivation is a complex process that includes evaluating, rewarding, and penalizing workers within a system that is accepted as fair by the workers themselves and in such a manner that employees and employers share common goals. Since production takes place in a dynamic setting, workers must be trained, rewarded, and disciplined in a context of fluctuating market demand and continually changing information, which requires well-developed communication systems. Consequently, the HR system must accomplish four main goals—motivation, skill development, communication, and goal congruence.

The components of an HR system must be internally consistent and mutually reinforcing to prevent them from working at cross-purposes and producing unintended or undesired results. For this reason, individual parts of an HR system usually cannot be established or modified successfully in isolation from the others. Instead, the system must be modified as a whole to ensure that the parts remain consistent and reinforcing.

A worker's long-run earnings profile in a firm will depend on access to career ladders and training. Career ladders are defined within an HR system by the development of an employee's skill, knowledge, and responsibility and by the earnings that accompany this development over the employee's tenure. To the extent that skills, knowledge, and responsibility are transferable to jobs outside the firm, career ladders include opportunities both within and outside a particular firm. Although mobile career paths are observed most often in professional and craft occupations, they can be extended under the right circumstances to other occupations as well.

Since each job requires some initial on-the-job training and skills are developed and deepened through work experience, training and job assignment are interrelated. Even if management does not plan or structure career paths, work assignments translate into an earnings profile and a job path for the individual over time. A job path becomes a career path when it includes increasing skills, responsibility, and pay.

In the United States, employees usually have some influence over their job assignments. Rules that constrain managers' decisions concerning assignment, promotion, and upgrade often include a post-and-bid procedure and a role for seniority in ranking equally qualified candidates.

The compensation structure provides the primary means, other than the threat of job loss, for motivating workers. Consequently, the compensation structure includes short-run elements (i.e., current pay) and long-run elements (i.e., future opportunities). These elements can include:

- Job-based pay: the returns to effort and formal and on-the-job training that are tied to a job classification
- Skill-based pay: the returns to the acquisition and certification of specific skills, whether or not the skills are used
- Seniority-based or age-based pay: the returns to seniority, which reflects an automatic progression up a pay schedule
- Performance pay: the reward (or penalty) for individual performance, which includes effort as well as making suggestions, voicing complaints, or having a helpful attitude; performance may also be rewarded through job assignment or promotion
- Incentive pay (including piece rates): the reward for individual output
- Profit or gain sharing: group-based pay that relies on some measure of firm performance

Two Prototype HR Systems

To analyze how an HR system accomplishes a firm's goals and how the component parts operate within an HR system, we set up two prototypical systems: one represents a system based upon high-performance (or high-commitment) management practices; the other is based upon job specialization and economies of scale.

Our field work identified three key elements in addition to compensation in the high-performance work organization that we call SET (for security, employee involvement, and training): (1) a high degree of employment security based upon flexible job assignment and continuous skill development; (2) employee involvement in problem solving, continuous improvement, and knowledge sharing; and (3) continuous training or retraining of all employees. These three elements of SET are central to what has been described as the prevailing system in large Japanese firms (Aoki, 1988; Koike, 1988; Cole, 1989, 1995). Goal congruence is achieved by security, employee involvement, and compensation; skill accumulation and deepening are achieved through training; communication is achieved through employee involvement and training; and motivation is achieved through all three components plus compensation. The compensation system may include motivational rewards for company performance (profit sharing), team performance, or skill acquisition (pay-for-skill). In unionized settings, the union and company enjoy a cooperative relationship, and grievances are often settled informally at the first level. In the United States, until the 1990s, the SET system could be found only in a small subset of large companies or only among salaried employees in some large and mid-sized companies (Foulkes, 1989), although it is now said to be spreading to more firms and to more hourly employees (Lawler et al, 1992; Osterman, 1994).

The SET system contrasts with the employment system that has prevailed since the 1940s for American unionized workers (but not for their nonunion professional and managerial colleagues). In this system, which we call JAM (for job classification, adversarial relations, and minimal training), security is determined by seniority, employee involvement is impeded by a traditionally adversarial relationship between the union and management and by narrowly defined job classifications, and firms make only minimal investment in training hourly workers for tasks that are highly specialized and circumscribed. The union's short-run power is largely situated in its ability to enforce job classification rules. In a traditional nonunion setting for nonexempt workers,[1] the power of the supervisor over workers is not constrained by the union, and so the adversarial relations are individualized and a worker's main recourse is quitting rather than grieving. Goal congruence and motivation are achieved through close supervision; communication comes from the top down through the supervisor; and skills can be quickly learned.

SET systems have two major variants for nonexempt employees, depending upon the type of compensation system used: an individual-based pay system, where *career ladders* are founded upon skills and performance; or a job-based pay system with *post-and-bid* job allocation (Table 1.1). Japanese SET systems take the career-ladder form for all regular employees, while American companies typically adopt a post-and-bid SET system for their production (nonexempt) employees and a modified career-ladder version for their professional and managerial (exempt) employees.

The Japanese system is characterized by management control over individual career paths: job assignment determines skill development and skill use in the short run and determines career ladders and pay in the long run. Pay has components

TABLE 1.1. Characteristics of the Employment Systems

Dimensions of the Employment Systems	JAM	SET—Career Ladders	SET—Post and Bid
Security/job assignment	Job security determined by seniority, rigid job classifications, and employee control over job assignments.	Employees grant managers discretion in job assignments and skill development in exchange for employment security.	Employee input into job assignment through the post-and-bid system. Security through seniority.
Compensation	Pay determined by job classification. Wage differential mainly between new hires and regular workers.	Pay rewards experience, job skills, and performance. Increasing pay with seniority reflects skill deepening with increasing tenure.	Experiments with forms of skill-based and performance-based pay. Some pay increase with seniority, but does not usually reflect skill deepening and acquisition.
Training/skill development	No overall connection between job paths and skill development. Long career ladders with continual skill acquisition and deepening for managerial workers only.	Well-developed job paths that engender skill acquisition and deepening for both production and managerial workers. Continual training for all workers.	The post-and-bid system results in inefficient job changes and career paths. Job changes within the firm are often accompanied by lost firm-specific human capital.
Employee involvement	Employees perform well-defined, narrow jobs and have little involvement in making improvements or solving problems.	Continual employee involvement in improving product quality and the production process.	Continual employee involvement in improving product quality and the production process.
Voice	Employee voice exercised through union and grievance procedures.	Voice at the individual level is virtually absent.	Employee voice through request for assignments and grievance procedures.

rewarding experience (age), job skills (job grade), and performance. Most large Japanese companies have only one comprehensive (and complex) pay-grade schedule covering all employees, from new entrants through executives. The job grade reflects the worker's experience and skills and indicates the types of job tasks and responsibilities the worker is eligible to do, but the job grade does not reflect the actual job the worker does. Each employee will also have an occupational title, but the fit between the occupational title and the job grade is not exact.

Seniority works differently in the Japanese and U.S. SET systems. Although seniority is not explicitly rewarded in Japan, age pay reflects seniority since workers are seldom laid off and tenure is long. Job-grade pay also reflects seniority as the vast majority of unionized workers move through the job-grade chart at nearly the same predetermined rate. Only performance pay, which usually increases the pay or promotion rate for the top performers, does not reflect seniority. Rewards for performance of Japanese union workers remain limited, but pay and promotion based on performance become more important after an employee leaves a union and enters management ranks. Private-sector professional employees in the United States seldom belong to a union, and the SET system covering professional and managerial employees in U.S. companies is based on individual performance even more than the Japanese SET system is.

While seniority increases pay in Japan, it does not increase voice as it does in the United States, where seniority is used in job assignment and vacation scheduling. Voice at the individual level is almost absent in the Japanese system: workers have the potential to file grievances through their unions, but grievances are rare—perhaps zero to three per year per company. Those who grieve are seen as troublemakers by both the union and the management.

In Japan, production work is not divided into craft and assembly or operator jobs, so long career ladders can be formed for male production workers as well as for male managerial and professional workers. From entry until retirement, male production workers continually deepen their skills in a systematic and planned progression. As a result, experience translates into increased ability to perform certain skills, which over time include basic operations, problem solving, cost reduction, quality improvement, and maintenance.

In traditional U.S. employment systems, production workers have well-defined, specialized tasks and move up a ladder of job titles differentiated by small increments in pay and more desirable characteristics. The traditional system in the United States emphasizes production employees' preferences in job assignment. Seniority is used as the basis for fairly assigning the detailed jobs among those workers who apply for a job or shift opening, with skill the deciding factor only if there is a noticeable difference in relevant skills. Although seniority is likely to play a more prominent role in unionized firms than in nonunionized firms, this post-and-bid system with the use of seniority is widespread throughout both types of firms for nonmanagerial workers in the United States. The result is a hodgepodge of possible job paths, which reflect workers' individual preferences concerning improved working conditions (e.g., work that requires less physical effort, is off the production line, or involves no exposure to toxic materials), overtime availability, or supervisors or teammates.

Although each job will require some on-the-job training, there is no overall connection between job paths and skill development, and pay differences between job classifications are usually small or nonexistent. Some traditional systems include incentive pay based upon individual output. Pay goes with the job classification, and perhaps with individual output, but the variations within one occupational group are quite small. Long career ladders that provide skill acquisition and skill deepening with pay increases generally do not exist for production workers. The major wage increment occurs between new hires and regular workers, with the catch-up period typically one to three years. Workers have a great deal of voice in this system, and their voice increases with seniority. When a union is present, worker voice through the grievance system ensures fair application of the rules.

The SET system adopted by U.S. companies is a combination of the Japanese SET system, with its emphasis on employee involvement and training, and the traditional U.S. system, with its reliance on job-based pay and on seniority for worker voice and security. Workers still have input into job assignment through post-and-bid systems and through the use of seniority, although managers usually have more input into the job assignment process than in the traditional system.

When companies make a transition to a SET system, the number of job classifications usually is reduced dramatically to provide managers with greater flexibility in deploying workers. When present, individual incentive pay is dropped to facilitate team activities and employee cooperation. As a result, production workers' potential for improving earnings and ascending career ladders is actually reduced in many companies. Although many U.S. SET companies are experimenting with forms of skill-based or performance-based pay, these innovative pay systems usually contain only a few steps. Skill-based pay systems in the United States are not similar to the age-grade-performance pay systems in Japan. Unlike the Japanese pay system, they do not form long career ladders for production workers and so do not encourage and reward continuous skill acquisition and skill deepening. Skill broadening, but not skill deepening, seems to be the result in U.S. SET companies.

Some researchers suggest that American firms, both with and without unions, should move toward SET on the grounds that SET will make U.S. producers more competitive in world markets (Walton, 1987; Dertouzos et al., 1989; Womack et al., 1991; Kochan and Useem, 1992), maintain high wages and living standards (Cohen and Zysman, 1987; Commission on the Skills of the American Workforce, 1990), and provide more satisfying working conditions as well as a more equitable distribution of employment and income (Osterman, 1988). Some studies explore the role the union plays in the transformation of SET practices (Kelley, 1989; Mishel and Voos, 1992; Cooke, 1994). Other researchers have been more critical of

SET (Cooke, 1990; Tabb, 1995). Criticisms include the argument that flexibility called for in SET is not required by new technologies (Pollert, 1991); that increased flexibility can erode union power (Fucini and Fucini, 1990; Eaton and Voos, 1992); and that SET systems increase employee stress and effort (Parker and Slaughter, 1988). Yet recent surveys of the literature by Bailey (1992) and Appelbaum and Batt (1994) conclude that the empirical studies of SET systems show positive results overall.

Much of the existing literature, whether positive or critical of SET, examines the effectiveness of individual reforms in workplace systems without sufficient consideration of the interrelationship among the elements of an employment system or of the role of the external environment. Here we turn to a theoretical discussion of the interdependence of the component parts of an employment system and the relation between the employment system and the external environment.

Interdependence of HR Components

In a capital stock and wage structure, the productivity of individual workers and their flexibility in deployment determine total output and unit labor cost. An effective employment system must provide an efficient use of labor, and it must be viewed as fair by the workers. Both goals can be achieved in a SET system or in a JAM (traditional) system.

Companies with a JAM system may achieve flexibility by adjusting the size of the work force according to production needs and by breaking jobs into minute tasks that can be quickly learned. Efficiency is accomplished through workers' proficiency, which results from specialization in job tasks and from automation. Quality is sought through reduction of defects that accompany changes in job tasks and by computer monitoring of work in process. Fairness is rooted in the seniority system and the detailed job classifications, which constrain supervisors' arbitrary decisions regarding job assignment and promotions and the application of work standards.

Companies with a SET system achieve efficiency by combining employment security with broadly defined jobs, flexible job assignments, transfers within a plant and across plants, and a buffer stock of unprotected labor. Productivity is enhanced by employee involvement in ongoing problem solving and in suggesting and implementing improvements. Quality is achieved by training workers to perform each job well, by cross-training workers, by training them to do inspection and maintenance tasks with each job task, and by retraining workers when they are transferred as a result of changes in demand or technology. Fairness is rooted in job security, the implementation of employee suggestions, and the continual development of workers as they move up career ladders, as well as the more traditional means of equitable job assignment and application of rules.

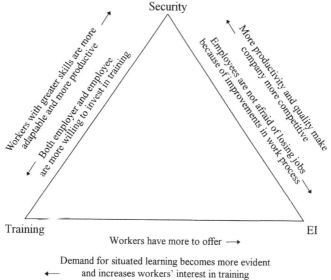

FIGURE 1.2. SET Theory

   The interdependence among the three elements of SET is illustrated in Figure 1.2, which shows how each part reinforces the others. Employment security enhances employee involvement because employees are more willing to contribute to improvements in the work process when they do not fear that they or their co-workers will lose their jobs. Employment security contributes to training as both employer and employee have greater incentives to invest in training when they expect their relationship will endure. At the same time, training reinforces employment security because workers with greater skills will be more productive and adaptable to new conditions, and training strengthens employee involvement because better-trained workers have more ideas to offer. Employee involvement contributes to increased training by making the need for situated learning more evident and by increasing employees' interest in training. Finally, employee involvement also enhances employment security as higher productivity and quality make the company more competitive.
   Both systems depend upon a group of unprotected workers who serve as a buffer to absorb changes in demand or technology and who help lower labor costs. Under SET, unprotected workers are usually separate from the protected SET workers who have job security and an expectation of retraining. Unprotected workers include the employees of suppliers as well as those hired "temporarily" or part-time within the plant to perform tasks similar to those done by protected workers. In a JAM system, the buffer stock includes "outsiders" (i.e., the subcontracted work force) and "insiders" (i.e., the junior regular workers with less seniority). The in-

ternal division between protected and unprotected workers is not clear since it depends on the relative concept of seniority rather than on the absolute concept of occupation. Since traditional companies can lay off workers according to production needs, the use of nonunion temporary or subcontracted workers is more important for reducing wage costs than for providing flexibility.

Under a traditional system, the union has short-run power over its job control on the shop floor. In a well-functioning system, where union and management have a good relationship, workers engage informally in solving problems and making improvements. Foremen also have the cooperation of the union in using workers in a flexible manner as needed. If workers are dissatisfied, however, they can work in a routine manner and resist reassignment; they will not solve problems or make improvements. In this case, the production process does not work smoothly, many defects occur, and the line is down frequently. In the short run, the company is at the mercy of the goodwill of the union and workers. But the company has long-run power since it has total control over plant location and product placement. With a good relationship between union and management, the union may influence decisions about plant location and capital investment; but, in the long run, the union and workers are at the mercy of the goodwill of the company.

Under SET, the union and workers are exchanging some of their short-run power on the shop floor for increased power in the long run, mainly through improved security. The company is increasing its short-run power by having more flexible use of workers and by having employees involved in solving problems and making improvements. In exchange, the company makes training and employment commitments to the workers. This usually entails not moving jobs elsewhere as soon as the company otherwise would.

In the contemporary economic context of rapid changes in production technology, the information sharing of SET is thought to produce greater advantages than the specialization of JAM. Aoki (1990) offers a theoretical formulation in which a JAM system is efficient under production conditions using prior planning and economies of specialization and in which a SET system is efficient under production conditions requiring horizontal coordination among operating units that share information and learned results. The comparative advantages of the two systems depend on the ability of employees to learn, the development of communication systems among units, and the degree of economies of specialization. The two extremes of a stable planning environment or a highly volatile or uncertain planning environment, coupled with economies of specialization, support a JAM system; an intermediate external environment that is continually changing but not too volatile, coupled with returns to learning that outweigh returns to specialization, support a SET system. Our research results are consistent with Aoki's formulation. However, the returns to learning and to specialization depend upon the effectiveness of the HR system in which they are embedded. In addition, the trade-off between returns to learning and returns to specialization depends upon the product market and the technology, as well as economic institutions.

For these reasons, there is no single "best practice" for HR management; rather, alternative HR systems may reach similar performance goals. A high-performance HR system, however, must have integrated, consistent components, and the overall HR system must be consistent with the external economic environment and labor market institutions.

The Interrelationship between Employment Systems and the Macroeconomy

The relative costs and benefits of the prototypical systems described above depend critically on several aspects of the economic environment. For instance, lifetime security pledges within an erratic and volatile macroeconomic environment will entail large costs in the form of retaining redundant labor during recessions and losing trained workers during periods of labor shortage. Moreover, if publicly provided income insurance drives a significant wedge between material well-being and labor market participation, the value of employment security to the worker will be minimal and employees will be unwilling to make the concessions necessary under the SET system. Under such conditions, the SET system becomes unrealistic as the erratic product demand requires greater flexibility in adjusting total labor costs.

In the contrasting situation of a relatively stable macroeconomic environment, the value of being able to adjust labor costs through layoffs is minimal and is outweighed by the dynamic efficiency gained under the SET system. Since security pledges are more credible with macroeconomic stability, workers are free to participate in improving the efficiency of the production process without the fear of losing their jobs. Moreover, employers are more willing to invest in the training of their work force as minimal variation in product demand minimizes the loss of training resources both through permanent layoffs during recessions and through excessive interfirm labor mobility during periods of labor shortage.

The Japanese SET system, with its fixed labor costs and high break-even capacity points, thrives when product demand is maintained at a high and growing level. This minimizes the costs of retaining redundant labor since lifetime security systems often entail no-layoff pledges. At the same time, hiring and wage-setting practices constrain inflationary wage pressures, even with labor shortages. Quitting is limited because of seniority wages and promotion from within. Meanwhile, the labor market power of large firms in the national wage-setting process has prevented the upward spiraling of wages under conditions of high-level employment. Finally, enterprise-based unions have been content to allow gains in compensation to accrue to their members primarily through the operation of internal systems of promotion and seniority pay in the interest of long-run firm growth and employment security.

In contrast, the JAM system still prevalent in the United States can be regarded as a response to a more fragile economic and institutional environment. Chronic unemployment and publicly provided income security have reduced the feasibility of employment security within the firm, while a historically mobile work force has dampened the prospects for extensive employer-financed training. Adversarial industrywide unions have participated in the determination of "conditions of work" within the firms, including job classifications and production standards, and these have constrained management's use of labor. These relationships between the economic environment, labor market institutions, and HR systems will be discussed in detail in several of the following chapters.

Layout of the Book

The case studies analyzed here include only large companies in the United States and Japan. These companies appear to be representative of management practices at large companies in these two countries. The practices observed at the Japanese plants are fairly uniform within a company. However, within U.S. companies, practices and performance are not uniform across plants. We witnessed wide variation in how corporate policy is carried out at each plant, and so the U.S. electronics and automobile companies could be classified as SET or JAM according to the plant selected. In the data presented here, the high-performance or SET plants are used, with occasional reference to practices at traditional plants. For this reason, the six prototype cases used here represent various types of SET plants. Contrasting examples are given from other plants within the industry (and perhaps the same company). In addition, we compare the case study outcomes to national data whenever possible.

In Chapters 2 and 3, examination of the most distinctive components of the SET system—that is, employment security, extensive employee involvement in operations, and continuous training—shows how the effectiveness of each depends on the presence of the others. Chapter 2 evaluates the role of security in the employment systems of Japan and the United States. The chapter argues that lifetime employment requires mutual risk sharing on the part of employers and employees: employees do not leave their jobs during periods of high employment and firms do not lay off workers during downturns. Such a system moderates short-run wage demands and requires both full employment and high growth since workers are rewarded by promotion according to their tenure within the firm. This chapter also considers the relationships among employment security, specific labor market institutions, and the publicly provided income insurance systems in the United States and Japan. The security systems offered by Japanese and U.S. employers are shown to be consistent with their respective institutional environments.

Chapter 3 provides an analysis of the prevalence and importance of employee-involvement and training programs and an assessment of how these two programs function in Japanese and U.S. work places. Employee involvement and training differ significantly in SET and traditional firms since SET firms not only do more training but also do it differently. In contrast to traditional firms, in which minimal training is required for minutely divided job tasks that are quickly learned, SET firms find ways to build continual learning into the work process itself. Furthermore, we argue that the career-ladder SET system does a much more effective job of training and involving workers than does the post-and-bid SET system since a worker's job tasks and skill development build on what the worker already knows. This formation of career ladders ensures that a worker's skills deepen over time.

Just as it is unsatisfactory to attempt an analysis of security, employee involvement, and training in isolation from one another, so is it unsatisfactory to examine any or all of them without taking wage determination into account. By the same token, analysis of wage behavior that fails to take explicit account of nonwage factors could exaggerate the role played by wages in, for example, forming economic incentives. Chapters 4–6 address wage determination, examining in particular how wages are affected by national institutions governing industrial relations, labor mobility, and economic performance.

Chapter 4 focuses on wage structures and the distribution of earned income. Pay systems in Japan are generally organized to reflect experience and the associated development of deeper and broader skills. Age thus accounts for a much greater share of wage variation than is the case in the United States. Distinctions between university and high school graduates segment workers in Japan but not to the extent found in the United States. Gender barriers are greater, however, in Japan. Taking all sources of variation into account, Japan has both more wage growth and less inequality in earnings than the United States.

Chapter 5 considers how the Japanese system of management–union relations has contributed to economic growth by fostering productivity growth in excess of real wage growth. The bargaining power of large firms in the private sector has contributed to these outcomes, as have the cooperative and security-conscious enterprise-based unions.

Chapter 6 analyzes how Shunto—the annual spring labor offensive—became transformed from a wage-boosting mechanism in the high-growth period of the 1960s and early 1970s into an engine of restraint since the mid-1970s. In response to the demise of industrywide bargaining during the 1940s and to the weakness of enterprise-based unions, militant union leaders introduced a system of coordinated bargaining across firms and industries on an economywide basis. Shunto was intended to redress the power imbalance and advance real wages to Western levels as rapidly as possible. The transformation of the system occurred after a violent wage explosion in the wake of the 1973 oil crisis threatened the economy with inflation, unemployment, and a loss of international competitiveness. With the power of the leading large firms supported by accommodating authorities, Shunto was used to restrain wage movements below productivity growth, assuring the international competitiveness of the export sector.

Finally, in Chapter 7 we offer our conclusions about how firms' practices and national institutions contribute to different outcomes in growth, security, and equality in Japan and the United States. We discuss the lessons that the firms of each country can learn from the employment practices of the other and the extent to which these lessons are constrained by union and government practices. We end with a discussion of how we expect the Japanese and U.S. employment and wage systems to continue to evolve.

NOTE

1. Nonexempt workers include workers who are covered by the national Fair Labor Standards Act and are eligible for overtime pay. Exempt workers are those who are not covered by the act. In general, professional and managerial workers are not covered since they have supervisory tasks.

2

Security

The provision of security is an intricate concept since economic reliability or protection takes on many dimensions over a person's lifetime. Certainly it involves the assurance of income, both within the labor market and through social programs. This chapter focuses on the role of security within a firm's employment system while also referring to the interaction between employer-provided security and public income-support programs. Since the type and degree of security provided affect the functioning of the labor market, the economy, and society, security has economic importance even above satisfying the human need for stability.

In the United States and Japan, security is provided in part through a company's HR system. Security provisions affect the company's hiring and training decisions and the workers' efforts, as well as the company's costs and workers' income. In this chapter, we first analyze the benefits and costs associated with two types of security—employment security and income security—and then examine how a firm's optimal security structure is shaped by macroeconomic and institutional constraints. Next, we discuss how security works in Japanese and U.S. companies and analyze the interaction of security with the other components of the employment system. In particular, we look at how the employment system as a whole motivates workers and provides flexibility in total labor costs over the business cycle for the firm. Finally, we discuss how the Japanese security system performed during the recession in the early 1990s.

Analyzing Security

Costs and Benefits to Firms and Workers

A firm can provide varying degrees of two types of security: income and employment security. At one extreme, employment security assures workers of a lifetime job with the same company. This usually takes the form of a pledge on the part of the company of no layoffs except under conditions of extreme financial distress. At the other extreme, income security guarantees workers a minimum weekly income through a combination of earnings and unemployment insurance (UI) benefits. Between these two extremes, varying degrees of income and employment security are provided by combining firms' employment systems and the government's social welfare programs.

Security provides benefits to both the firm and the worker while also extracting a cost. The benefits of income security for the firm consist of flexible labor adjustment and the elimination of excess labor; the cost depends on how many days workers must be paid for time not worked. The benefits of employment security are lower turnover, flexible assignment of labor, and the elimination of payments for unemployed time, while the cost depends on the firm's rate of capacity utilization in the short run and on its ability to train and utilize the worker in the long run. For both types of security, the cost is affected by the workers' efforts and willingness to do a good job. In general, the firm faces a trade-off between flexibility in using workers on the job and flexibility in adjusting total employment; the net cost of the trade-off depends on dynamic macroeconomic conditions. Employment security has a higher net benefit than does income security to the firm in tight labor markets and to the worker in slack labor markets. Income security has a higher net benefit than employment security to the firm with slack or highly variable product demand and a higher net benefit to the worker in tight or highly variable labor markets.

The optimal security system for the firm depends also upon the economy's demographics. When birthrates are high and the work force is young, firms benefit from providing employment security since they need to retain their experienced workers, who are in relatively short supply. When the work force is aging, however, the security system coupled with seniority results in an excess of higher-priced senior employees and a reduced chance of promotion. These senior employees may become idle when new technologies are introduced since the returns to training are higher for younger workers.

The value of a firm's security policy to a worker depends on several factors. Available job opportunities, which reflect the state of the economy, workers' skills, and the norms governing job change all determine the value workers place on the freedom of mobility between employers. In addition, other aspects of a given worker's situation, such as the worker's desire for locational flexibility, the availability of other family income or savings when the worker is unemployed, and the percentage of the worker's earnings that go toward nondiscretionary expenditures,[1] will determine the relative benefits of employment versus income security.

For the worker, both income and employment security provide peace of mind. Income security is preferred if the work is not rewarding since it usually provides paid time off while the worker is temporarily unemployed. However, employment security is usually provided over a longer period than income security, and so it provides less risk while fully engaging a person's paid time. In return for employment security, the worker is expected to be committed to the firm and to accept reassignment (including relocation) and retraining. In addition, workers must also give up flexibility and freedom associated with absenteeism and quitting since part of the quid pro quo is full utilization and commitment of the work force. If the company minimizes its protected work force, excess regular workers are not available to fill in for absent workers and some overtime will be the norm. With income security, the worker must accept periods of unemployment and usually must search for another job and change employers several times during a work life. However, income security is consistent with a worker's right to quit without penalty or constraint, just as the employer retains the right to decide how many employees to keep on the payroll.

Outside the firm, a worker's transferable skills, which include skills that can be used in other organizations, determine employment and earnings opportunities.[2] Transferable skills include behavior (e.g., communication skills, discipline), job tasks (e.g., craft or certified skills), and knowledge (e.g., problem-solving skills). Transferable skills provide the most reliable form of security in a fully employed market for those skills since workers have the power to demand a wage at least equal to their contribution and do not have to rely upon promises made by any one employer.

In general, employers and employees both want flexibility—the employer to adjust payroll to product demand and the employee to be mobile in order to take advantage of better opportunities. When a firm offers security, it expects in return assurances that labor can be used in a flexible and efficient manner and that workers will be motivated without the threat of layoffs. However, a firm does not want to bear all the risk of the business cycle. In return for granting security to workers during a downturn, the firm must be compensated by some combination of fewer quits during an upturn and the ability to reduce payroll costs during a downturn through flexible compensation and adjustment of hours.

Both parties can benefit by giving up some flexibility and sharing the implicit costs or risks over the business cycle. As a consequence, employees receive improved security during recessions and firms have reduced quits and reduced wage pressure when the economy is robust. The employer also wants effort and commitment from the employees, who in turn want career development and earnings growth. These latter goals, which are related to employee involvement, training, and compensation, will be analyzed in detail in the following chapters. Here, we will analyze the provision of security and the issues of employee mobility, firm adjustment of total labor costs, and employee effort.

The Institutional Framework and the Provision of Security

The relative costs and benefits of providing alternative degrees of employment and income security will depend on the institutional structure of the economy. Although the institutional structure can be taken as given in the short run, over time institutions change in response to the needs of firms and workers. The dynamic interaction of the institutional environment, firm practices, and worker responses is beyond the scope of this book.[3] Here, we will focus on how a firm's security practices are constrained and supported by institutions. For example, extreme fluctuation in aggregate demand conditions may render no-layoff pledges untenable. Alternatively, a generous UI system reduces the potential benefits of employment security to workers. Clearly, the optimal security structure of a given firm will depend on the larger institutional environment within which the firm operates. Three basic institutions shape and constrain a firm's security structure in the United States and Japan (Figure 2.1): (1) macroeconomic policies, which affect the business cycle and long-run growth; (2) labor market norms governing status, individual rights, management rights, fairness, and nonpirating agreements; and (3) the social welfare system, especially UI and retirement programs.

Macroeconomic policy affects a company's net security costs through short-run as well as long-run approaches. Cyclical variation in product demand determines the firm's short-run flexibility requirements in adjusting labor input. If policy makers as a rule pursue a full-employment macroeconomic strategy, the firm's risk of having to bear the costs of idle labor during a cyclical downturn is diminished. In addition, through its effect on the firm's long-run performance, macroeconomic policy will determine the size of the work force to which the firm is able to extend long-run security coverage. In general, the net cost to a firm of providing employment security relative to income security increases with large cyclical swings and decreases with strong long-run growth and tight labor markets. The effect of macroeconomic policy on overall labor market tightness also affects the firm's ability to hire and the employee's ability to change jobs. Security systems, in turn, work for the public good by affecting the overall stability of the economy. If all firms provide security, a more stable economy results, and the costs of providing security to the individual firm are lowered. However, if only one firm provides security, no stabilization results and the firm is penalized by deeper recessions (Levine and Tyson, 1990).

The impact of labor market norms and the UI system is best analyzed within a macroeconomic framework (Figure 2.1). Norms concerning loyalty, status, fairness, and competition for workers will modify the impact of labor market tight-

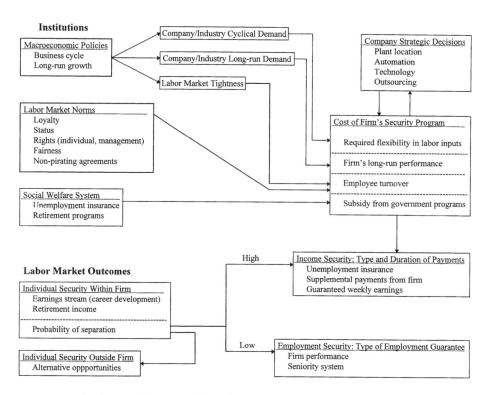

FIGURE 2.1. Institutional Structure of Security

ness on the optimal security structure. For example, if workers expect to remain with a company for their careers and do not quit during upswings for better wage offers, then a tighter labor market can be maintained with less upward pressure on wages. If workers expect to lose their jobs during recessions and quit their jobs for higher wages during recoveries, then a higher unemployment rate is required to keep wage and price inflation in check.

The UI system, coupled with the institutions of labor market norms, also influences a company's security costs by affecting turnover and by providing a public subsidy to income security policies. For example, UI in the United States encourages companies to make short-term layoffs during periods of sluggish demand since the payroll tax is not fully experience-rated, and so high-turnover companies are subsidized by low-turnover companies. In contrast, Japanese programs directly pay companies for surplus workers who are kept on company payrolls. Companies with surplus workers are subsidized by companies with lean work forces.

While the institutional framework strongly influences the firm's optimal security policy, the economic environment, which reflects macroeconomic policies and industry demand characteristics, also plays an important role (Figure 2.1). For example, the degree of security provided over the business cycle or in response to long-run structural changes varies by industry and size of firm. In industries with steady growth and incremental technological change, workers do not have to rely on company policy for security since employment security is already provided by a propitious economic environment. Company policy makes a difference only when the economic environment is not so favorable and produces short-run or long-run declines in labor demand. In addition, relatively large firms may have greater resources and better access to capital markets and will be better equipped to bear the costs of security commitments during cyclical downturns. Since the company's security policy is one of many factors that affect the company's strategic decisions on investments in capital and plant, the economic environment in which the company operates interacts with its security policy.

A company's security policy also varies with the occupational structure of the firm's work force. Since variation in transferable skills alters how workers value various earnings and employment security mixes, the optimal security policy the firm provides will depend on the overall transferable skill level of its work force. When a firm's modal occupation category embodies a relatively high level of transferable skills, the firm may be forced to offer more earnings security in order to retain workers. In addition, a company may have different security policies for production, clerical, and professional workers, and this may affect the willingness of employees to accept various parts of the employment system. The status or importance of the company and occupation and relative level of earnings in the industry, which together determine how a worker's current job compares to alternative jobs, will also affect the value of the firm's security policies to the employees.

The interaction between security and economic environment can be seen in the actions taken by Japanese and American companies in planning the location of plants, the introduction of new technology or automation, and the subcontracting of production. Together, these factors determine the company's demand for various types and amounts of labor. For example, when automobile or electronics plants located abroad do not provide as much employment or income security, foreign plants may offer a way either to circumvent costly security provisions or to accommodate domestic demand changes by adjusting production offshore. Outsourcing, which has long been a part of the Japanese automobile production system, is increasingly used by American automobile companies to shift production to smaller companies that provide less security and lower earnings.

In general, automation and technological innovation have reinforced the provision of security for employees. The introduction of expensive capital stimulates firms to reduce swings in production, as well as to add shifts for continuous production, since any periods of unused capital are costly. Automation increases the skill levels of most of the reduced labor force, who are trained to run and maintain the machines. In addition, automation dramatically increases the value of reliable and trained workers, who do not (intentionally or unintentionally) harm the equipment and who increase equipment uptime and lifetime. Security arrangements become more valuable as the company wants to increase tenure of its trained employees, even as the company may downsize with the automation.

Technological innovation and downsizing especially have characterized telecommunications, an industry historically known for its security provision. The challenge for the large telecommunications companies has been to increase the flexibility of their security policies without losing the benefits derived from employee loyalty and commitment. Both CommEx and CommSun were downsizing as labor-saving technology became part of the new computerized and digitized systems. However, downsizing at CommSun proceeded at a slower pace and in a methodical manner. Management was in charge of which workers were relocated, transferred, or "retired to second careers." In contrast, CommEx used a series of costly "early retirement" buyouts to downsize at a relatively rapid pace. Both unionized and exempt employees were in charge of determining who "retired," and management had no control over the outcome. A plan would be announced, then the company would wait to see how many and who responded. Although CommEx was able to shed workers more rapidly, the downsizing had a noticeably negative impact on worker morale and on relations with the union; no such reactions occurred at CommSun. Overall, we cannot even conclude that the more rapid shedding of employees resulted in lower long-run costs at CommEx relative to CommSun because CommEx's lack of control over who remained employed forced it to hire back many former employees as consultants.

In summary, both firms and workers must make trade-offs between flexibility and security. The net benefit of these trade-offs depends on the institutions shaping labor demand and labor turnover. Moreover, the economic environment, which varies within the institutional structure, influences the optimal security structure for both firms and workers. Now let us examine how firms' security policies work within these institutional structures in Japan and the United States.

Security in Japan and the United States

Institutional structures, which are historically rooted and continue to evolve, contain the provision that a company can offer and shape how the security provisions perform. We present the broad differences in security practices, rooted in basic institutional differences in Japan and the United States. The analysis of the security practices of specific firms in each country follows.

The United States and Japan provide very different macroeconomic outcomes within which companies structure security for their employees. We argue that these macroeconomic outcomes reflect the wage-determination systems in the two countries. The United States relies primarily on monetary policy to restrain inflation in a decentralized and largely nonunion wage-setting system, while Japan relies upon an implicit social contract among the large firms, trade unions, and government to provide employment security, wage restraint, and full employment with growth, respectively (see Chapter 6).

Japan has less volatile business cycles and higher long-term growth than the United States (Figure 2.2). As a result, Japan has less variation in labor market conditions and tighter labor markets, as measured by the unemployment rate. Although the U.S. unemployment rate is typically three to four times the Japanese rate, the disparity primarily reflects differences in short-term unemployment. The

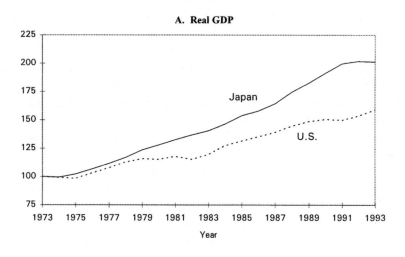

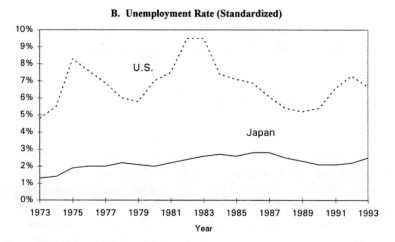

FIGURE 2.2. GDP and Unemployment in the United States and Japan, 1973–1993

Sources: A: OECD (1994a). B: OECD (1995a).

Note: A: Indexed to 1973 = 100; data at 1990 price levels.

United States has large movements both into and out of unemployment, with the monthly inflow approximately 2 percent of the population and the outflow between 37 percent and 49 percent of the unemployed.[4] In Japan, the comparable inflow into unemployment is around 0.3 percent and the monthly outflow between 20 percent and 24 percent. Long-term unemployment rates between the two countries are remarkably similar. In 1989, a year of relatively strong labor demand, the long-duration unemployment rate was 0.4 percent in Japan and 0.3 percent in the United States.[5] Growth and cyclical measures by Abraham and Houseman (1993a) for manufacturing in the United States and Japan over the period 1970–1977 show similar growth in the two countries, with slightly more cyclicality in Japan. Over the period 1978–1985, the United States had only one-half the growth rate of Japan, and Japan's cyclicality dropped by one-half.[6]

These broad macroeconomic trends influence and are influenced by the security policies that firms offer to workers. The Japanese lifetime employment policy both requires and supports full employment policies, which minimize the costs of employment security. The American approach of laying off workers and paying them some portion of their income allows volatile and slack labor markets, which facilitate wage moderation. The salient differences in macroeconomic outcomes result in distinct patterns of labor adjustment to demand cyclicality. Generally, Japan's lifetime employment system relies on adjustment of regular workers' hours (rather than of their employment status), adjustment of the number of temporary or contract workers when their contracts expire, adjustment of the number of part-timers, and adjustment of new hiring, if necessary. However, reductions in overtime can provide a cushion adequate for most large firms in the typical recession to decrease per capita labor costs as labor productivity declines. Only during crises, such as in 1974–1975 and in 1992–1994, do companies undertake the unusual tasks of changing patterns of scheduled time, part-time workers, and new hires in order to survive a deep recession (Dore, 1986). In periods of financial crisis, such as the crisis some automobile and electrical firms experienced during the 1990s, firms also have some flexibility in compensation through the bonus system. In general, however, wages for workers in large firms are not cyclical, and bonuses are only slightly cyclical.

The flexibility in labor costs achieved in the Japanese automobile industry between 1983 and 1993 is shown in Figure 2.3. Labor costs per worker moved with labor productivity primarily through adjustment of hours. Declines were made in the bonus only during deep recessions (1983–1985 and 1992–1994). Change in regular wage remained fairly constant throughout this period. This pattern was also exhibited in the national economy during the first half of the 1990s, when reductions in overtime hours began early in the recession and provided most of the adjustment in labor costs. Constant or slightly declining bonus payments and a slowdown in wage increases provided some adjustment after the first year of the recession. The Shunto wage increase was 5.9 percent in 1990, 5.6 percent in 1991,

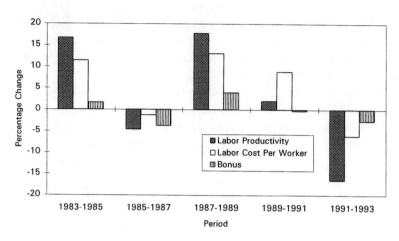

FIGURE 2.3. Changes in Japanese Labor Productivity, Labor Costs, and Bonus Payments in Autos, 1983–1993

Source: Calculated by Y. Nakata for twelve major automobile companies from Confederation of Japan Automobile Workers' Union (JAW) and Bank of Japan materials.

5.0 percent in 1992, and 3.9 percent in 1993, while bonus payments increased 6.2 percent in 1990–1991 and then *declined* in the following three years by 0.7 percent, 2.7 percent, and 0.3 percent, respectively.

In contrast, U.S. employers tend to rely on employment adjustment. These are the main findings of a detailed analysis of manufacturing industries during the period 1970–1985, which found less total labor market flexibility in Japan than in the United States (Abraham and Houseman, 1993a).[7] In general, employment in American manufacturing was found to be highly sensitive to fluctuations in demand, while employment in Japanese manufacturing was much less sensitive. Hours adjustments were found to be similar in both countries.

Job tenure and retention rates, as well as labor adjustment, are affected by the different security policies employed in the United States and Japan. One in ten Japanese workers had less than one year of tenure, and one in five had more than twenty years. The numbers were almost reversed for the United States, where two in seven had less than one year of tenure and one in twelve had more than twenty years. On average, tenure is higher for Japanese men and women compared to their American counterparts. The median tenure was 10.1 years for Japanese men and 4.8 years for Japanese women in 1990; it was 3.5 years for American men and 2.7 years for American women in 1991. Tenure also varies by education, firm size, and age. Japanese university graduates have noticeably higher tenure than high school graduates, while the differences for Americans are much smaller. The average tenure for workers in large firms compared to small firms is considerably higher and increases with age in both Japan and the United States (OECD, 1993a).

The differences between tenure (holding age structure constant) in the United States and Japan have been remarkably stable since the early 1970s for men, with American men averaging 60 percent of the tenure of Japanese men (Table 2.1). In contrast, American women increased their average tenure during the 1980s relative to Japanese women, whose average tenure declined slightly. American women's tenure rose from 50 percent of the Japanese average in the 1970s to 60 percent in 1987. Overall, the tenure data show that security for Japanese and American men and women has not weakened since the early 1970s and may have even improved for men in their 50s; security for Japanese women has weakened somewhat.

These tenure figures are reflected in retention rates by industry. Japanese male employees in government, finance, and utilities have retention rates (i.e., they will still be at the company in five years) of over 80 percent, even for junior workers (i.e., those with less than five years' experience). Even industries providing less security, such as manufacturing, agriculture, and trade, have 60 percent retention rates for junior workers. In contrast, retention rates are bifurcated for male workers in the United States. American junior workers have only a 25 percent to 35 percent chance of being with the same employers five years hence, while workers with five to ten years' experience have 90 percent retention rates in the utility, transportation, and service industries and 60 percent to 70 percent retention rates in government, finance, manufacturing, and agriculture (Nakata, 1990).

Job quitting and layoffs, the underlying forces creating these national outcomes in tenure, are different in the two countries. The average tenure for workers who separate from their employer in Japan is higher than for workers who stay. (For example, among men aged 45 to 54 years, the tenure for stayers was nineteen years and for leavers was twenty-four years during 1977–1987.) In the United States, the opposite is true; the tenure of stayers is higher than the tenure for leavers (for example, among men aged 45 to 54 years, the tenure for stayers was eighteen years and for leavers was nine years) (Nakata, 1990). These patterns reflect the Japanese practices in medium and large firms of compulsory retirement at age 55 to 60 years (*teninen taishoku*) and of transfer of workers to other firms (*shukko*) and the Amer-

TABLE 2.1. Age-Adjusted Mean Tenure (Years)

Year	Male			Female		
	U.S.	Japan	U.S./Japan	U.S.	Japan	U.S./Japan
1973	7.93	12.75	0.62	5.25	10.13	0.52
1978	7.95	13.19	0.60	5.07	10.12	0.50
1981	7.88	13.31	0.59	5.27	9.51	0.55
1987	7.87	13.01	0.60	5.52	9.22	0.60

Source: Nakata (1990).

Note: 1983 U.S. worker age composition is used for age-composition adjustment. The years stated are for the U.S. data; years for Japan are 1974, 1977, 1982, 1987.

ican practice of layoffs by seniority. In general, younger workers bear a larger share of employment adjustment in the United States; workers in large firms share equally in the hours adjustment, and older workers, temporary and part-time (female) workers, and workers in smaller firms bear the employment adjustment in Japan.

Transfer to another firm or relocation within the company is an accepted part of the Japanese lifetime employment system. In a 1987 survey, 20 percent of men and 5 percent of women reported being transferred, and 27 percent of men and 18 percent of women experienced a relocation or personnel shake-up (*Japan Labor Bulletin*, April 1993). The use of temporary transfer to another company is widespread, with over 90 percent of large firms (more than 5,000 employees) and 50 percent of medium firms (300 to 1,000 employees) using it in 1987 (*Japan Labor Bulletin*, April 1989).

Since American firms tend to adjust to demand changes by laying off surplus workers, U.S. unemployment rates are more sensitive to demand changes than are Japanese unemployment rates. Japanese institutional arrangements tend to minimize the observed unemployment rate, especially for short-term unemployment. For example, large Japanese companies carry excess regular workers during downturns, and the UI system pays benefits to the company so that "unemployed" workers are kept on the job. In addition, women workers are encouraged to drop out of the labor force when unemployed,[8] and some workers are absorbed into family businesses.[9] In contrast, U.S. institutions might bias upward the short-term unemployment rate. The UI system in the United States encourages people who have dropped out of the labor force to report that they are unemployed so they can collect benefits. However, this bias may be offset by many women who enter and leave employment without reporting a spell of unemployment while they search for jobs. Two out of three women who were separated from a job (both voluntarily and involuntarily) dropped out of the labor force in the following month, and three out of five who began a job were out of the labor force in the previous month during the 1990–1992 period.[10]

The UI systems in Japan and the United States differ significantly (Table 2.2). In general, benefits and durations are higher in Japan than in the United States. Japanese employers and employees split the payroll tax of 1.1 percent, while American employers pay the entire UI payroll tax, which is experience-rated and averages 0.7 percent of payroll. Since the benefits are higher and the costs are not experience-rated (i.e., not related to the firm's own record of layoff) in Japan, one might conclude that UI would encourage layoffs and unemployment more in Japan than in the United States. However, we can see that the institutions constraining layoffs keep the proportion of the work force collecting UI benefits in Japan at a much lower level than in the United States (6.8 percent vs. 2.1 percent).

Costing less than 0.03 percent of what the UI program costs in the United States, the Japanese UI program for individuals is not an important source of security. More significant is the existence of UI for companies, known as Employment Ad-

TABLE 2.2. Unemployment Insurance Systems in the United States and Japan

Individual Benefits	U.S.[a]	Japan
Eligibility requirement	20 weeks worked in previous 12 months; min. earnings during period range from $150 to $3,640	Regular worker insured 6 out of 12 preceding mos.; 55% of employment or 73% of non-agricultural regular employees covered
Total beneficiaries during year as		
% of work force	6.8	2.1
% of unemployed receiving benefits	36	40
Benefits		
Average amount	50% of previous wage, up to ceiling of 50% of avg. state wage; avg. weekly ceiling of $447; $162 avg. weekly benefit	¥2,390 to ¥9,040 basic daily allowance (regular workers); avg. total benefit is ¥1,638,000 ($16,380 at $1 = ¥100)
% of wage	35 to 45	60 to 80
Average duration	13.4 weeks	—
Financing		
Payroll tax rules	Experience rated; max. rate 5.4% to 8.0%; min. rates 0% to 1%; .73% of total payrolls or 1.95% of taxable payrolls actually paid	1.1% of wage split between employer and employee; plus Japanese Treasury pays 25% of benefits
Total cost of benefits (1992)	$39.2 billion	¥944.82 million ($944,000 at $1 = ¥100)

Sources: U.S. Department of Labor (1993); Blaustein (1993); Japan Ministry of Labor(1993a); Japan Institute of Labor (1992), pp. 22, 24, 28, 29; *Japan Labor Bulletin*, March 1992; U.S. President (1994).

Note: Unless otherwise noted, the figures are for 1990 for the United States and for 1992 for Japan.

[a] In the United States the unemployment insurance program is a state program. Each state has its own set of eligibility requirements and benefits, and there is tremendous variation across states. This table only reports averages, typical program rules, or variations across states.

justment Assistance (EAA).[11] The employment adjustment aid covers one-half of the wage in large companies (two-thirds in small and medium-sized companies) for surplus workers who remain on the payroll but do not go to work (*kyugyo*), for transferred workers (*shukko*), and for employees who undergo education and training (*kyoiku*) (plus, companies receive ¥1,500 per person per month for training costs). Before 1992, eligibility for this assistance was determined by whether the firm had experienced an annual drop of over 5 percent in both production and employment in the pervious three months. This condition was relaxed in 1992 to require only that the number of employees did not increase over the previous year. This criterion was geared toward including large firms during the 1990s recession. In October 1992, 171,000 establishments and 4 million workers received subsidies. These numbers were still far below the all-time high in June 1975, when 297,000 establishments and 7.8 million workers received subsidies.

The use of EAA by the two major export industries, automobiles and electronics during 1993–1994 is shown in Table 2.3. Firms were assisted primarily by being paid a wage subsidy for the surplus workers. On average, these workers remained at home only two days per month. Employee participation in EAA for education and training was only a small fraction of the participation in the wage subsidy; and assistance to firms for transferring workers was almost nonexistent. Although EAA participation by the automobile and electrical companies was high in December 1993, participation had fallen sharply by December 1994, and participation in education and training grew in relative importance. We can see that EAA provided only minor assistance to these industries as a whole. However, we saw confidential documents that showed EAA assistance was very helpful to the weaker companies, whose financial position was precarious.

In 1994, the Ministry of Labor instituted a "total employment support program" to assist companies in maintaining employment by making more companies eligible for the subsidy and by expanding the subsidy to companies for temporary transfers, to assist companies who hire new workers as a result of opening a new establishment, and to encourage laid-off workers to find new jobs. The ministry expected to spend ¥331.1 billion ($3.31 billion) during the fiscal year ending in March 1995 for these programs (*Japan Labor Bulletin,* January 1993, May 1994).

The actual participation, benefits, and costs of this program are not well documented, and until earnings and profits plummeted in 1992–1993, large companies viewed participation in this program with disdain, as we learned in our interviews with managers. However, many automobile and electrical companies accepted EAA subsidies in 1993 and 1994, especially for surplus workers.

In general, Japanese companies have faced relatively stable product demand, higher long-run growth rates in product demand, and tighter labor markets than U.S. companies. Provision of employment security in Japanese companies and provision of income security in U.S. companies are reinforced by the UI systems in the two countries. Since lifetime employment policies result in fewer quits, security provisions have benefited Japanese companies in their tight labor markets during the 1980s. In contrast, American companies attempting to provide employment security have been penalized by large variations in cyclical demand, long-run structural shifts, and slack labor markets during the 1980s.

Security in the United States

In the United States, workers have been more concerned with annual income than with long-term employment in a particular company since money income rather than company affiliation is important in marking success. Income security is largely provided by government-mandated programs since the ability of the company to determine the size of its labor force and the ability of the individual to change jobs have been considered basic rights.[12] For this reason, even with the persistence

TABLE 2.3. Employment Adjustment Assistance

	December 1993			December 1994		
	Automobile Assemblers	Automobile Body and Parts Maker	Electrical Industry	Automobile Assemblers	Automobile Body and Parts Maker	Electrical Industry
Kyugyo (employed but not at work)						
# of firms participating	21	381	396	14	81	139
# of workers participating	26,785	66,117	50,334	8,761	8,807	5,268
Average # of days per participant	2.2	1.7	2.2	2.2	1.5	3.5
Kyoiku (education and training)						
# of firms participating	3	26	26	7	9	17
# of workers participating	360	1,600	1,800	2,434	331	1,397
Average # of days per participant	2.5	2.3	3.1	3.7	2.3	5.0
Shukko (transfer to other firm)						
# of firms participating	0	2	1	0	2	1
# of workers participating	0	12	1	0	45	1

Source: Japan Ministry of Labor, Bureau of Employment Security, unpublished data.

of slack labor markets, unions have sought to improve unemployment pay or to guarantee income rather than prevent layoffs.

The focus in the United States on income security rather than employment security (with skill enhancement) has several detrimental effects. Once workers have guaranteed incomes (i.e., income security rather than employment security), they have no incentive to accept changes in work assignments. The connection between the economic welfare of the company and earnings of the workers has been broken. In addition, companies have already paid large sums of money into funds to pay for UI benefits and supplemental unemployment pay, and so plant managers have an incentive to lay off workers when demand falls in order to reduce their immediate payroll costs. Management has no incentive to provide training programs during periods of slack demand since this increases marginal costs and may increase a worker's employability elsewhere during an upturn. Workers do not have an incentive to participate in training programs since this requires effort on their part without improving their pay or security. For these reasons, income security sets up economic incentives that are often less efficient than those provided by employment security, and income security provides less security in the long run than employment security.

Fairly large and unpredictable business cycles result in what is viewed as capricious, and therefore unfair, layoffs across firms, and so the "objective" rule of seniority is often used to distribute layoffs in both union and nonunion companies. In the absence of a policy of employment security, job security has developed through seniority. Seniority rights historically grew out of the need to constrain the power of the supervisor to make arbitrary and unfair decisions, especially about termination and job assignment (Jacoby, 1985). The use of seniority provides stability and norms of fairness in rationing jobs through ordering layoffs and recalls as well as assigning jobs through post-and-bid and transfer rights. The use of seniority as a factor in making promotions, as well as layoffs and recalls, is widespread in the United States. The majority of companies—ranging from 80 percent of plant/service jobs to 53 percent of professional/technical jobs to 42 percent of office/clerical jobs—used seniority as a factor in promotion decisions in a 1977 national survey (Bureau of National Affairs, 1978).[13] Posting of vacancies is the most common method of publicizing job vacancies (four out of five companies post blue-collar vacancies; two out of three companies post office/clerical jobs; one half post professional/technical jobs).[14]

For the firm, however, the use of seniority to ration jobs involves costs associated with retaining or promoting inferior employees, and the costs depend on the degree of skill required and the variation among workers eligible for the job. For this reason, firms have resisted using seniority to ration higher-skilled jobs that require discretion and responsibility for decision making, but they have used seniority in the assignment of jobs that are fairly routine.

Prior to 1973, variations in demand usually resulted in temporary layoffs and not plant closings. A production worker's security depended primarily on the presence of supplemental unemployment benefits and not on the overall health of the company or industry, which was taken for granted. With increased international competition accompanied by structural shifts in manufacturing, American workers' security has come to depend more on the health of a particular company and seniority rights. However, even workers who have sufficient seniority rights to transfer to another plant if their plant closes face inferior working conditions and possibly lower wages since they lose their plant seniority.

In contrast to blue-collar workers, Americans with professional skills, such as managers or lawyers, have traditionally had more security since they have skills that are transferable to other jobs. With the restructuring process under way, white-collar workers as well as blue-collar workers have faced layoffs. However, white-collar workers are able to handle the transition to another industry, or even occupation, more easily than blue-collar workers.

Security in Japan

The Japanese security system intertwines flexible and rigid components. Regular employees with lifetime employment compensate their large employers by accepting flexible job assignment, transfers (including relocation), retraining, temporary or permanent assignment to a related company, second careers after retirement before age 60, and overtime hours. Employers also have a contingent work force consisting of temporary workers, seasonal workers, part-timers, and contract workers. In addition, the lack of vertical integration results in large firms using small and mid-sized firms as suppliers, which also provide a buffer for adjustment. The extent of employment security and the wages and benefits provided are less at mid-sized firms and decline even further at small firms.

The provision of security to a core of employees creates a dual structure of employment that segregates workers by age, sex, and, to a lesser extent, ethnicity. Since security requires a buffer stock of unprotected workers, the social and work roles of the regular and nonregular (contract and seasonal) workers must be consistent. Accordingly, the Japanese security system is embedded in a socioeconomic system that includes a family wage system. Each family requires a regular worker who receives security, a "living" wage that increases with seniority, and benefits. The extreme sex segregation of jobs and strict restrictions on immigration support the security system. Foreigners, women, and elderly men are employed as nonregular workers. Wives' lower, less secure wages supplement husbands' earnings as regular workers. Furthermore, up to ¥1 million of a wife's earnings are exempt from income taxes. If the security system is revamped, then other parts of the system, such as gender segregation, seniority-based wages, and the UI system, must be changed accordingly. Likewise, providing equal access to jobs in the Japanese labor market will require a restructuring of the security system and of the social and economic roles of men and women.

The number of Japanese workers covered by "good jobs" that provide security is debatable, since the available jobs lie on a continuum of gradual declines in security, working conditions, and wages. For example, the degree of security depends upon the firm's financial resources, which declines with firm size. Similarly, earnings decline with firm size, and male earnings in small firms (10–99 employees) average three-fourths of male earnings in large firms (over 1,000 employees). Koshiro (1995) considers good jobs as employment in banking, public service, and any of the 924 companies listed on the Tokyo First Class Stock Exchange, and he calculates that 17 percent of all employees (excluding the self-employed) held such jobs in 1993, compared with 25 percent in 1974.[15]

Since this calculation is subjective, we provide two alternative calculations of the coverage of core jobs in the Japanese economy. In 1992, men working as regular employees in private companies with ten or more employees or in government made up 64 percent of all male workers (including the self-employed) and 78 percent of all male employees (excluding the self-employed); regular male workers in medium and large companies (more than 100 employees) or in government made up 43 percent of all male workers and 52 percent of all male employees.[16] Since the Japanese labor market is still based on the concept of a family wage, we also estimated the number of Japanese households in which the breadwinner worked in a regular job. Approximately 75 percent of nonfarm, nonretired households had men working as regular employees (firms with more than 10 employees) in 1992; 50 percent had men working as regular employees in medium or large firms (more than 100 employees).[17]

The coverage of core jobs had actually increased since the height of the endaka period (the bubble economy) in the mid-1980s. In 1987, men working as regular employees in companies with ten or more employees or in government made up 62 percent of all male workers and 78 percent of all male employees; regular male workers in medium and large companies or in government made up 41 percent of all male workers and 51 percent of all male employees. Approximately 71 percent of nonfarm, nonretired households had men working as regular employees in 1992; 47 percent had men working as regular employees in medium or large firms.

Since many self-employed families have high incomes, these figures are conservative estimates. In summary, the large majority of Japanese households have a breadwinner in a regular job with some security, and this coverage has not declined in recent years.

Core workers are primarily concerned with employment security since identification with a company is important in marking status. The system of lifetime employment became more prevalent after the Productivity Accord of 1955, which spurred the importation of new technology while it protected workers' jobs.[18]

Japanese security provisions are backed by dismissal restrictions formed primarily through court rulings and socially accepted practices rather than legislation. In general, the court will not support collective dismissals of regular employees unless the company supplies substantial proof that the dismissals were made on "obviously reasonable and socially appropriate grounds."[19] Companies are expected to use their reserve capital to endure a deteriorating business environment and to allow an orderly reduction in employment without layoffs. Before accepting a certain number of dismissals, the courts consider the employer's efforts to prevent dismissals by reducing overtime, retraining and transferring within and outside the company, stopping recruitment, and not renewing temporary contracts (Hanami, 1991). This type of protection against the abuse of dismissal rights has been extended even to part-time and temporary workers who have been employed over a period of years.[20] As a result, Japanese firms spend a great deal of time and money on screening and recruiting workers, given that they are hiring them for the long term.

Conversely, the employer's broad discretion in deciding upon the employees' work place to meet business needs has legal backing in the courts. Employees are expected to make considerable sacrifices for their companies, including transferring to another city and leaving their families behind. Family needs such as care of elderly parents, desirable schools for children, or employment of spouse are not considered valid reasons for declining a transfer.[21]

At Star Electronics, we were told of one case in which a worker suffered hardship because of a transfer that forced him to live apart from his family, which included a sick child. The union intervened on the worker's behalf and was able to negotiate the worker's return to his former plant after one year. This case shows the obligation of workers to provide flexibility for the company and the role of the union in helping mitigate some of the hardships transfers cause.

Under a system of employment security, cost minimization encourages internal training of workers, wages that increase with experience, and performance-related pay. Such a system takes advantage of a fixed labor force while providing individual motivation. A system of employment security can function over time only in a fully employed economy, and so the government is obligated to moderate the business cycle. In a lifetime employment system, firms can implement wage structures that do not match productivity to wages at particular points in time without being penalized by turnover or without penalizing the employees by unequal treatment. Since the pay level is connected to the worker on the basis of tenure, skills, and performance and pay is not attached to the job, workers can be transferred within plants and between plants without their earnings being affected. The allocation of labor is a management right, while workers' rights are grounded in employment security and seniority pay. Once these rights can be taken for granted, workers are perhaps more mindful of their obligations to the group or company than of their individual rights.

Since pay is not determined by job assignment and since workers are rarely laid off, seniority loses its importance as a security device. Seniority is also not used for job assignment, which is usually viewed as a management right in Japanese companies. Therefore, jobs need to be perceived as somewhat equal in terms of working conditions. Job rotation and team work help achieve this. But it also means that work is organized so that jobs are not seen as being either extremely undesirable or extremely desirable. Great efforts seem to have been made to get rid of the worst jobs, especially through automation.

A Comparison of Japan and the United States

Seniority functions differently in Japanese and American employment systems. In the United States, especially among production workers, seniority is used to provide security by ordering the layoff queue. In Japan, seniority is used to guide the acquisition of skills and responsibility over the worklife of the employee. Although seniority is also used to order the job assignment queue in American companies, this mechanism is supported on grounds of fairness rather than efficiency. In Japan, the long-term employment relationship results in seniority being viewed as a measure of the training received by the worker. The automatic wage adjustment with age (*nenko*) and increase in job grade with firm tenure reflects this assumed increase in skills and responsibilities.

Although blue-collar workers face less secure jobs in the United States than in Japan, security systems for professional and managerial employees are fairly similar in the two countries. In Japan, employment security and the demands it makes upon workers to be flexible in accepting training and job assignments are applied to both blue- and white-collar workers. As they pass 50 years of age, Japanese managers face less security than production workers in Japan or managers in the United States since they may be "retired" and forced to pursue a second career at another company at a lower wage. At least one Japanese company reported to us that some older union workers would not accept promotion to a management job because of this decline in security.

American workers highly value their input into job assignments and their ability to change jobs. The American emphasis on freedom and individual autonomy conflicts with the emphasis on stability and the collective good that underlies the Japanese security system. The automobile industry provides a good example of why employment security cannot function in the United States as it does in Japan. Unlike their Japanese counterparts, American autoworkers resist being relocated when a plant shuts down, cuts production or moves. When the UAW secured the equivalent of lifetime employment for workers with ten or more years of experience, the auto industry did not simultaneously achieve the ability to transfer or relocate workers. Instead, the auto makers can only require workers to transfer to another plant within 50 miles. As a result, GM is paying 8,300 laid-off workers close to full pay while it hires temporary workers or pays overtime. For example, 1,100 idled workers in Van Nuys, California, have turned down jobs at other plants and drawn almost full pay since August 1992. Meanwhile, the Arlington, Texas, plant is short 250 workers and the Baltimore, Maryland, plant is short 200 workers. GM is now offering Van Nuys workers up to $60,000 in cash and moving expenses if they transfer to another plant.[22] Even so, in fall 1994 and winter 1995, GM workers in the Detroit area staged two successful strikes to force the company to hire new regular workers in order to reduce overtime hours.

We observed similar resistance to relocation by American workers at CommEx, which had a security pledge with the right to transfer workers within a commutable area. In practice, though, workers were not transferred without their consent. Experienced crafts workers often refused to transfer to another location within the same suburban area. The company finally forced a strike over the issue in order to gain more flexibility in assignment.

Although Japanese companies must discuss relocation plans with their unions, and although the unions resist permanent relocation that requires workers to move their place of residence, Japanese workers are more amenable to relocation. For example, when Toyota moved a production line from its Motomachi plant to a new Kyushu plant in 1993, the management met with the union to discuss the relocation of 300 production workers to other plants in the area. All 300 workers agreed to relocate. In another example, when Nissan closed its Zama plant in 1995, a union–management special committee was formed to oversee and facilitate the relocation of union workers. Special attention was given to relocating workers nearer to their hometowns when possible. Before the plant closing, 400 workers left voluntarily. Of the remaining 2,000 union workers, all of whom were relocated, approximately one-half had to move their residence. Approximately 1,000 workers were transferred to the remote Kyushu plant, and the company and union established special programs to ease the relocation of the reluctant families. The union made maintenance of employment their principle requirement and strongly preferred relocation to early retirement.[23]

The Japanese and American constraints on relocation have two important differences. First, the meaning of "voluntary" is not the same in the two countries. In the United States, workers must step forth to volunteer; in Japan, workers who are asked and do not decline are volunteers. When we asked whether a particular activity was voluntary in Japan, the reply was often, "It is 'mandatory voluntary.'" Second, U.S. automobile workers who do not volunteer to relocate are usually eligible for close to full pay while they are not working. Japanese workers continue to work whether or not they relocate. In practice, then, U.S. workers must request to be relocated to another plant in lieu of receiving close to full pay without working, while Japanese workers agree to their company's request that they relocate, which may result in a better job because of their helpfulness.

Now that we have investigated how the firm's security structure functions within the overall institutional structure of the country, let us examine how the security structure functions as a component of the firm's employment system.

Consistency of Security within the Employment System

Because they influence each other, a company's security policies must be consistent with its training, employee involvement systems, and mechanisms for adjusting total labor costs. Security and training structures are integrally related since tenure determines returns to training and retraining is required for long tenure employees. Security and employee involvement are integrally related since employees must feel secure and believe that they will share in the gains before they are willing to improve productivity. Workers will resist deepening skills, learning new skills, making suggestions for improvement, or solving problems unless they are assured these activities will not result in possible job loss and unemployment.

While the worker is concerned that expectations of wage growth and security are realized, the firm is concerned about employee effort and commitment. In particular, a firm wants hard-working employees who continually improve their skills and do not quit. The extent of a firm's motivational problem depends upon what types of activities are influenced by a worker's effort. In today's computerized work places, both the quantity and quality of work are often monitored automatically, and so the worker has little control over these outcomes. In the following chapters, we will consider how certain types of employee activities (e.g., participating in problem solving or making improvements, maintaining equipment, teaching or assisting others, learning new skills) are affected by motivation and how sufficient motivation might be achieved. Here, we examine the relationship between security, motivation, and quitting. Then we look at how workers within the same firm work under different security provisions and how firms adjust labor costs under different types of security provisions.

Worker Motivation

A potential conflict exists between the provision of security and the ability to motivate workers. Managers may properly be concerned about how to motivate workers if security is provided without a compensation or promotion system that rewards performance. This problem may be aggravated if pay rises with tenure in order to discourage quits and to provide pay consistent with life-cycle needs. The motivation of senior workers, who expect to earn high wages relative to productivity and outside opportunities, may become a serious problem if promotional opportunities within the firm diminish. Companies offering security, and their unions, will want to promote policies that support growth of output and market share so that promotion opportunities do not diminish. The option of using early retirement for adjustment when needed becomes more costly with an aging work force. Firms may need to restructure work and compensation for older workers in order to bring their compensation in line with their productivity as early retirement becomes less viable to a society with an aging population.

The Japanese family wage system, in which workers face a rising wage structure as their family obligations grow and a declining wage structure as their family obligations decline, provides economic security in a "fair" manner (i.e., according to life-cycle needs). Meanwhile, the Japanese system motivates younger workers with promotions and rising wages and rewards experienced workers, who serve as trainers. The junior workers know they can look forward to a wage transfer from future junior workers, and the experienced workers do not feel threatened by their trainees. Over time, the system provides not only job security but also income security and skill enhancement. In return, the system demands loyalty: workers accept the jobs assigned by management (including relocation) and do not quit during periods of labor shortages.

The Incidence and Consequences of Quits and Layoffs

Employment security requires that workers reciprocate by remaining with a company and not quitting when opportunity knocks, especially in periods of high demand. If employees exercise the right to quit whenever they please, the employer must bear the cost of providing security during periods of slack demand without being compensated by lower turnover costs in periods of high demand. In the absence of institutions that restrain quitting, firms face a disincentive to provide employment security.

An employee's propensity and ability to change jobs are affected by the institutional structure, including the social evaluation of quitting and the economic returns to changing jobs. The U.S. labor market does not have social norms that restrain quitting. In the United States, management and workers both view mobility as a right—the right of managers to lay off workers when necessary and of workers to quit when desirable. Younger workers have much higher rates of job mobility than older workers since layoffs are usually by seniority and workers usually quit to improve labor market position.

Overall, job mobility is twice as high in the United States as in Japan[24] and is more likely to be involuntary in the United States than in Japan.[25] One-quarter of all U.S. workers separated from a primary job during 1990 (Table 2.4); three out of five separations were voluntary and two out of three separations were permanent (i.e., the employee did not return to the same employer within twelve months).[26] Sixty percent of involuntary separations were layoffs, another 20 percent were temporary jobs that ended,[27] and the remaining 20 percent were discharges (for cause).

TABLE 2.4. Job Leavers in the United States by Voluntary–Involuntary Status, 1990

	Total	Permanent	Temporary
Separations as a % of the labor force			
Total	23.5	15.8	7.7
Voluntary	13.8	10.0	3.7
Involuntary	9.7	5.8	3.9
% of voluntary separations due to			
Quit for other job	36	23	14
Quit for other reason	56	34	18
Other	8	43	65
% of involuntary separation due to			
Layoff	63	43	20
Other	37	57	80

Source: Calculated from the 1990 Survey of Income and Program Participation.

Note: Separations are classified as permanent if the worker does not return to the employer within twelve months of the separation.

Sixty percent of the involuntary separations were permanent. Voluntary separations were dominated by quits for another job (one in three), quits for another reason (over one in two), and quits for retirement (one in twelve).[28]

The Japanese worker operates within an institutional structure that views leaving one's company as disloyal and shameful. In addition, a Japanese worker's mobility is constrained since within-company experience pay is not fully transferred to midcareer hires; job changers also lose entitlement to a corporate pension plan.[29] This constraint on mobility supports the HR system in large Japanese firms, where the cohesion and unity of the team as stressed. Midcareer hires usually have specific talents or skills that current employees lack, so they are seen as complements rather than competitors to members of the team. Lower mobility in Japan reflects workers' constrained opportunities to move from smaller to larger firms, as well as the lower dismissal rates throughout the economy.

In contrast to the rate in the United States, the total job separation rate is between 14 percent and 15 percent in Japan. For regular male workers[30] in large firms, the separation rate is around 6 percent, with approximately two-thirds voluntary (Table 2.5). Although managers at large firms complained to us about the turnover of new operators during their first year,[31] after the first year, separations are very low until retirement age. In general, the male turnover rate for small firms is over twice the rate for large firms.[32] Women leave jobs more often than men in Japan, but the women's differences in turnover between large and small firms are not very great. Although Japanese workers usually have to switch to a larger employer in order to improve their earnings and labor market prospects, the opportunities to quit for a better job as well as the threat of job loss are much more limited in Japan than in the United States.

TABLE 2.5. Japanese Separations by Firm Size

	Total[a]	Voluntary[b]	Involuntary[c]
All Employees			
1992			
All firms	14.55%	12.18%	2.37%
Large (>999)	11.30	9.57	1.73
Medium (100–999)	15.11	13.34	1.77
Small (5–99)	15.70	12.84	2.87
1988			
All firms	14.32	12.04	2.28
Large (>999)	11.90	10.22	1.68
Medium (100–999)	14.69	12.39	2.30
Small (5–99)	15.97	13.46	2.50
Male Regular Employees			
1992			
All firms	10.26	7.82	2.44
Large (>999)	6.23	4.39	1.83
Medium (100–999)	10.04	8.34	1.69
Small (5–99)	13.09	9.84	3.25
1988			
All firms	9.30	7.86	1.44
Large (>999)	5.25	3.55	1.69
Medium (100–999)	9.66	8.16	1.49
Small (5–99)	12.23	11.02	1.21

Source: Japan Ministry of Labor (1994b, 1989b).

[a] Includes voluntary and involuntary.

[b] Left by own choice, illness, injury, or fixed retirement age.

[c] Contract ended, employer's convenience, or fired. Excludes temporary transfers.

Although Japanese employees do not usually leave large firms, which rank at the top in status and pay, this is not true in smaller companies. The majority of new hires (57 percent in 1991) are workers with experience; only one in five are new graduates. Two-thirds of new male hires and one-half of new female hires in 1991 were experienced workers. The 1991 pattern is similar to the 1971 pattern, but the pattern in the recession year 1981 showed fewer new hires (50%) with experience (*Japan Labor Bulletin,* June 1993). In 1992, 3.5 percent of employees at large firms (more than 1,000 employees) moved to jobs at another firm: 1.0 percent moved to another large firm, 1.1 percent moved to a medium-sized firm (100 to 1,000 employees), and 1.3 percent moved to a small firm (5 to 100 employees). However, 8.2 percent of employees at small firms moved to jobs at other small firms (5.3%), medium firms (2.2%), or large firms (0.6%); and 6.4 percent of employees at medium firms moved to small firms (2.5%); other medium firms (2.5%); or large firms (1.1%).[33]

Male separations in large Japanese firms are less likely to be voluntary than male separations in smaller firms. Overall, job separations in Japan are reported to be over 80 percent voluntary, and separations exhibited little variation as the unemployment rate rose between 1988 and 1992. Although temporary or contract workers do not have the security rights of regular workers (or, to a lesser degree, of part-timers), in practice, many contract workers have long tenure with their employers. Contract termination accounted for only 6.5 percent of leavers in Japan in the low unemployment year of 1988, and it rose only slightly to 8.5 percent in the higher unemployment year of 1992.

Table 2.6 presents a comparison of the percentage distributions of wage changes realized by voluntary job leavers in the United States and Japan.[34] The most striking difference between the two countries is the relatively low dispersion in wage changes in Japan. In addition, Japanese male job leavers are in two distinct age groups—those over and those under 55 years of age, with the older group more likely to experience wage decreases and less likely to experience wage increases. Overall, nearly 90 percent of voluntary male job leavers in Japan realize a wage

TABLE 2.6. Distribution of Wage Changes for Voluntary Job Leavers

Age Group	Percentage Wage Change Realized				
	Less than −30%	−30% to −10%	−10% to +10%	+10% to +30%	Greater than +30%
United States, 1990					
All ages	.117	.149	.325	.173	.235
19 years or less	.088	.140	.405	.181	.186
20–24 years	.111	.154	.315	.176	.244
25–29 years	.121	.182	.308	.178	.211
30–34 years	.120	.163	.294	.181	.242
35–44 years	.155	.123	.288	.163	.271
45–54 years	.110	.133	.320	.171	.265
55–59 years	.054	.162	.297	.162	.324
60–64 years	.214	.071	.393	.071	.250
65–over	.053	.053	.474	.105	.316
Japan, 1991					
All ages	.057	.104	.432	.349	.059
19 years or less	.031	.095	.348	.408	.118
20–24 years	.047	.101	.373	.391	.088
25–29 years	.032	.098	.418	.370	.081
30–34 years	.038	.107	.392	.415	.047
35–44 years	.036	.102	.465	.347	.050
45–54 years	.051	.079	.490	.340	.040
55–59 years	.119	.138	.492	.237	.014
60–64 years	.248	.179	.454	.105	.014
65–over	.122	.061	.659	.153	.004

Sources: Wage changes for the United States are computed from the Survey of Income and Program Participation, 1990 Panel for all workers. Wage changes for Japan are computed from Japan Ministry of Labor (1992a) for males.

change between −30 percent and 30 percent. A full 43 percent realize wage changes between −10 percent and 10 percent. The comparable figures for the United States indicate broader dispersion: 65 percent realize wage changes between −30 percent and 30 percent, and 33 percent realize changes between −10 percent and 10 percent. Approximately four in ten Japanese male job changers increase their wages by at least 10 percent, often because they move from a smaller firm with lower wages to a larger firm with higher wages. Only one in six experiences a wage decline of over 10 percent. Although job changers will often earn less than same-age co-workers at the new firm, changers will improve their own earnings. For this reason, the firm's "wage penalty" for job changing (i.e., the wage differential between a mid-career hire and the standard worker) does not usually transfer into a decline in earnings for voluntary job changers.

Faced with a fairly flat tenure-earnings profile, many American workers change jobs to improve their earnings, especially during the early phase of their careers. In a study of white male high school graduates, Topel and Ward (1992) found considerable returns to "between-job" mobility.[35] On average, workers in the sample held approximately seven jobs over the first ten years in the labor force. While the average quarterly wage growth within jobs was 1.8 percent, the average wage gain between jobs was 12 percent, yielding an average net wage gain of 10 percent associated with changing jobs. Overall, changing jobs accounted for approximately one-third of the earnings growth realized during the first ten years in the labor force. The role of mobility is particularly relevant in light of the fact that nearly two-thirds of lifetime wage growth for male high school graduates is realized during this period (Murphy and Welch, 1992).

Table 2.6 also shows the important role of voluntary job change in the United States for wage growth. One in four voluntary changers realizes more than a 30 percent wage increase. However, one in four also sees a wage decrease of over 10 percent. For prime-aged (35–54 years old) voluntary changers, 27 percent of Americans versus 5 percent of Japanese men increase their wages over 30 percent while 13 percent of Americans and 4 percent of Japanese men decrease their wages over 30 percent (*Japan Labor Bulletin,* September 1992).

The implicit wage penalty in Japan is greater for high school than for college graduates (*Japan Labor Bulletin,* September 1992). Furthermore, the implicit wage penalty increases with age, as older mid-career hires lose more seniority pay in the job change. In 1991, the penalty was 5 percent (or less) for high school graduates who change jobs before age 25 and for college graduates who change jobs before age 35. However, the penalty was 30 percent for high school graduates aged 35–44 and 24 percent for college graduates aged 40–49.

In the United States, the potential wage penalty does not increase as drastically with age, reflecting the relatively flatter earnings-tenure profiles than in Japan. Overall, the wage penalty in the United States is lower for older job changers and higher for younger job changers than in Japan. A 40- to 44-year-old college graduate in the United States with less than one year of tenure will earn 70 percent as much as a colleague in the maximum tenure category (or a 30% wage penalty); a similar 30 to 34 year old new hire will earn approximately 78 percent as much as a colleague with the maximum possible tenure (or a 22% wage penalty). The comparable calculated wage penalties for the Japanese job changer are 38 percent and 12 percent, respectively.[36]

In the United States, voluntary job changers experience improved earnings, while workers who lose their jobs experience decreased earnings on average. Several studies document the substantial economic consequences of job loss (Farber, 1996; Kletzer, 1989; Neal, 1995). In our own calculations made to compare the United States and Japan, the average decline in weekly earnings for job losers increases with age and tenure, as expected (Table 2.7).[37] The wage decline is less in service occupations than in managerial, technical, or production occupations. The decline in earnings for many groups is, after 5 years, somewhat less than in the first year; however, this difference would be greater if the unemployed were included in the calculation. On average, a young person (aged 25–35 years) who is laid off has a 13 percent decline in earnings after 1 year and a 3 percent decline after 5 years.[38] A middle-aged person (aged 45–55 years) who is laid off experiences a 22 percent decline in earnings after 1 year and a 29 percent decline after 5 years.[39]

The high degree of mobility of the American work force, which reflects desired

TABLE 2.7. Average Percent Change in Weekly Earnings for All Involuntarily Displaced Workers, United States

	Years since Displacement		
	4 or 5 Years	2 or 3 Years	1 Year or Less
Current age			
25–35	−2.9	−11.8	−13.2
36–45	−14.9	−14.6	−14.6
45–55	−28.9	−29.0	−21.9
55–65	−34.5	−28.6	−31.4[a]
Tenure at time of displacement			
0–5 years	−7.8	−12.7	−13.5
6–10 years	−20.1	−20.1	−24.5
10–15 years	−25.1	−29.1	−19.7[a]
More than 15 years	−35.6	−34.1	−36.1[a]
Occupation at time of displacement			
Managerial and professional specialty	−15.6	−15.8	−18.7
Technicians and related support	−12.7	−18.8	−18.5[a]
Services	6.7	−19.5	−15.8
Precision production, craft, and repair	−11.1	−9.9	−16.9
Operators, fabricators, and laborers	−20.4	−21.0	−15.5

Source: Current Population Survey, January 1990 Displaced Workers Supplement.

[a] Cells contain fewer than fifty observations.

adjustments by workers (quits) and employers (layoffs), seems to result in increased earnings dispersion. As we saw above, mobility results in substantial wage decline for a large proportion of job losers and a substantial wage gain for a large proportion of job quitters. This wage dispersion resulting from mobility adds to the earnings dispersion that is already higher in American companies than in Japanese companies, as we discussed in Chapter 4. Compared to Japanese workers, U.S. workers face greater variations in earnings in addition to higher mobility (both voluntary and involuntary) and its accompanying wage changes.

The impact of pensions. The Japanese pension system presents another penalty for quitting in Japan since most employees depend upon a private pension until they are eligible for the public pension at age 65.[40] Among private employers with more than 30 employees, 92 percent have a private pension program. Typically, private retirement benefits are paid out as a lump sum, which is a multiple of the final monthly salary, although one-fifth of company programs provide a monthly payment and one-third provide both a lump sum and monthly payment (Japan Ministry of Labor, 1993a).

Approximately one-half of workers who leave voluntarily are not eligible to receive a private pension; this includes women who retire to marry or to raise children. In the predominant private pension plan (Tekkaku Nenkin), 56 percent of voluntary leavers are not eligible to receive a pension based upon age and tenure. For workers who are requested to leave by management, the majority of companies (63 percent) require that workers be at least age 60 to receive a pension; 19 percent have a minimum age of 55; only 12 percent provide a pension for those under 55. The minimum age requirement is less stringent for voluntary leavers: 44 percent of companies allow pensions for leavers under 51, while 44 percent pay a pension to leavers aged 55 or over. The minimum tenure conditions for eligibility have a wider variation across companies. For workers requested to leave by management, one-fifth of the companies require that they have 9 years of tenure to be eligible to receive a pension; two-fifths require at least 20 years of tenure. More years of tenure are required for voluntary leavers: one-half of the companies require 20 years of tenure to be eligible to receive a pension, and only one-sixth pay a pension to leavers with less than 10 years of tenure (Japan Ministry of Labour, 1993a).

The portability of private pensions is limited. One in six Japanese workers is covered by the type of pension system that allows leavers with fewer than ten years to move their fund to an association to be accumulated for eventual payment (Yamazaki, 1988). One study found that the Japanese private pension system deters voluntary leaving when workers are young, but the deterrence is less for older workers. The effect varies by industry, and deterrence for quitting peaks at a younger age in firms with steeper wage profiles (Seike, 1995).

In contrast to Japanese legislation, U.S. federal legislation over time has liberalized vesting rules, and today's workers have full vesting rights after five years.[41] Pensions are offered by the majority of large American employers but are less likely to be offered by small firms. Private retirement plans account for 2.9 percent of total compensation costs, which is one-half as much as the legally required Social Security.[42] During the 1980s, private pension coverage declined and vesting rights improved, which mitigated any negative effect private pensions had on quitting.

Overall, then, Japanese workers are more dependent upon private pensions than American workers for retirement income, and those who leave an employer before age 50 usually forfeit their pensions.

Trends in Mobility and Security in the United States

Although the popular press highlighted the downsizing of large corporations, overall mobility patterns in the United States appear to have been stable over the past fifteen years. While there are no data for the post-1982 period on job separations by reason, studies that examine different aspects of job mobility show that overall stability (i.e., retention) has not changed in the United States during the last decade and provide indirect evidence that voluntary labor mobility has been stable (or possibly has increased) over the period. Evidence of stability in the incidence of layoffs (including job loss due to plant closings) over the business cycle coupled with stability in the distribution of tenure imply that quit behavior has remained stable during the post-1979 period.

Farber (1996)[43] shows that the incidence of job loss is up slightly in the 1990s compared to the 1980s, primarily because of the rise in the last several years of downsizing ("position or shift abolished"). The increase in displacement is larger for older and more-educated workers, but younger and less-educated workers continue to bear the brunt of job loss. Earlier, Farber (1993) showed that the incidence of displacement during the *troughs* of the last two recessions (1982–1983, 1990–1991) was roughly the same, and Farber (1995) showed that the prevalence of long-term jobs had not declined over the period 1973–1993, although since then more are held by women and fewer by less-educated men.

Two studies of retention rates (or job security) found mixed results. A study by Diebold et al. (1994),[44] comparing retention rates from 1973 through 1991, found relatively stable retention rates. Those with fewer than six years of tenure experience a slight decline in retention, and blacks experience a decline relative to whites. Another study by Swinnerton and Wial (1995), using the same data and time period, shows a small downward trend in job stability, especially for low-seniority workers. Although the reason for the difference in results of these two studies is unclear, the general consensus is that job stability from 1971 through 1991 did not decline (Farber, 1996). Given the relative stability of overall retention rates and the stability of layoffs, one can infer stable quit rates (or slightly increased rates for low-seniority workers) since the mid-1980s.

Divisions among Workers within the Firm

When a firm provides security to a core of workers, its need to create a buffer stock of workers external to the firm is well known. However, security provisions also create divisions among employees within the firm. A firm's security system can create insiders (with vested interests) and outsiders within the firm. The insider–outsider problem (Lindbeck and Snower, 1988) results from the need to designate which workers are protected by rules that are perceived as fair. Employment and income security divide workers in different ways within the firm. Employment security separates those who are protected from those who are not (e.g., temporary or part-time workers, subcontract workers). Income security, with its use of seniority to order layoffs, creates divisions within the union by seniority. Under both types of security, protected workers and vulnerable workers will favor different strategies in responding to a decline in demand. Under employment security, protected workers and vulnerable workers are clearly delineated since they work under different rules or conditions.

In Japan, temporary, part-time, and seasonal workers, as well as employees of subcontractors, know that they provide the buffer stock when adjustments are required in severe recessions. Even though they often work alongside regular union workers, such workers' status is marked by a stripe on a hat or sleeve. Even some subcontracted employees may do their jobs, such as subassembly, within the plant. When we asked what the union thought about such a group of workers at Star Electronics, one union leader told us that those were not his workers, but he went on to say that the union improved the subcontract workers' conditions through such workplace improvements as better air circulation. Overall, however, the buffer stock of workers is not represented by the company union. Indeed, the union workers' security requires a buffer stock. During a recession, protected workers will want to take over tasks performed by unprotected workers, including temporary or part-time workers, and take back subcontracted work before protected jobs are threatened. They may also prefer these alternatives to having protected workers reassigned to other locations or companies. Even among protected workers, rules for allocation of work during a downturn (e.g., by skill level or seniority) may create vested interests and result in different effects on groups of workers (e.g., those who will have to relocate, those who will be reassigned to lower-skilled work, those who will receive training). However, the differences in interests among core workers are usually slight compared to those between core workers and a firm's buffer stock.

Under income security, workers with ostensibly the same rules or conditions are divided by their seniority. Senior workers, whose seniority provides them with some degree of employment security, will resist a decline in compensation or working conditions or other plans to "share the misery" among workers during a period of reduced profitability for the firm. In several U.S. auto plants, we interviewed senior workers who complained that the move toward employee involvement (the

SET system) would make their jobs harder. For them, it was a no-win situation. Senior workers' interests are protected, at least in the short run, through layoff of junior employees. However, junior employees, who may have sufficient work experience to qualify for unemployment benefits for only a short period and who are uncertain about when they will be recalled, will want to find ways to reduce costs or shorten hours in order to share the misery with the senior workers. On long-run issues of work restructuring, the division between senior and junior employees may be even wider. If senior employees are eligible for retirement in a few years, or are eligible for guaranteed income until retirement, they will usually resist restructuring plans to improve productivity. Since their economic future is no longer tied to the plant's future, they will not support a plan that changes their working conditions in an uncertain (or negative) way. Junior workers, who are not protected if the plant is closed, will back the restructuring plans in order to make the plant more competitive.

Although both countries use buffer stocks of labor, temporary workers in the United States primarily perform a cost-cutting function rather than a flexibility function, as in Japan. In the United States, temporary workers are less expensive than permanent workers because they receive lower wages and seldom receive benefits such as health insurance and private pensions. Although temporary workers do not receive fringe benefits or bonuses in Japan, they have contracts with the companies for which they work and may make higher monthly earnings than part-time or even regular younger workers, as we observed at several plants.

Unlike Japanese companies, American companies can rely heavily upon temporary layoffs of regular workers for flexibility, and income security allows employers to adjust the work force in response to demand changes. The buffer stock is internal to the firm, and the work force varies in its vulnerability, depending upon seniority rules. Unions in the United States tend to constrain the use of temporary, part-time, and subcontracted workers. Even nonunion companies seldom have subcontractors performing production jobs within the plant. However, the practice of subcontracting parts and some maintenance jobs within American plants has been gradually expanding both to reduce costs and to improve flexibility. The situation varies across plants. At Together Manufacturing, the union agreed to the hiring of temporary workers (who were usually relatives) during the summer to replace workers on vacation. However, the union was less happy with the contracting out of cafeteria work and grounds keeping. At the U.S. plant of Agile Auto, the union and company disagreed over the use of temporary workers on Mondays and Fridays, when absenteeism was high.

The use of temporary employees in Japan has remained at approximately 10 percent of nonagricultural employees over the period 1983–1994 (OECD, 1996).[45] The use of part-time workers grew much faster—from 3 percent of total employees in 1975 to 12 percent in 1992.[46] Most part-timers are women (95 percent in February 1994), and 28 percent of female employees are part-timers. Most part-timers are found in wholesale and retail trade (46 percent of total), manufacturing (25 percent), and services (22 percent). Part-timers' share of employees in these industries are 24 percent in trade, 10 percent in manufacturing, and 13 percent in services in 1992 (Japan Institute of Labor, 1992), pp. 24–27.).

Part-time workers in the United States, unlike their counterparts in Japan, have remained a stable component of the work force over the period 1979–1992, with approximately 10 percent of male workers and 25 percent of female workers working part-time (i.e., less than 35 hours) (OECD, 1993a).[47] Although the popular press has speculated that temporary employment has grown in the United States, no data exists to measure temporary workers over time. A special 1995 Current Population Survey survey including questions about contingent employment found that 4.9 percent of workers (including the self-employed) did not expect their jobs to last for an additional year. Women were 50 percent and part-time workers were 43 percent of these contingent workers. The survey also identified 1 percent of employed workers as being paid by temporary help agencies, another 0.5 percent as working for contract firms, 6.7 percent as independent contractors or freelance workers, and 1.7 percent as on-call workers and day laborers (U.S. Department of Labor, 1995a).[48]

In summary, we can say that temporary and part-time work is more prevalent and is much more likely to be done by women in Japan than in the United States. The use of part-timers, and of temporary workers to a lesser extent, has grown in Japan. The use of part-timers and temporary workers appears to have grown more in Japan than in the United States, where the use of part-time laborers has not grown and less than 3 percent of the work force consisted of temporary workers in 1995.

Flexibility in Total Labor Costs

By providing employment security, employers are forced to respond to demand changes in ways other than laying off their core employees. Flexibility usually is provided by adjustment in hours (especially overtime), reduced compensation growth to include slower promotion rates and lower bonuses, as well as reduced wage-rate growth, and reduction in the overall level of employment for both regular workers and the buffer stock of labor. Demand is stabilized within the company by reducing demand at the supplier or subcontractor level or at a plant located abroad, although these moves may increase the parent company's costs and may harm relations with suppliers or foreign governments.

Changes in hours is the easiest way to reduce labor costs quickly. Both U.S. and Japanese companies rely upon the use of overtime to make small and quick hours adjustments, with U.S. companies paying a 50 percent overtime premium by law and large Japanese companies paying a 30 percent premium by agreement with the unions.[49] In addition, the long work year in Japan has allowed companies also to reduce total work hours over time. Regularly scheduled work hours had fallen in the early 1970s but remained steady from the mid-1970s throughout the 1980s before falling again after 1988. The government, urging companies to decrease the hours of work because of international pressures, decreased the regular work week (i.e., the number of work hours before overtime is paid) from 48 to 44 hours beginning in April 1991. Small and medium-sized companies were allowed to continue with a 46-hour work week until March 1993, and the continuation was later extended to March 1994 (Japan Institute of Labor, 1993). Still, the hours of Japanese workers are longer than those of workers in other OECD countries. In 1990, Japanese workers averaged 1,905 scheduled working hours plus 219 overtime hours (2,124 hours total), compared to 1,756 regular hours and 192 overtime hours (1,948 total) for U.S. workers.

The main difference in hours for U.S. and Japanese manufacturing production workers is not in the average hours worked per day but in the number of days worked. Japanese workers have fewer "holidays," which includes weekends, than American or European workers. On average, Japanese workers had 85 weekend holidays (compared to 104 in the United States and Germany) plus 21 holidays, 9 vacation days, and 3 absences for a total of 118 days off. Production workers in the United States averaged 9 holidays, 19 vacation days, and 7 days of absence for a total of 139 days off. German production workers had 12 holidays, 29 vacation days, and 12 absences for a total of 157 days off (*Japan Labor Bulletin*, September 1992, April 1994). Japanese companies favor holidays over vacation days since the latter present scheduling problems.

Changes in the number of protected or regular workers can be accomplished through fewer new hires, early retirements, turnover, reassignments, and outplacements. However, changes in the expected outcomes for the protected sector cannot be too dramatic, as the stress upon the system may force major structural adjustments and union unrest. For example, if large Japanese companies curtail their hiring of new university graduates, one cohort of university graduates will not obtain their expected placements in the labor market. Many will be forced to work for smaller, lower-status companies. This outcome will require modifying the norms of hiring at "mid-career" so that "recession" graduates can be properly integrated into the labor market when the economy recovers.

These changes in labor input are sometimes viewed differently by the worker and the firm. From a worker's viewpoint, expected earnings and the family budget are reduced by a cutback in standard hours or overtime hours. For the family, the decline in work time does not compensate for the decline in income, and so reductions in hours are similar to reductions in compensation. The firm considers the decline in hours to be compensated by the increase in time off. In contrast, a reduction in bonus or in wage-rate growth affects norms relating effort to reward, and the firm realizes such reductions can cause inequities over time. However, the firm is not likely to share the worker's sense of entitlement to an expected wage-rate growth since the worker's family is not being asked to reduce its budget. Workers' willingness to share the burden of the recession with the employer depends upon whether the recession is short term and followed by an economic recovery.

The Japanese Security System under Pressure: The Challenge of the 1990s

The deep recession in Japan in the first half of the 1990s put the adjustment mechanisms to a test. As expected, large firms protected "lifetime employment" by slashing overtime, relieving temporary employees, reducing new hires, and making use of early retirements. Many large Japanese companies introduced restructuring plans that were major by Japanese standards, although they appear insignificant by American standards. For example, Nissan Motor Company closed the Zama plant in spring 1995 (with two years' notice) and reduced jobs by 5,000 out of 53,000 in three years (by March 1996) through reducing new recruits. NTT launched a program in 1990 to cut employment by 40,000 over four years to 230,000 by introducing early retirements and limiting new hires. This program was extended to cut employment by another 30,000 to reduce the work force to 200,000 in 1996 (*Japan Labor Bulletin,* April 1993, July 1993). Toyota Motor Corporation reduced hiring and eliminated part-time employment—in 1992, Toyota had 2,700 part-timers; by 1995, it had none (*Japan Times Weekly International Edition,* May 9–15, 1994, p.13).

In the fifth year of stagnant growth (1995), the unemployment rate was slightly over 3 percent and there were only 65 job offers for every 100 job seekers. As would be expected, the groups providing the buffer stock bore the brunt of the recession. Part-timers, foreigners (who must leave if they lose their jobs and their spouses are not Japanese), and workers at small companies most frequently lost their jobs. The number of women in the work force fell 0.8 percent during 1993. The estimated number of in-company unemployed, who are still paid but have little or no real work (*madogiwa-zodu,* or "those who sit next to the window"), ranged between 400,000 (Labor Ministry) and 1 million (private economists) in 1993 (*Japan Times Weekly International Edition,* May 9–15, 1994 p. 14).

Nevertheless, a systematic look at the data on these changes do not confirm the major transformation dramatized by the popular press. Instead, Japanese companies adjusted to the long and painful recession by using the adjustment mechanisms described earlier. In the earlier years of the recession, minor adjustments in hours and buffer stocks were made. As the recession continued past three years, seldom-used adjustments to new hiring, bonuses, and wage growth were made. Specifically, the companies did the following.

In industries where overtime had become standard practice, Japanese companies realized large and immediate declines in output and labor costs by reducing overtime. This was especially important in the automobile industry, where the average work hours of union members in the twelve major firms fell 11 percent from a high of

2,253 hours in 1989 to 2,012 hours in 1993. Earlier, automobile makers had resisted the government's pressure to reduce hours, but the recession resulted in their achieving significant reductions in work hours. Hours fell 5 percent between 1992 and 1993, which translates into a 7 percent salary saving since the overtime premium is 30 percent. The amount of reduction varied by company. For example, between 1992 and 1993, a relatively stronger Toyota saved 7 percent in labor costs by reducing hours and a relatively weaker Mazda saved 10 percent by reducing hours. Toyota, Nissan, Honda, and Mazda had annual working hours below 2000 in 1993. Nationwide, scheduled hours fell 1.7 percent (to 1,780 hours) and overtime hours fell 11.3 percent (to 133 hours) in 1993 (calculated from *Japan Labor Bulletin,* September 1992, April 1994). Although American companies decreased overtime during the recession, since early 1991, they have been increasing overtime rather than increasing employment.

Large Japanese companies reduced hiring . In the tight labor market of the late 1980s, large firms increased their annual hiring by 2 to 3 percent and complained about labor shortages. After the early 1990s recession persisted past the second year, new hires declined, especially for large firms and for less-educated workers and women. Leading exporters like Toyota, Mitsubishi, and Matsushita Electric instituted programs in cutting recruits (*Japan Times Weekly International Edition,* May 2–8, 1994, p. 4). However, the recession was a boon for some small businesses, who were able to improve the quality of new hires. In 1993, large firms (more than 1,000 employees) decreased hiring by 15 percent, while small firms (fewer than 99 employees) increased hiring 15 percent. For firms listed on the Tokyo Stock Exchange, recruitment of university graduates graduating in March 1994 dropped by 21 percent for men and 40 percent for women. In 1992, 38 percent of university graduates went to work for these listed companies, but only 27 percent of the university graduates in 1994 expected to land such jobs (*Japan Labor Bulletin,* October 1993, October 1994).

Overall, companies relied on internal transfers to other company locations to provide flexibility. Temporary transfers to other companies (*shukko*) did not increase, but transfers to more distant locations within the same company did increase during the recession. The number of workers who transferred to a new location without taking their families (*tanshinfunin*) increased in 1993 to 481,000, or 1.5 percent of all male workers (up 15 percent over five years before). Over two-thirds of transfers without their families are between 40 and 60 years of age. Large firms were more likely than small firms to have such transfers, and 2.3 percent of male employees in large firms (more than 1,000 employees) and 1.5 percent of male employees in mid-sized firms (100 to 1,000 employees) were on transfer without their families (*Japan Labor Bulletin,* April 1994).

Medium-sized companies were more likely than large companies to cut their work force, primarily by reducing part-timers, temporary workers, foreigners, and seasonal workers. Beginning third quarter 1992 and continuing into the mid-1990s, employment at large companies (500 or more employees) declined, with separations exceeding new hires. Employment at medium-sized companies began declining three quarters earlier. However, employment at small companies (30–99 employees) remained steady, with separation and accession rates roughly equal (*Japan Labor Bulletin*, March 1994, July 1992).

Earnings flexibility developed in the bonus and wage structure in the third year of recession. In 1993, for the first time since 1975, bonuses for major firms decreased 0.3 percent from the year before, including −4.6 percent in printing, −4.5 percent in autos, and −3.1 percent in electric appliances. Some industries reported positive annual bonus growth, including 5.6 percent for oil products and 3.6 percent for telecommunications (*Japan Labor Bulletin*, February 1994).[50] NEC and Sanyo paid part of the winter bonuses to managers in coupons for the company's products. One problem with this approach is that the employees must pay (cash) taxes on the coupons. NEC also suspended pay increases for executives and decreased summer bonuses by 5 to 10 percent for managers (*Japan Labor Bulletin*, January 1993).

In 1993, workers' average monthly wages in *real* terms showed the first year-on-year decline since 1980. Average monthly basic salaries of workers at companies with 30 or more employees increased 2.7 percent from the year before, but special allowances (including bonuses) declined 1.6 percent and payments for overtime work dropped 5.6 percent. As a result, workers' total monthly wages averaged $3,896, up 1 percent from the year before but slightly below the 1.1 percent increase in consumer prices in fiscal 1993 (*Japan Labor Bulletin*, January 1993).

Households experienced a 1.1 percent drop in average annual real income in 1994, the first decline since 1980. This deterioration reflected growth in wage-earning householders' regular income of only 1.0 percent declines in special income (bonuses) and spouses' income of 6.1 percent an 5.9 percent, respectively, and employment adjustments by corporations (*Japan Labor Bulletin*, July 1995).

Employment adjustments increased as the recession continued. By third quarter 1993, 46 percent of manufacturing, 36 percent of trade, and 24 percent of service establishments reported reducing overtime, reducing or suspending mid-career hiring, and/or relocating employees (*Japan Labor Bulletin*, February 1994). How five major electrical companies adjusted their work force during 1989–1993 is shown in Figure 2.4.[51] The number of regular workers rose slightly during the downturn, and the number of part-time workers fell slightly. However, the use of temporary workers rose sharply at one company while it fell slightly at two others. The fall in the buffer stock of workers was not sufficient to offset the small rise in regular workers, and so overall employment did not fall during this period.

The lack of any major shifts in the employment relation in the electrical or transportation equipment industries in Japan during the 1990s recession is confirmed by preliminary results provided by Susan Houseman that updated her earlier work with Abraham on employment adjustment in Japan (Table 2.8). Overall,

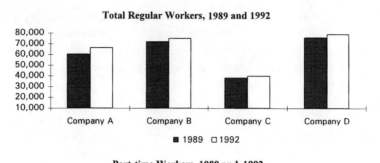

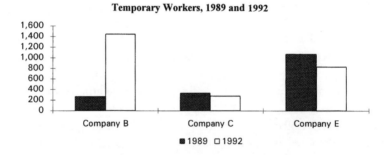

FIGURE 2.4. Employment Adjustment in Electrical Companies

Source: Data collected by Denki Rengo at our request from selected companies by written survey.

adding the years 1990 to January 1993 to the period of estimation (1970–1993) did not affect the employment adjustment in manufacturing or in electrical equipment, and it *lowered* the employment adjustment in transportation equipment.[52]

Helped or hurt by demographic trends? The adverse cyclical forces of the 1990s will be followed by secular declines in labor supply, which should mitigate the pressures from the long-term forces of global competition and slower domestic growth. Since immigration is almost nonexistent, the birth rate determines the long-run labor supply. The Japanese labor market faces a dramatic decline of younger workers in the late 1990s, and the male work force will decline by two million during the 1990s. Similarly, declines in the number of young people and increases in the num-

TABLE 2.8. Total Employment Adjustment in Japan, 1970–1993

Industry	Current Month	Twelve Month
Manufacturing		
1970–Jan. 1993	.018	.213
	(.008)	(.038)
1970–1989	.017	.220
	(.008)	(.038)
Electrical equipment		
1970–Jan. 1993	.036	.321
	(.010)	(.035)
1970–1989	.033	.336
	(.010)	(.043)
Transportation equipment		
1970–Jan. 1993	.015	.300
	(.007)	(.043)
1970–1989	.022	.316
	(.008)	(.043)

Source: Estimations provided by Dr. Susan Houseman, W. E. Upjohn Institute for Employment Research.

Note: The numbers in the table are estimates of the elasticities of total employment over the subsequent month and year following a change in production. They are the coefficients from a differenced regression of ln(employment) on ln(production) and a time trend. Standard errors are in parentheses.

ber of elders will translate into a net decline of 1.4 million male workers in the first decade of the next century (*Japan Labor Bulletin,* February 1994, January 1994).

While the aging work force will partially relieve some of the pressure placed on the lifetime employment system by reducing the number of new entrants to the labor market, it will also place upward pressure on average salaries. Japan's aging work force poses special challenges for a system of lifetime employment with a seniority-based wage structure since wage costs rise with the average age of the work force. The potential slowdown in promotion rates is especially critical for large Japanese firms, where all regular male workers expect to reach the equivalent rank of supervisor before retiring. In some large Japanese companies, workers can even expect to reach the first level of management, which is the American equivalent of third-level manager. In response to the aging of the work force, large companies set up two-track management systems, one for line managers and one for staff managers (i.e., those without a subordinate staff), in order to partially offset the reduction in managerial positions relative to those eligible.[53] However, many companies in 1993 reported having surplus managers and clerical workers and reported the major causes were lack of posts commensurate with age and high seniority-based wages (*Japan Labor Bulletin,* February 1994).

Although this approach mitigates morale problems, it does not alleviate the problem of rising average salary costs. Financial pressures have pushed companies to revise pay and promotion systems to be more performance based, especially at the higher nonmanagerial job grades and in the managerial grades. For example, Nissan Motor Company reported a plan in which 15 percent (down from 40 percent) of a manager's pay would be seniority based and 85 percent performance based, with greater variance in managerial wages (*Japan Labor Bulletin,* January 1994). Many Japanese managers told us that they would like to increase performance-related pay, which awards pay increases to individuals who show more effort or a better attitude. However, we observed the actual implementation to be occurring at a much slower rate than company proclamations suggested, especially for union members. A Japan Productivity Center survey in March 1993 showed that few companies had adopted "the annual pay scheme," in which employees' annual raises vary by performance and the attainment of targets. Only 10 percent had such a scheme and only 30 percent planned to implement one. Partly because of the Labor Standards Law and union resistance, the system is directed mainly toward those in management positions (*Japan Labor Bulletin,* June 1993).

Although Japanese companies weathered the 1990s recession without major changes in their employment systems, we question their ability to weather the secular trends of slower growth and increased global competition without modification of their employment and wage systems to offset the rise in labor costs as the work force ages.

Summary

We conclude that security is shaped more by external environment, including macro-economic policy and labor market norms, and less by idiosyncratic company policy.

Security practices vary more between Japan and the United States than they do across companies within each country, reflecting the importance of the economic institutions and macroeconomic conditions in shaping a company's security system and a worker's decisions to change jobs. The Japanese system of employment security is embedded in a rigid labor market where transfers to new and better jobs are limited, where workers have traded some control over their work lives for more security, and where women and younger and older workers bear the burden of adjustment. The Japanese employment system gives managers control over workers' job assignments and requires workers to accept flexibility in transfers, overtime hours, and earnings growth. The U.S. system of employment security is embedded in a mobile labor market where earnings improvements are often made by changing employers; where workers highly value their input into their job assignment, their ability to change jobs, and their autonomy; and where managers highly value their ability to control the size of their work force. Workers and companies have opted to exercise control over jobs and work force rather than to seek long-term employment relations. Security comes from seniority and income support programs, especially unemployment insurance.

Increased international competition has put pressure on U.S. firms to restrict the proportion of workers with income or job security and to increase the contingent work force. Similar pressures are at work in Japanese firms, and we expect this trend to become more visible as a secular adjustment when the Japanese recession ends. Overall, the labor market institutions in Japan have changed much more slowly than in the United States, and a much deeper economic crisis seems to be required before firms make adjustments in their practices to reduce costs. Even then, their adjustments tend to be marginal compared to the changes undertaken by U.S. companies facing intense global competition.

The 1990s recession has brought renewed emphasis to the benefits of employment security in the United States and to the costs of employment security in Japan. After analyzing the employee involvement, training, and wage systems, we will return in the concluding chapter to the question of what type of employment system, including security, would be effective in the United States, given its emphasis on mobility and individual autonomy and its macroeconomic institutions. We also discuss to what extent American (in)security practices are transferable to Japan.

NOTES

1. Nondiscretionary expenditures are those that maintain a family's normal daily life and cannot be changed without disrupting the family's life-style. For a more complete discussion, see Vickery (1979).

2. We distinguish this individual human capital, often referred to as general human capital, from organizational capital, which refers to skills and knowledge that are developed through experience on the job, are related to organizational activities, and are valuable only within the organization. Organizational capital includes relationships among employees; workers' knowledge of the firm's culture and structure; workers' knowledge of rules and procedures; workers' experience in teaching certain skills to others; the firm's knowledge of workers' skills and talents; and proprietary knowledge (e.g., research-and-development secrets, financial data, supplier information). Although organizational capital might be thought of as specific capital, it is not solely embedded in one individual and may not become lost to the organization when that person quits or retires. Rather, organizational capital is embedded in groups and is learned incrementally. Therefore, the loss of capital to the organization when one individual leaves is quite small and can quickly be replaced with a minimal amount of job experience for the person who is transferred to the vacant job. However, if several people in a work group leave at one time, the training costs can be high since the natural training structure embedded in the work process has been destroyed.

3. On the origins and dynamics of institutions in Japan, see Upham (1987) and Campbell (1992), and in the United States, see Jacoby (1985).

4. These figures are for 1979, 1989, and 1991. The inflow is given as a percent of population aged 15–64 minus the unemployed; outflow is given as a percent of the total unemployed (OECD, 1993a, pp. 88–89).

5. Long-duration unemployment rate equals the number of those unemployed continuously for at least twelve months as a percent of the labor force (OECD, 1993a, p. 83). The 1989 conventional unemployment rate was 2.3 percent in Japan and 5.3 percent in the United States.

6. These measures are from regressions of seasonally adjusted monthly ln (production) on a time trend. Growth is the time-trend coefficient, while cyclicality is the standard deviation of the regression results.

7. For a discussion of the speed of employment adjustment in Japan relative to other economies, see Koshiro (1994).

8. Since 1977, Japanese women are less likely to leave the labor force when unemployed. Meanwhile, the phenomenon of women being "involuntary part-time workers" has grown (Tachibanaki, 1987).

9. *Japan Times,* May 9–15, 1994, p. 13. The practice of using unemployed family members in a family business has declined over the years as the number of family businesses has declined. Even so, in 1992, 9.8 percent of nonagricultural female workers were family workers and 9.4 percent were self-employed (Japan Institute of Labor, 1992, p. 24).

10. The numbers are also high for men: two out of five men who began a job or were separated from a job were out of the labor force in the preceding or subsequent month, respectively (Masumura and Ryscavage, 1994).

11. The Employment Insurance Law was amended in 1974 and in 1978 to subsidize training programs for employed workers and increase the number of authorized upgrade education and training programs provided "in-house" by corporations. Employers contribute 0.35 percent of their payroll toward this program (*Japan Labor Bulletin,* June 1992).

12. Although companies have fairly broad powers of dismissal, large companies and unionized companies have formal procedures for termination. However, smaller nonunion companies often use their right to "terminate at will." State courts and federal legislation (e.g., the Civil Rights Act of 1964, the Americans with Disabilities Act of 1990) have limited these rights to terminate if the cause is unfairly applied to certain groups (e.g., women, minorities, older workers, or the disabled) or occurs under certain conditions, such as when a worker refuses to commit an illegal act or opposes unsafe working conditions (Braconi and Kopke, 1994; Gould, 1984).

13. See also Ng and Maki (1994).

14. Employees eligible for promotion are identified through a skill inventory or employee information system in less than one-third of the companies for office/clerical and plant/service jobs and less than two-fifths of professional/technical jobs. Proficiency or aptitude tests are required for promotion in only one-fourth of the companies for office/clerical jobs, in one-sixth for plant/service jobs, and in one-ninth for professional technical jobs (Bureau of National Affairs, 1978, p. 1).

15. Self-employed workers accounted for 22 percent of all workers in 1970 and 17 percent in 1990. In addition, family workers accounted for 16 percent of all workers in 1970 and 8 percent in 1990. Many of the self-employed and family workers are in agriculture, trade, and eating places. The agricultural work force has declined from 17 percent of total employment in 1970 to 7 percent in 1990, but the proportion of the work force in wholesale and retail trade and eating and drinking places rose slightly from 20 percent in 1970 to 23 percent in 1990 (Japan Management and Coordination Agency, 1996, Tables 3–3, 3–4).

16. Estimated from Japan Management and Coordination Agency, (1987, 1992). The figures include regular male staff plus executives in private industry plus regular male staff in government service.

17. The assumption is made that each household had no more than one male regular worker. Households with the head working for pay are included.

18. See Noda (1988) for a good review of the literature on this issue.

19. Japan Institute of Labor (1994a, pp. 93–94).

20. See the Tokyo Shibaura Electric Case, 1974 and the Sanyo Electric Case, 1990 (Japan Institute of Labor, 1994a).

21. See the Toa Paint Company Case, 1981, the Kowa Company Case, 1980, the Hitachi Seiki Company Case, 1981 (Japan Institute of Labor, 1994a).

22. *Wall Street Journal,* April 21, 1994, p. B4.

23. From interview with union official by Y. Nakata in May 1995 and *Japan Labor Bulletin,* (July 1993).

24. OECD estimates annual job-leaving rates of 19.4 percent for the United States and 10.9 percent for Japan. Moreover, 29 percent of American workers have less than one year of firm-specific tenure, compared to 10 percent in Japan (OECD, 1993a, pp. 121, 124, 126, 136, 141).

25. An important exception, however, is the involuntary turnover rates of workers over age 55. Koshiro (1994) cites an involuntary separation rate for Japanese male workers ages 55 to 64 of 5.9 percent, compared with 4.2 percent for U.S. workers in this age category.

26. The figures shown for the United States are not inclusive since they include only a worker's first job separation from a primary job. The sample is for employees aged 18–64 years old, not in school or the armed forces. These calculations were made from the 1990 Survey of Income and Program Participation by Steve Raphael. Voluntary separations include retirement or quitting; involuntary separations include layoffs, discharges, the end of a temporary job. Another study of turnover in the United States between 1980 and 1983 found very high levels of separation—23 percent *per quarter,* with one-quarter of them temporary. Turnover was negatively related to firm size and to average payroll per worker. Compared to other industries, manufacturing relied more on temporary layoffs and less on permanent separations (Anderson and Meyer, 1994).

27. Although both U.S. and Japanese contract or temporary workers accept jobs with the understanding that they will (or might) end, we still list this type of separation as involuntary because in practice many workers stay on whenever possible. Some separations from temporary jobs may be voluntary since workers may have wanted to work only for a short time or for a season. Often workers return to the same temporary job over many years. This results in a conservative measurement of the rate of voluntary leaving. In the United States, separations from temporary jobs are only 7 percent of all separations, and less than half (44 percent) of them are permanent.

28. Some retirements may not be voluntary. The rate of retirement rises rapidly after age 58, and one-quarter of retirements are before age 59.

29. See excerpt of the Nikkeiren's guidelines for overhauling the employment system, as reported in the *Daily Labor Reporter,* December 23, 1993, pp. A4–5.

30. Regular workers exclude temporary or daily workers but include part-timers. Regular male employees are over 95 percent of all male workers and 60 percent of all employees.

31. The rate of separation in the first year of a job was 22 percent in 1988 for all high school graduates, compared to 17 percent in 1980 (*Japan Labor Bulletin,* May 1993).

32. Higuchi (1994) reported annual separation rates of 7 percent for men and 15.5 percent for women in 1987. Less than 5 percent of male Japanese workers in large firms voluntarily separated, and another 2 percent involuntarily separated. Dore (1986, p. 93) found similar rates in an earlier period. These numbers are consistent with the finding that turnover rates in small Japanese firms are lower than in large American firms (Blinder and Krueger, 1990).

33. This includes nonregular (contract and seasonal workers) as well as older workers who "retire" to a second career. Calculated from Japan Ministry of Labor (1993d). Agriculture, forestry, and government sectors are excluded.

34. The figures represent men and women in the United States and men in Japan since Japanese women tend to leave the labor force when they leave their jobs for marriage or childbirth.

35. The authors analyze a white male sample from the Longitudinal Employee Data (LEED) taken from Social Security records that cover quarterly earnings data from the period 1957–1972.

36. Implicit wage penalties for the United States are calculated from the January 1991 Current Population Survey, Job Training Files, and for Japan from the 1991 *Survey on Employment Trends.*

37. Four years after displacement, job losers earn 10 to 13 percent less than job stayers (Ruhm, 1987). Relative to stayers, job losers average a 9 percent wage loss up to two years out (Farber, 1993).

38. The data are calculated from the Current Population Survey, January 1990 Displaced Worker Supplement, by Steve Raphael. The sample of displaced workers includes all workers 25 years of age or older who, during the five-year period prior to the survey date, lost their jobs because a plant closed, a position or shift was abolished, or work was slack. Only workers who were full-time employees at the time of layoff are included. Thirteen observations (out of 2,892) were dropped because the postdisplacement earnings were more than three times their predisplacement earnings.

39. Similar earnings declines accompany layoffs arrayed by years of tenure. In general, young men did better and older men did worse than their female counterparts after layoff.

40. Private pensions are an important source of assets for seniors. The typical private pension for a person who has worked 30 to 35 years for a company is 30 to 40 times the final monthly salary (or approximately two times annual salary, including bonus.) The private pensions averaged ¥20 million in large companies ($200,000 if $1 = ¥100) and ¥10 million in medium-sized companies ($100,000) in the early 1990s. Public pensions have a flat-rate basic benefit and an earnings-related benefit. The maximum monthly basic benefit in 1991 was ¥58,500 ($585 if $1 = ¥100) for those retiring at age 65. The average monthly earnings-related benefit for private employees retiring at age 60 was ¥206,000 ($2,060), or 55 to 60 percent of annual net earnings (Takayama, 1992).

41. The 1974 Employee Retirement Income Security Act (ERISA) introduced minimum vesting, participation, and funding rules. The 1987 Pension Reform Act further restricted funding flexibility (Ghilarducci, 1992). See Ghilarducci (1992) for an excellent analysis of the private pension system and how it functions in the United States.

42. In 1991, 59 percent of full-time employees in large and medium private firms (over 99 employees) were covered by a defined contribution pension, and 48 percent were covered by a defined contribution pension (including employee stock ownership and deferred profit sharing). In 1992, 22 percent of employees in small private companies (fewer than 100 employees) participated in defined benefit pension plans and 33 percent in defined contribution plans. Employers can offer more than one type of plan. However, only 48 percent of full-time employees (age 15 and older) reported participating in an employer-provided pension plan in 1992; 62 percent of employees in large firms (more than 1,000 employees) and 30 percent in small firms (25 to 99 employees) reported participation in a pension plan (U.S. Bureau of the Census, 1994, Tables 672, 673).

43. Farber analyzes even year Displaced Workers' Survey supplements to the Current Population Survey to cover job loss between 1981 and 1993. He also found that the consequences of job loss have not changed systematically over time and that more-educated workers suffer a smaller decline in earnings from job loss than do less-educated workers. See also Gardner (1995).

44. The authors use consecutive Current Population Survey Job Training Supplements for the period 1983–1991. Retention rates are defined as the probability that a worker with a given level of tenure will accrue *t* additional years of tenure.

45. Temporary workers usually have a contract for more than one month and less than one year. Our own calculations show temporary workers growing slowly from 6 percent of total employees (excluding self-employed and family workers) in 1980 to 9 percent in 1992, when three out of four temporary workers were women. Day laborers, who are not included as temporary workers, accounted for 2.3 percent of employees in 1993, and 43 percent were men (Japanese Institute of Labor, 1992, p. 24).

46. Part-time employment also has a cyclical component, and part-timers reached a high of 13 percent of total employees in the trough years of 1989 and 1991. "Part-time" workers in Japan may actually work more than 35 hours, which is the traditional designation used in the United States. They may actually work a 40-hour week, but they have less security than regular workers and they are not union members. Japanese workers who actually worked less than 35 hours in the 1992 survey week included 11 percent of males (up from 8 percent in 1979) and 35 percent of females (up from 28 percent in 1979), and 75 percent of the part-time employment was female (OECD, 1993a). Part-timers do not include those who are called *Arubaito,* which are usually students with a "side" job. See Houseman and Osawa (1995).

47. Our own calculations of workers who were working part-time during the survey week totaled 23 percent of the work force with 4 to 5 percent working part-time involuntarily. Calculated by Steve Raphael from the 1989–1993 Current Population Survey March Demographic Files.

48. Women accounted for one-third of the independent contractors and the workers provided by contract firms and for one-half of the on-call workers/day laborers and the temporary help–agency workers. Our own calculation from the March Current Population Survey found 0.8 percent workers employed in the "personnel supply services" industry in 1989, 0.5 percent in 1991, and 0.6 percent in 1993.

49. The legal overtime premium in Japan is 25 percent. In both countries, unionized companies pay more for holidays and shifts by agreement. For example, the late-night pre-

mium negotiated across large companies in Japan is 60 percent, the holiday premium is 45 percent, and the late-night premium on holiday is 75 percent. In the United States, unionized companies usually pay 2.5 times for holiday work; the shift-work premium is usually in the range of 10 to 15 percent.

50. Rengo reported the winter bonus averaged ¥701,263 (2.59 months of regular income), down 0.8 percent. Nikkeiren reported the winter bonus averaged ¥774,193, down 0.9 percent (*Japan Labor Bulletin,* February 1994).

51. Our thanks to Denki Rengo for administering a survey to the five major companies to collect this information.

52. Our appreciation to Dr. Houseman for supplying us with these updated estimations.

53. Based on interviews in summer 1994 with leading companies in the automobile and electronics industries by Clair Brown, Jim Lincoln, and Yoshi Nakata. This research was funded by the Japan Society for the Promotion of Science.

3

Employee Involvement and Training

Introduction

It is widely believed that the employment system in Japan is structured to generate more employee involvement (EI) in production tasks and more skill training of workers than in the United States. Thus, Japanese workers are said to contribute hundreds of individual suggestions per year to improve productivity, to participate wholeheartedly in quality circles, and in general to be unlike U.S. workers, who rarely make above-norm efforts to increase company performance. Japanese employers are said to provide many more hours of formal training each year to their workers, enabling continual skill growth. These characteristics are believed to account for much of the faster productivity growth rate of the Japanese economy documented in Chapter 1. They provide much of the basis for U.S. management's initiatives in the 1990s to increase the use of teams, job rotation, quality circles, and other well-known Japanese management practices on the shop floor, and they underly repeated calls for U.S. employers to step up sharply the training of their work force.

As we noted in the last chapter, many observers attribute these better outcomes to a key institutional characteristic of the Japanese system: the lifetime employment commitment afforded to many Japanese workers. In this view, a lifetime employment commitment means that the productivity and other cost improvements that are generated by EI do not place the existing work force at risk of a layoff, so that high-performing workers know they will not hurt their peers.[1] Long-term employment security is similarly invoked as a means to enhance skill training, as workers are then not likely to renege on their commitment to their employers; if trained workers are not likely to leave, the company can recoup its training invest-ment.[2] The institution of employment security, in other words, is sufficient to over-come the free-rider problems associated with EI and skills training in a market economy and to lift the economy from a low-skill, low-commitment equilibrium to one of high skills and high worker effort.

Our argument builds partly upon this logic while revising it in critical dimen-sions. In our view, the United States—and not just Japan—sustains much higher levels of EI and worker training than has been recognized. The common view that the U.S. system does not provide the correct amount of EI or training goes wrong by not asking whether EI and training are of the right type and whether they are embedded in a supportive environment. We find that the crucial differences be-tween the two countries inhere in the structure of each country's EI and training and the extent to which each is integrated coherently into the overall employment system. In other words, employment security, while it may be necessary, is not by itself sufficient to transform one system into the other.

The chapter begins with definitions and a conceptual typology of EI and then discusses its role in alternative HR systems. EI in Japan is oriented more to em-ployee communication, to the development of shared goals among workers and managers, and to the attainment of specific cost-reduction targets, and it tends to be highly integrated into the company's overall HR system. In contrast, EI in U.S. companies is oriented more to worker well-being—issues such as ergonomics, health, and safety. While problem solving and cost reductions also motivate EI poli-cies, these policies are often embedded in an adversarial labor-management system and tend to be organized very simply, with little connection to the rest of the com-pany's HR system.

The second part of the chapter addresses worker training, beginning again with definitions and a typology and continuing with an examination of differences in the character and quantitative levels of training in each country. Training in Japan is primarily on the job and planned, while training in the United States is more like-ly to occur off the job and to reflect only short-term planning. We then consider how EI and training in SET companies, as observed in both Japan and the United States, contribute to employment security. We describe how the compensation and performance appraisal systems in Japan stimulate continual involvement and learning and how employee involvement programs provide a motivational and dis-ciplinary structure that complements the Japanese compensation system. The Japanese and U.S. compensation systems themselves are discussed at length in Chapter 4.

Our comparison in this chapter emphasizes the Japanese strategy of moving workers from one job to another in a coherent sequence. Over a period of years, workers accumulate knowledge and skills in a gradual and systematic manner, thereby enhancing their performance and permitting employers to increase pay with experience. The Japanese approach acknowledges the importance of job assignment for skill development, and managers are responsible for assigning jobs and developing careers for their subordinates. In the United States, creating long-term career ladders within the firm is more difficult, because workers move more freely among firms and managers have less control over individual job assignments within a firm.

From a U.S. perspective, the strengths of the Japanese system of EI and training often appear to be based upon elements that are problematic: weak grievance and voice mechanisms, restrictions on individual mobility and independence, an emphasis on implementation of management goals of cost reduction rather than on development of worker autonomy and creativity. We shall suggest that these problems stem from the historical context in which the Japanese system evolved; they are not necessary elements of the system. Many weaknesses of the U.S. system similarly arose in a specific historical context that has long eroded; substantial improvements can be made in the U.S. system as well. We discuss these issues for both countries and consider how Japanese EI and training might be modified for the U.S. context.

Employee Involvement in the United States and Japan

The premise of EI is, of course, that the traditional Tayloristic system of work organization can be made more productive by incorporating the active input of workers into the production process. This input, if it is to be called EI, must involve individual workers doing their daily tasks, but it is not limited to individualistic involvement or to daily tasks. EI can also be constituted through small work groups or teams, as well as through plantwide or companywide organizations. Generally, the higher the level at which EI is constituted, the more it is oriented to longer-term management issues.

Although EI can be integrated into the activities of a collective worker organization, EI is distinct from traditional forms of worker representation or voice, such as U.S.-style collective bargaining, Japanese-style enterprise unionism, and European-style works councils. Indeed, many U.S. unions have expressed concerns that EI constituted an attempt by employers to communicate directly with their work forces, to bypass existing forms of union voice and representation. This traditional U.S. labor approach regards independent union power, as structured and recognized in the National Labor Relations Act, as a necessary condition for successful EI. An alternative view suggests that EI addresses issues of work organization that are not part of traditional collective-bargaining contracts. The fact that some U.S. unions have embraced EI programs while others remain hostile suggests the enormous diversity of policies that are labeled as EI in the United States.

Definitions and Typology

The purpose of EI, from an employer's point of view, is to enhance workers' motivation in their work by getting them to improve the work process and thereby company performance, by getting them to identify with the company's general welfare, and by encouraging receptivity to change. EI programs may be top-down or also bottom-up. A top-down program is structured by management and mainly involves communication of decisions to workers, with little or no opportunity for workers to make or influence decisions through a process that moves upward in the organization.[3] The program can involve nothing more than exchange of information, often labeled consultation or communication, with varying relationships to resultant decisions based upon the responses to the consultations. They can occur at the top levels of management as well as at the small-group level on the shop floor.

EI programs can be integrated with other HR practices (as when the compensation system rewards participation in EI programs or when workplace training addresses communication skills needed for effective EI), or they can remain separated (as in most U.S. companies' traditional suggestion programs). EI programs can therefore be categorized according to their level of centralization within the organization, the resources and power accorded to EI activities, and the fit between EI programs and other elements of the HR system.

EI in Unionized Systems in the United States

In unionized U.S. companies, traditional labor-management systems have led to widespread seniority rules for job assignment, employee transfers and promotions, and layoffs. In addition to giving these important roles for seniority, unions generally have compressed pay increments with seniority in order to enhance member solidarity. In order to protect their members against arbitrary actions of supervisors, unions have successfully narrowed job classifications and reduced the role of supervisory appraisals in determining employee pay increases or job promotions.

In a traditional union-management system, employee and union voice generally play a limited direct role in EI. A major exception concerns the overseeing of job assignments. In the United States, employees usually are included in the job assignment decision, often through a post-and-bid system. In most work places, a set of rules delineates how job assignments and promotion or upgrade decisions are made. These rules usually include a skill requirement (before training), an employee application for a specific job openings, and a role for seniority in ranking equally qualified candidates. Employee satisfaction in the assignment of work seems to be at least as important as skill or career development for nonexempt employees.

Other important areas of union involvement in EI concern health and safety issues (Weil, 1991), structured apprenticeship programs (Mills, 1984), and the recent development of joint union-management training programs (Ferman et al., 1991). Yet the traditional model remains: management structures the workers' EI and training, and unions focus on monitoring job assignments and on increasing the proportion of training programs that are accessible to union members.

The traditional union–management system in the United States affects EI indirectly by creating some employer and employee incentives for employee training and career development. The rewards of greater seniority—which include improved protection from layoffs and preferences in job assignments—induce employees to remain with the firm, to acquire skills, and to train junior workers. At the same time, the relatively flat age-earnings profile can reinforce employers' long-term commitments to workers as employers are less likely to want to replace senior workers with junior workers who receive relatively similar pay.

EI in Nonunion Systems in the United States

In the much larger nonunion sector, collective EI is of course less important and outcomes are more varied across individuals than in the union sector. Yet the similarities rather than the differences between the union and nonunion sectors are most notable. Like the union sector, the nonunion sector exhibits relatively flat age–earnings profiles for frontline workers; often uses job evaluation schemes that attach pay to jobs rather than to individuals; often uses post-and-bid systems to fill job vacancies internally and permits employees to transfer within the company; generally uses narrow job classifications with a small number of well-defined tasks and separates production jobs from craft jobs; and rarely designates to EI programs the power to assign jobs and oversee training. These five characteristics create inadequate training incentives and constrain career development in both the union and nonunion sectors. They especially inhibit skill deepening and broadening because pay does not adequately reflect long-term skill development. As a result, job progressions do not form career ladders in which skills are developed and deepened over a series of job assignments.

Incidence and Consequences of EI

Although numerous studies have documented the high incidence of EI programs in the United States, the estimates vary widely.[4] Moreover, many of the initial quality circle programs were found to have short lives (Drago, 1988), and there are virtually no large-scale longitudinal studies to provide a confident estimate.[5] The key question, of course, is, Under what conditions do EI programs survive and make a positive contribution? Studies comparing union and nonunion firms point to the importance of trust between both sides, which would be mediated by security commitments. Such studies find significant differences in the adoption and implementation of EI programs (Cooke, 1994; Appelbaum and Batt, 1994). A careful study by Eaton and Voos (1994), for example, found that nonunion firms are more likely to use profit sharing than unionized companies, while unionized companies are more likely to use team production systems and quality circles. These findings have been interpreted to suggest that top-down EI programs are less effective than those implemented with the consent of the participants, and many case studies confirm this view, but the evidential basis remains preliminary at best.[6]

In some industries, such as the semiconductor plants we studied, all plants have some version of EI. Its universal presence and apparent survivability in the semiconductor industry indicate its positive impacts and perhaps augurs the future pattern. Some scholars suggest, however, that EI can be successful only when it is linked carefully to other components of the HR system.[7]

EI in the Companies We Visited

Employee involvement was an established program at each of the companies we visited in the United States and Japan, but the companies varied tremendously in how far along they were in implementing an EI policy. A typical example in Japan involves the plant of a leading automobile manufacturer. In 1991, this plant tallied over 100 suggestions per worker. Of these, 70 percent received at least a minimum reward. There were ten reward levels, ranging from ¥1,000 to ¥100,000. Unlike the case in many U.S. companies, where suggestions often involve such worker-oriented issues as the quality of the food in the cafeteria, at this company the suggestion system was explicitly limited to production, safety, and quality issues. Most of the top suggestions actually came from quality circle (QC) activity but were submitted individually for additional recognition and reward.

All workers were in quality circles; circles rotated themes every three to four months and were evaluated monthly. The company was about to begin paying overtime for time spent on QC activities, which usually took place after regular work hours but had been unpaid. This shift to paying for QC time was said to be occurring at many major companies. The director of QCs for the plant provided us with a chart of QC activity. In the previous six months, two different manufacturing lines had 287 circles, 2,011 members, and 266 different themes; they generated almost 2,400 suggestions, saved about 3,300 work hours of labor, reduced rejects by about ¥11 million, and saved ¥4 million in materials.

The unit leader was given a specific goal to reduce staffing and costs: in one case it was 5 percent. Targets and actual results were monitored on a monthly basis. One supervisor showed us a chart he had made to measure task times, with a green section for value-added work, purple for necessary but not value-added work (maintenance, for example), yellow for work in support of green and purple sections (and so also necessary), red for unnecessary movement that could be reduced, and black for waiting time that could be eliminated. This supervisor showed us the improvements made to standard work times; most of the improvements originated from managers, but half of the cases involved the workers as well. One operator on the welding line was a specialist in submitting suggestions for improvements, particularly regarding troubleshooting techniques when problems arose. Supervisors often had ideas for improvements, which they passed on to workers who then received the credit; this created a win-win situation between the worker and the supervisor. Workers gained because they received not only a one-time reward but also credits toward a permanent promotion in pay. Supervisors gained because in exchange they could expect flexibility from the workers when they might need it.

One union leader for this plant evaluated one of the supervisors as excellent because he did not try to make too many improvements and cost reductions. He did only what was required by his mandatory targets and was not interested in promotion. Nonetheless, the plant was operating quite smoothly.

At the same company's plant in the United States, employee involvement in improvements had become a dirty word. The workers' hostility concerned the direct reductions in overall staffing that were associated with the improvements, including the use of production workers in tasks that had been performed by skilled trades workers (but did not require high skill levels to perform). This plant also had large numbers of suggestions for a U.S. company—two per worker per year, with a participation rate of 50 percent and an adoption rate of 49 percent. About a year before our visit, the union local organized an effective three-month boycott of the suggestion program in response to management's decision to reduce the rewards provided. Sometime later, the company canceled the suggestion program altogether.

Another contrast comes from a plant in the same industry in the United States, also managed according to Japanese principles. The suggestion system at Together Manufacturing was supported by the union local and the workers and was generating large savings for the company. Workers received modest rewards on a one-time basis. The system was working, but it was not as integrated into the HR system as at the Japanese plants of this company. At High-Tech, the suggestion system was a shambles, poorly rewarded by management and disdained by engineers, who resented being asked to read and comment on the suggestions that were submitted.

From a U.S. perspective, a major issue concerns whether Japanese-style consultations and employer use of teams represent anything more than the infamous employer-dominated unions that prevailed in the 1920s. In the United States, labor law prohibits employer domination of labor organizations, as stated in Section 8a(2) of the National Labor Relations Act. This clause has led many observers to suggest that most EI programs in the United States may be illegal and to seek to amend the law accordingly.

EI in Japan

Employee involvement in Japan is embedded in a more cooperative relationship between workers and management. At the highest level, joint consultation committees are constituted at most large and medium companies, whether a formal union is present or not. In 1984, according to a Ministry of Labor survey (reported in Inagami, 1988, table 6), 72 percent of all companies had a joint consultation body, up from 70.8 percent in 1977 and 62.8 percent in 1972. Such bodies were widespread in very large companies—in 94.2 percent of companies with over 5,000 workers—but were also the norm in medium and smaller companies as well (for example, in 74.4% of companies with 300–999 workers and 57.6% of companies with 100–299 workers).[8] Again according to Inagami, over 40 percent of all nonunion companies have a joint consultation body.

These committees serve to communicate company plans and decisions on an early basis to labor and thereby to avoid surprises, a strategy that develops and maintains trust and provides a forum for the resolution of disagreements that may arise. Of course, not all communications from the company involve dialogue. Basic management policies, such as production and sales plans or a change in the company's organization, usually are announced by management with very little discussion or attempt to craft an agreement. On the other hand, changes in job content, revisions in scheduling or overtime, or revisions in health and safety or pay and retirement policies usually involve discussion by both sides and often result in modifications and a formal agreement (Inagami, 1988, Table 6).

Employee involvement at the individual and small-group level on the shop floor is virtually universal in medium and large Japanese companies. These EI activities generally involve individual suggestion systems as well as QCs, each of which is highly structured and rewarded.

The cooperation between unions and management in Japan and the lifetime employment commitment have not eliminated a need for labor discipline mechanisms. Although workers rarely are discharged, they can be demoted or transferred to smaller companies at lower pay. The pressures of work in Japanese companies are well known. According to one 1987 survey in the Tokyo area, over one-fourth of male respondents reported experiencing mental stress because they had not met their work targets or had difficulties with their supervisors or colleagues (Asakura 1993).

Training in the United States and Japan

Training systems can be categorized according to whether they serve new workers who are entering the labor force for the first time (schooling and apprenticeships), incumbent workers who already hold jobs (firm-based training), or displaced workers who need new or expanded skills to obtain new jobs. This chapter addresses the case of firm-based training for incumbent workers who are employed in private-sector companies and who make up the largest part of the work force.

Types of Firm-based Training

Firm-based training is often characterized as formal or informal. In the United States, formal training means off-the-job training and informal training refers to on-the-job training (OJT), supervised either by co-workers or supervisors. In Japan, formal training refers to both off-the-job training and structured OJT, and the latter comprises by far the largest component of the Japanese training system. Structured OJT is training received by an employee on site in a specified manner using a designated trainer and materials along with a plan for certification. The training is usually done one-on-one until the employee is certified to do the job alone. In the United States, OJT is usually unstructured training received by an employee by doing a job without having a designated trainer and usually without materials or a plan for certification. The inexperienced employee is expected to ask co-workers if a problem or question arises.

Firm-based training imparts skills that are characterized by theorists (Gary S. Becker, 1964) as general and transferable (useful to other employers) or as specific and nontransferable (useful only to the current employer). Training constitutes an investment in human beings, and standard economic theory suggests that the one who receives the returns to the investment pay for the training. With regard to transferable skills, employees, rather than employers, would pay for such general skills since they are portable and the returns accrue to the holder of the skills. With regard to nontransferable skills, the incidence of training costs of specific skills depends upon bilateral negotiations between the employer and employee. The length of a worker's tenure with the firm affects the return on the investment, and both the employee and employer suffer a loss of investment if a long-tenure worker separates from the firm.[9]

In practice, some of the costs of OJT are borne not by the employer or employee but by co-workers or supervisors, and the differentiation between transferable and nontransferable skills is often unclear (Brown, 1990). Even so, free-rider problems can exist because a firm can pay for investments in training only to have competitors benefit if workers quit. Some analysts argue that the free-rider problem results in an underprovision of firm-based training relative to its social returns (Stern and Ritzen, 1991).

Underprovision of Formal Training?

Unflattering comparisons of the incidence and consequences of training in the United States relative to those in Japan and Europe support the view of underprovision in the United States. Lynch (1994), for example, argues that the Japanese practice of lifetime employment in a single company eliminates the free-rider problem for employers who provide skills training. By allowing a long period to recoup investments in skill development, Japanese employment security practices coupled with low quit rates increase the rewards to employer-provided training, in both transferable and nontransferable skills, and encourage its use. Mincer and Higuchi (1988) argue that the higher return to training and its greater incidence in Japan generate steeper age–productivity profiles and therefore steeper age–earnings profiles than is the case in the United States. However, while Mincer and Higuchi document the steeper age–pay profiles, they do not provide any evidence that Japanese employers actually do more training.

A particularly distressing finding concerns the distribution of formal training in the United States. Although most medium and large establishments offer formal training for their employees, these opportunities are highly concentrated among managers and professionals. Nonexempt workers frequently receive orientation and job safety training when they are first hired, but only a few receive skills training, especially after the first year of employment (Bishop, 1994). Only 4 percent of young non-college graduates in one survey received formal training of at least 4 weeks' duration (Lynch, 1992), and over half of all U.S. establishments did not provide any formal job skills training in 1993 (U.S. Department of Labor, 1994).

The Prevalence of Formal Training in the United States and Japan

To compare the levels of formal training in the two countries on a national scale, Norman Bowers has analyzed survey data from U.S. and Japanese working adults. The U.S. data are from the 1991 Current Population Survey Job Training Supplement, which asked workers about training they had needed to qualify for their current job and training they had received to improve skills since obtaining their current job (U.S. Department of Labor, 1992). The Japanese data are from the 1989 Survey of Vocational Training in Private Enterprises (available in Japanese only), which surveyed establishments with thirty or more regular employees and included questions for both the employers and employees. In a chapter of the 1993 OECD *Employment Outlook,* Bowers compared the percentage of U.S. employees who had received training through a formal company program to improve their skills since obtaining their current job with the percentage of Japanese employees who had received formal, off-the-job training since being hired by their current firm.[10] The percentages, disaggregated by size of establishment, are presented in Table 3.1.

The large difference between the percentages for the two countries could simply reflect a broader definition of training in the Japanese survey. This might occur if respondents included as training some of the worksite activities that U.S. respondents would consider part of the job. To control for this possibility, Bowers also computed the percentages of U.S. employees who received any kind of training to improve their skills since obtaining their current job—whether through a formal company program, informal OJT, courses at a school or university, corre-

TABLE 3.1. Percent of Workers Receiving Training by Establishment Size, United States and Japan

	U.S.		Japan
Establishment size	Formal	All	Formal
25–99	10.6	34.5	
30–99			59.5
100–499	13.2	41.9	75.5
500–999	18.4	47.7	83.6
1,000 or more	26.2	52.2	89.5

Source: OECD (1993a).

spondence courses, or other means. Even with this broader definition, U.S. workers in both large and small establishments are less likely to report that they received training.

In another paper, Norman Bowers (1993) used the same survey data to obtain the incidence of training by age and by amount of schooling. Table 3.2 compares the percentage of U.S. workers who had received formal company training to improve their skills since obtaining their current job to the percentage of Japanese workers who had participated in formal, off-the-job training since joining the present firm. The levels of U.S. participation in formal company training are lowest among young workers—the estimated rate here is close to Lynch's (1992) calcula-

TABLE 3.2. Percent of Workers Receiving Training by Age and Education, United States and Japan

	U.S.	Japan
Age		
16–19	2.8	
20–24	9.9	
Under 30		73.1
25–34	17.5	
35–44	20.9	
30–44		78.7
45–54	20.1	74.7
55 and older	13.8	66.5
Years of schooling		
Less than high school	5.2	67.7
High school only	12.7	70.1
Some postsecondary	20.4	68.9
Four or more years of college	25.0	85.0

Source: Norman Bowers (1993).

tion based on the National Longitudinal Survey of Youth Labor Market Experience—and among employees with the least schooling. In every category of age or education, however, more Japanese than Americans had some formal training since obtaining their present job.

Challenges to the Underprovision View

Other survey evidence challenges the market failure or underprovision view of employer-based training in the United States. For example, several of the findings from a 1994 Bureau of Labor Statistics employer survey appear to contradict the free-rider argument.[11] Losing trained workers to other employers was not a fear of the respondents in over half of all surveyed establishments and in over three-fourths of the large establishments (250 employees or more) that provided formal job skills training. These employers reported training in order to *retain* their valued employees, and they did not distinguish between transferable and nontransferable skills in their training programs. Conversely, of the 51.4 percent of establishments that did not provide any formal training programs, only 3.1 percent responded that they did not provide training because of "fear of losing newly-trained employees to other firms" (U.S. Department of Labor, 1994, p. 2). Among the subset of establishments with 50 or more employees, the figure was 1.6 percent.

Most studies look only at formal training. Since it is informal, OJT in the United States is difficult to measure. The 1983 and 1991 Current Population Survey Job Training Supplements did include a question on informal OJT since obtaining the present job. The proportion saying they had taken such training was 14 percent in 1983 and 15 percent in 1991 (U.S. Department of Labor, 1992, p. 33). On the other hand, a 1982 survey of employers for the Employment Opportunities Pilot Project discovered that, in the first three months (520 paid hours), the average new employee spent 11 hours in formal training, 47 hours watching others do the job, 51 hours in informal training by management, and 24 hours in informal training by co-workers. A 1992 survey of employers for the Small Business Administration used similar questions and found averages of 19, 41, 59, and 34 hours, respectively (Bishop, 1994, p. 6). These findings imply that newly hired workers spend about one-fourth of their paid time on informal training during the first three months of employment. The same surveys find the intensity of training diminishes after the initial period. Even so, and allowing for the possibility that employers may exaggerate the amount of training they provide, it appears that a good deal of informal and unstructured OJT goes undetected in surveys of U.S. workers.

Training in the United States

Institutionally oriented case studies have long documented the importance of informal on-the-job learning in skill acquisition among nonexempt workers (Doeringer and Piore, 1971). Recent surveys of U.S. employers and workers consistently report that OJT constitutes the most important means by which workers learn the skills needed for their jobs and that OJT appears to be the most cost-effective form of skill development (Bishop, 1994). Among the establishments surveyed by the Bureau of Labor statistics that do not provide formal skills training, two-thirds of the respondents and over 80 percent of small establishments (under 50 employees) reported that OJT is sufficient for their needs (U.S. Department of Labor, 1994). In another formal training survey, almost one-half of the 58 percent of employers who did not offer training reported they already had access to an adequate supply of skilled labor, including skills developed on the job (Price Waterhouse, 1994). On the-job training has been found to have a positive and significant effect on wages and to reduce voluntary turnover (Brown, 1990; Lillard and Tan, 1992; Lynch, 1991; Bartel, 1994). However, the positive effect of OJT may result from permanent individual effects, and OJT may not be portable from employer to employer (Lynch, 1992).

Employer surveys on the hours spent on training have found that the hours recent hires spend in OJT exceeds, by multiples of eight to twelve, the hours spent in formal training.[12] In a 1991 Bureau of Labor Statistics employee survey, 57 percent of workers reported needing training to qualify for their current job. The major sources of this training were school (32%), informal OJT (27%), and formal company training (12%). Of the 41 percent of workers who reported taking skill improvement training in 1990, two-fifths reported informal company training as a source (Eck, 1993). As can be seen, data on formal training alone substantially underestimates the total quantity of firm-based training in the United States.

Little research has been conducted on the efficiency of structured versus unstructured OJT. One study of three tasks in a large truck assembly plant found that structured OJT required only one-fifth of the mastery time required for unstructured OJT across all three tasks. On average, unstructured OJT ended up costing twice as much as structured OJT when both direct and indirect costs (supervisor's time and reduced output or quality) were included (Jacobs et al., 1992). A report to Congress recommended that U.S. companies pay more attention to OJT and train supervisors to be instructors, as in Japan, in order to lower training costs (U.S. Office of Technology Assessment, 1990). Yet many companies pay little attention to OJT, and few managers are trained to plan and execute OJT successfully (Sloman, 1989; Rothwell and Kazanis, 1994).[13]

Claims about inadequate U.S. training need to be recast to reflect not the quantity but the efficiency of the U.S. training system. To understand the weaknesses of U.S. firm-based training, we must shift the focus away from classroom training and toward OJT and examine how to make OJT more effective.

Training in Japan

Although Japanese employers provide formal training for most employees, they do not spend a great deal of money on it. A 1989 Ministry of Labor survey found that enterprise expenditures per employee on off-the-job training ranged from ¥19,000 in establishments employing 30–99 workers to ¥31,000 in establishments employing 1,000 or more, with an overall average expenditure of ¥24,000 per employee.[14] At ¥120 to the dollar (approximately the exchange rate in 1989), the average amount would be $200 per employee for that year; at ¥100 to the dollar (the exchange rate in 1996), the average is still only $240 per employee. Either figure is considerably less than the amount per employee spent on formal training by U.S. companies for which data were available in the late 1980s (Stern, 1992). In Stern's admittedly nonrepresentative U.S. sample, most of the average training expenditures ranged from approximately $400 to $1,300.

Japanese employers' spending on off-the-job training also looks low as a percentage of total payroll cost. The 1989 General Survey of Wages and Working Hours found that firms spent only 0.5 percent of their payroll on facilities, in-house instructors, and outside trainers to provide off-the-job training. Although there are no precise comparable figures available for the United States, the total training budget of U.S. companies is usually considered to be in the neighborhood of $50 billion (Stern, 1992; U.S. Office of Technology Assessment, 1990), which is on the order of 1 percent of total payroll, or double the Japanese proportion.

Is it possible to reconcile the high apparent rates of Japanese workers' participation in off-the-job training with the low apparent rate of expenditure on training by their employers? The most likely explanation, formulated by Koike, suggests that off-the-job training is provided in short, periodic sessions that punctuate ongoing training on the job. It is more efficient to intersperse off-the-job training throughout an employee's career than to provide it all at the beginning, when "it is doubtful that new employees who do not know the practical content of a job can fully understand this type of detailed training. On the contrary, a worker's capacity to understand Off-JT effectively is much expanded after several years of experience on the job. Short, periodic Off-JT affords a worker the opportunity to theorize or systematize job experience and to form intellectual skills" (Koike and Inoki, 1990, p. 13).

The underlying principle here is just-in-time learning. Generally, off-the-job training should be more efficient when it is interspersed throughout the employee's career because the experience of daily work in a given environment will engender questions in the employee's mind that would not have arisen before having had that experience. A short interlude of off-the-job training then provides an opportunity to address some of those questions. Since people are more apt to retain and use information that relates to their own questions, this method of training is more efficient than delivering the information in one large batch at the beginning. Just-in-time learning, like just-in-time inventory control, minimizes waste and depreciation caused by storage.

Several of the Japanese companies we studied gave us copies of a document, sometimes called a training road map, that describes sequences of on-the-job and off-the-job training for different categories of employees. Evidently, these companies do adhere to the theory of interspersing the two kinds of training. We did not obtain sufficient data to test whether in fact they optimize the sequence for each employee. Koike has expressed skepticism about how well the model is implemented in practice.[15] But whether they execute the idea well or badly, it does appear that large Japanese companies see off-the-job training as something that occurs in the context of OJT.

Dore and Sako (1989) present a similar view while noting that the high level of literacy in Japan increases workers' ability to teach and learn from each other. On the job, "a lot of learning is based on informal production of job specifications and procedure manuals meticulously written out by supervisors and used as teaching material for self-teaching by newcomers to the job. You do not just stand by Nelly; you read what Nelly has thoughtfully and meticulously written about what she knows. . . . This helps to explain why Japanese firms' training budgets seem rarely impressive" (p. 80).

The career ladder, which forms the backbone of an individual's experience in a SET firm, can thus be seen as a mechanism for economizing on skill formation. Results presented later in this chapter indicate that this model often does describe the work histories of our sample of Japanese employees. Koike and Inoki note, however, that, despite its relative efficiency,

> OJT is not cost-free; its costs are related to the rate of production inefficiency or output of defective products while the workers are still in training. This cost can be enormous if the job is extremely difficult, but there is a way to lessen such cost, even for the most difficult jobs: the worker is given experience on simpler, but related, tasks before going on to the more difficult job. Obviously this decreases the inefficiency caused by inexperience on the main job. Formation of a career ladder thus emerges, in which workers start with the easiest job, move on to a slightly more difficult one, and finally come to the most difficult jobs. This ladder exists where the different tasks are closely correlated in job content. A cluster of such closely correlated jobs tends to be collected in one workshop or, at most, in two or three workshops. These jobs form the content of the ordinary span of a production worker's career. (1990, pp. 10–11)

Case studies by Koike and others have demonstrated that OJT in large Japanese firms tends to be more carefully planned, deliberate, and structured than in U.S. firms, where it tends to be more casual and haphazard. In fact, we encountered some difficulty in our field work because we followed U.S. usage in referring to "informal, on-the-job training" as opposed to "formal" instruction off the job. Pilot testing of the Japanese translation of our questionnaires revealed that the concept of "informal" training did not exist!

In sum, structured OJT constitutes the main vehicle for skill formation in Japanese companies. On-the-job training can be more efficient than off-the-job training because it allows the trainee to be productive while learning occurs. On-the-job

training can be tailored to individual employees and their specific work environments and allows new information to be given at just the time and place where
workers can use it.

Training in Japanese Firms

In SET companies, training is organized and ongoing. We once asked Together
Manufacturing's training director (who was Japanese) how the company justified
a major investment in training during a period of slack demand when the plant
was operating at only 60 percent of capacity. The director replied, "Training is like
breathing." As long as the company is alive, training continues. We observed a similar approach in Japan at an electronics manufactuer's residential training center,
which had delivered more than 32,000 person-days of instruction the previous
year. The then-gathering business slowdown was expected to shift a large proportion of the company's training activity from the training center to the production
plants. Yet instead of reducing the center's staff of forty professionals, management
assigned their extra time to developing new courses. The commitment to long-
term employment means that slack periods are seen as opportunities for more
training and preparation for the next upturn in activity.

The close connection between ongoing work and training in Japan is illustrated
by responses to questionnaires completed by 45 employees in 4 companies that we
visited during the spring of 1992. Thirteen were men belonging to 2 groups of assemblers in an automobile plant; they had been with the company for an average
of about 20 years. Another 4 men worked for a telecommunications company, also
with average tenure of about 20 years. Ten were women from 2 groups of assemblers in an electronics company; they, too, had an average seniority of about 20
years. From the same plant were 3 work-process engineers, all male, who had been
with the company about 8 years. Fifteen respondents, including 3 women, came
from 2 work groups in a new semiconductor plant belonging to Hi-Tech's Japanese
subsidiary; on average, they had been with the company for about 4 years.

The full sample consisted of 32 men and 13 women, with an average tenure of
12.7 years, somewhat more than the Japanese average of 10.9 years (OECD, 1993a,
p. 121). The average age was 33 for both males and females in the sample. Only 5
had not completed high school; all of these were from the automobile plant. Twen-
ty-six had completed high school but no further education, 4 had completed a
higher technical school, 1 had finished junior college, and 8 had university degrees.
Six of the university graduates were members of an engineering group at the Hi-
Tech semiconductor plant.

Aside from their initial training, 32 respondents, or 71 percent, said they had tak-
en courses provided by the company. Among the 26 high school graduates, the percentage was 73, which is quite close to the 70 percent reported at the beginning of

TABLE 3.4. Japanese Training Profiles

Male, 29, automobiles, high school, 11 years' tenure. Level 3, grade 7. Current assignment: body assembly. Previous: spot welder, body assembly. Skills learned in company courses: robot operation, inspection, handling low-current electricity, arc welding, gas welding, multipurpose motorized press. Correspondence courses: handling oil and air pressure devices, drawing manufacturing diagrams with Japanese Industrial Standards. National tests: molding level II, gas welding. New skills learned on the job in past year: new model front body, operator work. Most recent written suggestion: preventing slackness/slippage in rear floor overhead transport.

Male, 46, automobiles, primary school, 18 years' tenure. Level 4. Current assignment: body assembly. Previous: two in spot welding, three in body assembly. Skills learned in company courses: robot operation, inspection, arc welding. Correspondence course: automobiles in general. New skills learned on the job in past year: new model electrical robot, new line equipment, improved metal hammering. Most recent written suggestion: maintain the "matt switch" during movement of the conveyor belt.

Male, 45, automobiles, primary school, 23 years' tenure. Level 4. Current assignment: administration of pressurized painting dispersal room. Previous: sealer filling, sales outlet, sealer filling, painting room administration. Skills learned in company courses: quality control, beginning level. National test: metal painting, level I. Most recent written suggestion: improvements in dilution methods.

Male, 43, automobiles, high school, 20 years' tenure. Level 4. Current assignment: administration of painting tool room. Previous: finish paint, service paint, mix paint, painting tools. Skills learned in company courses: way of thinking about and proceeding with improvements. Correspondence course: handling dangerous things. National tests: metal painting, handling dangerous things supervisor, handling dangerous things trainer. New skills learned on the job in past year: vinyl. Most recent written suggestion: machine for supply of paint materials.

Male, 38, automobiles, technical high school, 19 years' tenure. Level 5. Current assignment: direct quality improvements in paint and painting equipment. Previous: paint shop, painting equipment office. Skills learned in company courses: technical worker core course. Correspondence course: engineering of paint on metal. National tests: engineering of paint on metal, workplace training leader. New skills learned on the job in past year: personal computer, word processing. Most recent written suggestion: measure for replenishing paint supplies to a constant level.

Female, 39, electronics, high school, 18 years' tenure. Level N2. Current assignment: writing ID documents for cordless telephones. Previous: portable radio adjustment, radio/cassette player adjustment, compact disc player adjustment, assembly work, outside inspection and repair of personal computers. Skills learned in company courses: small group activities procedure and QC methods.

Male, 26, electronics, high school, 8 years' tenure. Level N5. Current assignment: analysis of work process. Previous: overseas planning section, manufacturing section. Skills learned in company courses: personal computer, basic programming course. Correspondence course: practical business. New skills learned on the job in past year: practical methods of using "systems."

Male, 24, semiconductors, technical high school, 4 years' tenure. Level N2. Current assignment: analysis of MCU breakdowns. Previous: analysis of LOGIC breakdowns. Skills learned in company courses: English conversation, communication with different cultures. Correspondence course: electrical circuits. New skills learned on the job in past year: log analyzer operation. Most recent written suggestion: improving efficiency through setting up analysis.

Female, 40, electronics, high school, 22 years tenure. Level N2. Current assignment: exchange of parts. Previous: calculator manufacture, car stereo manufacture, cordless telephone manufacture. Skills learned in company courses: small group study meeting.

Female, 40, electronics, high school, 22 years' tenure. Level N2. Current assignment: high temperature "aging" inspector. Previous: process work, extraction inspection, unpacking and packing for inspection, high temperature "aging" inspection, oscillation test. Skills learned in company courses: small group activities.

(continued)

TABLE 3.4. (*continued*)

Male, 45, telecommunications, high school, 26 years' tenure. Section chief. Current assignment: customer service. Previous: installation, maintenance of customers' in-house switching machines,
switching maintenance, equipment maintenance, switching board design, budgeting. Skills learned
in company courses: engineering ("hard" and "soft") to improve functioning of switching board,
methods of proceeding in Total Quality Control activities. Correspondence courses: basics of tran-
sistors, wiring (transmitting) engineering. National test: handling dangerous things. New skills
learned on the job in past year: nothing in particular.

Source: Workplace surveys conducted by the authors.
Note: Responses are translated with minor editing from the Japanese written on the questionnaires.

required for carrying out particular operations. Company skill tests were in operating heavy robots and spot welding, each with two levels. The national tests were
in body hammering and metal forming, also with two levels in each.

The third and largest section of the chart showed specific operations that were
performed in this work area. Each of the approximately twenty-five separate
columns referred to the welding machine or robot at a particular work station. Tasks
were classified as A, meaning most difficult, or B, meaning difficult. (Class C, least
difficult, tasks exist elsewhere in the factory but not in this work area.) For each operation, the top of the column contained two numbers, one indicating the desired
number of qualified people and the other the actual number. Each individual's level of mastery was shown by a circle divided into quadrants, denoting 25, 50, 75, or
100 percent mastery. Circles were outlined in green for individuals who were scheduled to learn that particular operation in the current twelve-month period. This part
of the chart thus displayed not only skill status but also training plans.

Each worker's OJT plan was summarized in the fourth section of the chart,
which showed a time line for each person. The twelve months were marked off hor-
izontally, and a small arrow, typically three months long, indicated when the worker was scheduled to learn a particular operation, the name of which was written
above the arrow. At a glance, this section showed how the training plans for the
group all fit together.

These training plans and arrangements pertain to ordinary production workers.
Structured training in the United States, in contrast, most often occurs through apprenticeship and has traditionally been limited to skilled craft workers. It is offered
only to a small minority of production workers who are often described as "unskilled" or "semiskilled." In Japan, employers usually do not make such a distinction between craft workers and other blue-collar employees.

Training in U.S. Firms

These arrangements offer a distinct contrast with standard practices in the United
States. In most U.S. companies, which do not adhere to the SET model, on-the-job

training—indeed, training in general—does not usually have this structured, cumulative quality. In part, the lack of structure reflects the shorter average tenure of workers in the United States compared to that of workers in Japan. If employees are not expected to stay with the firm for a long time, there is less reason to make long-term training plans.[18] Moreover, most U.S. firms allow existing employees to apply for open positions within the company. In unionized companies, procedures for posting job openings, and employees' bidding rights, are often spelled out in collective-bargaining contracts. These practices give managers less control over workers' job assignments than in Japan, where workers may be asked periodically if they would like to move to a different section but managers decide where employees will be assigned. Therefore, in addition to knowing that employees will probably stay with the firm for a long time, Japanese managers also know that they can control workers' progression from one job to another. This control allows managers to arrange that individual employees will accumulate knowledge and skill through a coherent sequence of job assignments.

Despite the difficulties and disincentives of training, some U.S. firms do sponsor a substantial amount. One national survey of establishments discovered a bimodal distribution of training activity (Osterman, 1995). Although 63 percent of establishments reported that they provided formal, off-the-job training for less than one-fourth of their "core employees" (the modal group of nonsupervisory workers in each establishment), 19 percent reported providing such training to all their core employees. Osterman also found that provision of training was positively associated with employee involvement in total quality management, quality circles, and statistical process control.

United States companies that do promote training and EI have found creative ways to systematize on-the-job learning despite the relative lack of employment stability. During the 1988 downturn at Together Manufacturing, production workers were enlisted to design and teach courses for their colleagues, thus spreading the work of trainers, economizing on training cost, and providing instructors who were intimately familiar with the work problems facing the trainees.

Short-term job rotation represents another approach. At Together Manufacturing, for example, workers on many teams rotated among different jobs within the same working day. This pattern differs from the usual Japanese approach to job rotation, in which workers are assigned to new jobs once or twice a year. In addition to representing an adaptation to the risk of higher turnover in the United States, more frequent rotation can also be beneficial for ergonomic reasons—to prevent bodily harm due to repetitive motion. Also, despite management's efforts to balance jobs carefully, some tasks may still be less desirable than others, so job rotation is considered more fair.

Cross-training by co-workers within teams is another way to embed continuous training in the work process. We observed this approach at both Together Manufacturing and an insurance company, which we call Valley Life. Cross-training within teams can occur during slack time or downtime and thus minimize interference with the work process. Instruction can be given at just the time and place where it is needed, and it does not require that any member remain on the team for a long time. In fact, cross-training can be seen as an adaptation to worker mobility because it ensures that no individual is indispensable.

In Japanese fashion, the results of cross-training at Together Manufacturing have been displayed in skill charts showing workers' names and the extent of their mastery of each of the team's tasks. The extent of mastery was denoted by a circle divided into four quadrants corresponding to four levels of knowledge: knowing what the task is, knowing how to do it with supervision, knowing how to do it without supervision, and knowing how to teach it to someone else.

At Valley Life, cross-training was necessary because of the way teams were formed. A new customer service unit was created from three formerly separate groups, each of which had been responsible for one of three tasks: setting up accounts for new purchasers of insurance policies, making changes to existing policies, and computing premiums and taxes. In the new configuration, each group performed all of these functions for policyholders in a single geographic region. Every team included at least one member from each of the three previous, specialized groups. Cross-training ensured a fair division of labor within each team and prevented the team from being incapacitated by the absence or departure of one person.

Valley Life did not have skill charts on display, but it had instituted a pay-for-learning system to provide a material incentive for cross-training. The entire set of tasks to be performed by the team was specified in a written document, which also showed the pay increment for learning each task. A worker who learned the whole set of tasks would be paid approximately twice as much as one who knew none of them. Workers could learn new skills on the job by trial and error, reading operations manuals, learning from a co-worker, or consulting supervisors. Interviews with team members indicated that learning from each other was the preferred method.

Hi-Tech was also introducing skill-based pay in some of its U.S. factories but in a less far-reaching form than at Valley Life. There were only a few skills for which employees could earn more pay, and the pay increments were small. Osterman (1994, p. 185) found that 30 percent of the establishments in his national survey had implemented skill-based pay to some extent and that establishments that had adopted at least one of four innovative work practices (teams, job rotation, total quality management, or quality circles) were significantly more likely also to have implemented skill-based pay.

Another approach to just-in-time learning was observed at Hi-Tech in the early stages of implementation. Certain experienced workers were formally designated as trainers for others, not necessarily on the same work team. This is a variation on training by co-workers, modeled after the role of "Meister" in German work places. Finally, a practice observed at both Hi-Tech and Together Manufacturing had the effect of reducing the net cost of off-the-job training. The idea was simply to use

classroom instruction to generate possible solutions to real problems in the production process. For example, in a class on the concept of cycle time, production
workers developed concrete suggestions for reducing actual cycle time in their own
operations. Some of these proposals could be readily implemented. Similar results
were obtained from classes on quality control, continuous improvement, and
problem solving. If OJT involves learning by doing, the analysis of real work problems in off-the-job training can be called "doing by learning" (Stern, 1992). It
achieves just-in-time learning by making the classroom an extension of the work
process.

How EI and Training Enhance Employment Security

These accounts of EI and training in Japan and the United States indicate how they
may reinforce the SET practice of employment security. The broadening and deepening of skills and knowledge achieved by on-the-job and off-the-job learning
work to protect employment security by enhancing the firm's performance. Skill
broadening makes workers more interchangeable. If one worker becomes sick or
goes on vacation or retires, another can fill in. Or if one work group faces unusu-
ally heavy demands, individuals can be dispatched from other groups to assist. Skill
deepening enables employees to handle more nonroutine problems, as Koike and
Inoki (1990) have emphasized. Nonroutine problems arise from product change-
overs, introduction of new products, introduction of new machines or procedures,
and breakdowns of existing machines and procedures. Failure to solve any of these
problems results in downtime, delays, lower productivity, more defective products,
and possibly loss of customers, whereas EI and training that equip the employees
to deal with these difficulties promote employment security directly.

Although we have emphasized OJT and EI because these seem to constitute the
major activities aimed at upgrading employees' knowledge and skill in SET companies, we also note that these firms do not neglect off-the-job training. Hi-Tech,
Together Manufacturing, and every large Japanese firm we studied maintained formal training departments that offer necessary technical courses, as well as orientation for new employees and courses for people being promoted. One company requires that all of its employees spend at least forty hours a year in formal training
to keep their knowledge and skill up to date.

Some courses aim to strengthen EI. Most directly, company courses in quality
improvement, problem solving, group process, and communications are designed
to increase employees' capacity to participate in improving quality and efficiency.
In both Japan and the United States, SET companies provide such courses. Masahito Hashimoto (1990) has given particular emphasis to the importance of these and
other means of improving communications among workers and between workers
and managers, thus reducing "transactions costs" in Japanese firms.

A fundamental distinction can be made between two kinds of learning: assimilation of existing knowledge and production of new ideas. The former is contained in the usual concept of training. The latter becomes increasingly important as competition between firms increasingly depends upon faster introduction of new products and methods of production. In higher positions, the scope of new ideas extends to matters of longer-term strategy for the company. Yet an essential feature of SET firms is that all employees are engaged in producing new ideas on some scale. The writing of suggestions by production workers has been described in this chapter.[19] Employees with broader and deeper knowledge and skill are more likely to contribute valuable suggestions for improving procedures and products. The profiles of Japanese workers sketched above give an idea of how their suggestions grow out of their experience and training. By contributing to EI in continuous improvement of day-to-day operations and in promotion of longer-term change, training helps keep the company competitive and thus contributes indirectly to employment security.

Training enhances EI—and, indirectly, employment security—by keeping employees' minds engaged in their work. Job rotation, deliberate exposure to new problems, instruction on the job, and occasional courses that deal with work issues all provide stimulus for thought. Once the mind is engaged, it may keep working even when the person is not at the work place. One indicator of this pattern is visible in our Japanese sample—over 60 percent indicated that they "sometimes" think about ideas for improving quality or efficiency at work when they are not at work and not in a QC meeting, and over 10 percent stated they did this "often." Another 10 percent said "rarely" and only 16 percent said "never." Put more concretely, half indicated that they had written at least one suggestion in the previous month when they were not at work and not in a QC meeting; one-third of these had written three or more. Thinking about work when they are not there suggests that these workers are also using their minds on the job. Training enhances this intellectual involvement.

The effect of training upon deepening intellectual involvement was observed in the United States at Valley Life. The necessity for cross-training within customer service teams, and the incentive of pay-for-learning, focused conversation during slack periods onto work-related issues. When the telephones were not ringing or other tasks were not pressing, team members were free to talk, and instead of chatting about personal matters they could often be heard to be talking about work. Some of this exchange was direct instruction, as one team member would ask another how to do something. But some of the talk led to telling stories about interesting or puzzling episodes. These usually involved subtle or complicated situations that went beyond the cut-and-dried descriptions in the procedural manual or the pay-for-learning curriculum. The exchange of these anecdotes produced a sophisticated understanding embodied in an oral tradition that belonged to the team.

This kind of interchange, sparked by the training structure, seemed to enhance intrinsic motivation and effectiveness.

How the Japanese Compensation and Appraisal Systems Stimulate EI and Training

Just as EI and training support employment security, they can also be supported in turn by the compensation system. In the United States, where blue-collar workers are paid nearly as much when they are young as when they are middle-aged (see the following chapter), any reduction in young workers' productivity while they are being trained represents a cost to the employer. Studies that have measured U.S. training activity directly also found that employers bear most or all of the cost (Stern and Ritzen, 1991; Bishop, 1994). Pay for blue-collar workers in Japan, by contrast, rises more steeply with age. Therefore, the cost of initial training appears to be paid at least in part by employees, who collect the return on their investment in the form of higher wages later. Since employers in Japan are not paying the full cost, they can provide more training.

Employees in Japan are also stimulated to engage in EI and training, because their pay is immediately linked to performance as appraised by their supervisors, and good performance includes continuous learning. Dore and Sako (1989) note that workers' willingness to keep learning stems not only from their commitment to the firm's success but also from their desire to earn a good rating from their supervisors. Koike (1994) argues that the Japanese system for compensation and performance appraisal is particularly well suited to broadening and deepening employees' knowledge and skill. In this system, an individual's pay does not depend on the particular job being performed during the pay period, in contrast to the situation in the United States (and Europe), where compensation depends mainly on the job assignment. Instead, as the next chapter explains more fully, monthly base pay is awarded according to age and job grade, the latter being determined by seniority and the cumulative effect of frequent performance appraisals.

Each employee's share in the company's annual bonus payment also depends in part on performance ratings. Koike points out that this system is more conducive to developing employees' capacities than either job-based pay or payment by result, neither of which provides any incentive to pass along skills and knowledge to other workers. Both job-based pay and payment by result also inhibit skill broadening, which requires rotation through different jobs.

Our sample of Japanese workers indicates this system's effectiveness in motivating acquisition of new knowledge and skill. We asked workers which factors influenced their performance appraisal rating; their replies are presented in Table 3.5. The factor considered most important by the largest number of respondents was

TABLE 3.5. Japanese Workers' Perceptions of Appraisal Determinants

	Not at All Important	Slightly Important	Very Important	Most Important
Suggestions you submit	3	16	7	6
Your level of knowledge and skill	0	6	18	8
Your willingness to acquire new knowledge and skill	0	2	15	15
Your willingness to teach others	2	10	13	6
Your cooperation with supervisors	0	7	14	11
How hard you work	0	4	20	7
Your creativity and initiative in solving problems	0	10	14	6

Source: Workplace surveys conducted by the authors (N = 42).

Note: The table shows the number of individuals who gave each response. Ten respondents did not answer this question, four of these because the question inadvertently was omitted from their questionnaire. The three university graduates were excluded.

the willingness to acquire new knowledge and skill. If "most" and "very important" ratings are combined, this factor also attracted the most votes. Next in perceived importance were the level of knowledge and skill, cooperation with supervisors, and how hard the respondent works. As a group, the respondents regarded these three factors as roughly equal in weight, depending on whether one looks at "most" important ratings or "most" and "very" combined. The thirty-five individuals who responded to this question view the performance appraisal system as strongly rewarding their willingness to acquire new knowledge and skill and, to a somewhat lesser extent, their existing level of (old) knowledge and skill. Knowing is good, but learning is even better.[20]

Some Policy Implications

Employee involvement and training are more highly developed in SET firms. When employees stay with a firm for a long time and participate extensively in problem solving, EI and training are essential for both the transmission of existing know-how and the creation of new ideas. Moreover, on-the-job learning is also more extensive and systematic in SET companies, which have applied the just-in-time principle to the acquisition of knowledge and skill. In Japan, where SET is more extensively practiced, a greater proportion of employees participates in company courses than in the United States. Most important, both EI and OJT are planned, structured, and documented. The integration of training into the work process makes training more effective and reduces its cost in terms of reduced production. The cost of training may also be more affordable for Japanese employers because steeper age–earnings profiles suggest that workers pay for some of their own training when they are young.

Although this chapter describes EI and training in Japanese firms as generally superior to practice in the United States, there is room for improvement. We have noted Koike's observation that the coordination of off-the-job and on-the-job training is not optimal. Pressures for change are also growing with the aging of Japan's work force, the growing proportion of college graduates, and rapid automation.

Still, U.S. employers appear to lag behind their Japanese counterparts in both off-the-job and on-the-job training. The number of U.S. employees who said they had participated in a formal company training program to improve their skills rose from 11 percent in 1983 to 16 percent in 1991 (U.S. Department of Labor, 1992, p. 33), indicating that the gap in off-the-job training may be narrowing a little. But OJT remains more difficult to organize systematically in the United States than in Japan. Workers in the United States on average do not stay with the same employer as long as the Japanese do, and U.S. managers also have less control over the assignment of workers to jobs within the firm. Consequently, it is seldom possible for U.S. employers to arrange the kind of long-term career ladders that have been central to skill development in Japanese companies.

While the practice of EI and training is more advanced in Japan, a number of U.S. firms have implemented cross-training, skill-based pay, short-term job rotation, and mentoring in company courses. These practices tend to be adopted by firms that seek to take better advantage of workers' minds and involve them more in problem solving. Like the systematic Japanese approach to OJT, these U.S. practices inject continuous learning into the work process. But unlike Japanese career ladders, the U.S. approach does not require employees to stay with the same company for decades. This could signal a version of the SET model that does not depend on long-term employment security within the firm. At the same time, it provides constant upgrading of knowledge and skill for the substantial minority of workers who do in fact spend most of their careers with a single employer.

The development of more and better skill formation for the U.S. work force must reconcile two conflicting considerations. First, the best place to acquire much work-related knowledge and skill is in the process of work itself. Second, while some U.S. employees spend a long time in the same work place, movement from one employer to another is frequent and widespread. The problem, then, is how mobile workers can capitalize on their experience. Recent policy initiatives have addressed this issue by promoting the establishment of skill certification procedures and standards for industries or occupations. By 1993, the U.S. Departments of Labor and Education had contracted with associations to write twenty-two new sets of certification procedures and standards (for example, see American Electronics Association, 1994). The Goals 2000: Educate America Act authorized a new National Skill Standards Board to coordinate such efforts. The main intent was to increase the portability of knowledge and skill acquired on the job, thereby encouraging greater investment in their acquisition. New skill credentials might also help to justify a steeper rise in earnings with experience for workers who remain with their employers, which could also stimulate greater investment in training for young employees.

While the development of new skill credentials is based on the recognition of widespread worker mobility in the United States, government action can also do more to promote training while at the same time preventing unwanted separations of workers from their employers. We have argued in Chapter 2 that employment security within the firm stimulates training directly as well as indirectly through greater employee involvement in problem solving. One particularly strategic public policy would therefore be to subsidize training for employees during business downturns so that firms can better afford to retain some valued employees who would otherwise be laid off. As described in Chapter 2, the Japanese government has provided such subsidies since the 1970s. In the United States, a number of state governments have created agencies to support training by and for firms, and some of this aid has been used to prevent layoffs. For example, a $5 million training grant from the state to Together Manufacturing helped avoid layoffs when the company was operating at 60 percent of capacity for several months due to slack demand. This example illustrates how targeted public support for training can enable companies to maintain all three mutually reinforcing elements of SET.

Summary: Employee Involvement and Training in the SET Model

Employee involvement and worker training constitute interrelated elements of the SET model. We have argued in this chapter that SET firms involve workers more actively in the daily tasks and decisions of the work place and that better workplace-based training facilitates this form of work organization. Firms modeled on SET structure each of these elements carefully and integrate them closely into the company's HR system.

Firms structured on the SET model find ways to build continual learning into the work process itself. This "just-in-time learning" appears to be more efficient than off-the-job training. Unlike JAM firms, in which EI and OJT each tend to be unplanned, voluntary, and haphazard, SET firms create deliberate structures to recognize and support learning in the work process. These learning structures enhance the firm's productivity and flexibility by transmitting knowledge and skill efficiently from those who have them to those who need them. Because they are closely connected to the EI structures, these learning arrangements also stimulate a continuous flow of new ideas for improving the company's products, services, costs, and operating methods.

United States companies that have adopted the SET model, or are trying to adopt it, have developed practices that promote just-in-time learning but do not rely on long-term career ladders. These practices include short-term job rotation, cross-training by co-workers within teams, designation of certain workers as mentors for others, awarding extra pay to employees who demonstrate greater knowledge of work tasks, and using off-the-job training to solve actual problems arising from the work itself. Although it has become conventional wisdom to argue that such programs enhance company performance (Ichniowski et al., 1996), we find that such practices must be organized in a coherent ensemble in order to be successful.

NOTES

1. Levine and Tyson (1990), writing on the link between participation and productivity, represent an influential argument along these lines. It is worth noting that some economic theories (for example, Shapiro and Stiglitz, 1984) expect employment security to result in more shirking rather than more effort.

2. Influential statements along these lines by economists are Mincer and Higuchi (1988) and Lynch (1994). A contrary position is put forward by Heckman (1994).

3. This distinction is captured formally in the British Workplace Industrial Relations Surveys, which ask explicitly about the vertical direction of communication and decision making. See McNabb and Whitfield (1995).

4. For a sample of studies, see Levine and Kruse (1991); Lawler et al. (1992); Cooke (1994); Osterman (1994); Frazis et al. (1995); and Lynch and Black (1995). Osterman's survey of establishments with fifty employees or more found that about three-eighths were using multiple forms of EI. A 1993 survey by the Bureau of Labor Statistics of establishments with five employees or more obtained much lower figures, mainly in the 5–10 percent range (Frazis et al., 1995).

5. Lawler et al. (1995) surveyed the largest Fortune manufacturing and service companies in 1987, 1990, and 1993, but all of their respondents were at the corporate level, and they experienced a large attrition rate from one survey to the next.

6. Brown and Reich (1989); Brown, Reich, and Stern (1993). For an interesting British study, see McNabb and Whitfield (1995).

7. Voices in this chorus include Kruse (1993); MacDuffie and Kochan (1995); and Mc-Nabb and Whitfield (1995). Kruse argues that worker participation can be successful only when it is linked with profit sharing in pay, while MacDuffie and Kochan refer to the complementarities between technological change and organizational change.

8. Inagami (1988). See also Gould (1984, pp. 95).

9. Numerous empirical studies have found that firm-provided employee training is associated with higher pay (for a survey, see Bishop, 1994). A very small number of studies have direct evidence of the impact of training on productivity (Bartel, 1994; Baker and Lynch, 1996). Even their findings remain only suggestive since they confront difficult econometric issues involving who is chosen for training (selectivity biases) and the direction of causation between individual productivity and the receipt of training (simultaneity biases).

10. The U.S. survey asked workers about training since they had started their the current *job*, but the Japanese survey asked workers about training since they had joined their cur-

rent *firm*. In common U.S. speech, the phrase "since you obtained your present job" could be construed to mean "since you obtained a job with your present employer." In the U.S. survey, the training questions were preceded by a question asking how long the respondent had been working continuously for the present employer, and the survey instructions did not distinguish between the two concepts.

If the wording difference between the U.S. and Japanese surveys is important, the effect should be most pronounced among employees with the longest tenures at a firm. However, Table 4.8 in the 1993 OECD *Employment Outlook* indicates otherwise. Among workers who had been with the same employer for no more than five years, the Japanese percentage reporting formal training by the firm exceeds the U.S. percentage by 63 points. Among those with six to nine years' tenure, the difference falls to 52 points, and the difference remains at the same level in the ten-to-fourteen year group, suggesting that U.S. respondents construed "since you obtained your present job" to mean "since you obtained a job with your present employer."

11. The BLS's Survey of Employer-Provided Training (SEPT) sampled more than 58,400 private establishments with five or more employees and obtained a response rate of 71 percent, making it the largest and most representative survey of establishments in the training literature.

12. Holzer (1990); Bishop (1994); Carnevale and Gainer (1989); Black et al. (1993).

13. Based upon their management consulting work with numerous companies, Rothwell and Kazanis (1994) have developed off-the-shelf tools for companies to structure OJT.

14. The Survey of Vocational Training in Private Enterprises, conducted by the Human Resource Development Bureau of the Ministry of Labor, sampled 12,000 workers in 4,000 private firm units hiring 30 regular workers or more. The survey covers construction, manufacturing, transportation and communication, wholesale and retail sales, food, finance and insurance, real estate, and services.

15. "One of the defects of contemporary Japanese training systems is that these short, inserted Off-JT courses are not sufficiently arranged" (Koike, 1994).

16. Dore and Sako (1989) describe in detail the range of correspondence courses given in Japan.

17. An exception is number 3, who was sent to a sales office at one time, probably during a slack period.

18. Human capital theory implies that more training also leads to lower turnover by making wages increase with tenure in the firm and therefore creating a disincentive for senior workers to leave or for the firm to lay them off. Numerous studies have demonstrated that training does increase wages (see Stern, 1992). Mincer and Higuchi (1988) found that separations of individuals from their employers are less likely in industries where average wages increase faster with tenure.

19. Four employees in our Japanese sample, including three high school graduates, stated that they had worked on pilot teams to help design or develop new products.

20. The Japanese compensation and appraisal system also supports learning by requiring applicants for promotion to supervisory and managerial positions to write an essay on some problem facing the company. Sometimes running to forty or fifty pages, these essays demonstrate the applicant's ability to contribute important new ideas.

4

Pay Systems, Career Paths, and Earnings Inequality

Introduction

Compensation systems and wage structures, which provide incentives and construct income differences among workers, constitute essential elements of any employment system and economy. If they are to function well, pay systems must be coherently integrated with the other elements of the employment system. In this chapter, we examine the structures of compensation in the United States and Japan and their relation to the broader institutional structure of each country's employment system. Our discussion of pay systems in the two countries begins with the stylized facts that motivate our analysis.

Stylized Facts

Six stylized facts that characterize economic outcomes in each country provide the starting point for this chapter. Each fact summarizes an important aspect of the level and distribution of earnings in Japan and the United States. We present these facts briefly and then return to discuss them in more detail later in the chapter.

The first stylized fact concerns the much faster growth of real wages and productivity in Japan than in the United States. When one makes this comparison, it is instructive to review both the long-term trends and the figures for more recent years. From 1970 to 1990, real wages in Japan rose 71 percent but increased only

7 percent in the United States. Over the same period, worker productivity rose 211 percent in Japan and only 23 percent in the United States.[1]

The more rapid growth of living standards and productivity of Japanese workers has continued. In the six years from 1985 to 1991, real earnings in Japan rose 11.2 percent while the comparable figure for the United States was 1.8 percent. During these same six years, worker productivity rose 35 percent in Japan, compared to only 4.8 percent in the United States.[2]

The second stylized fact concerns inequality levels in the two countries. The overall level of earnings inequality among all workers is much smaller in Japan than in the United States. Earnings inequality among white male workers in the United States is greater than among *all* workers in Japan (Green et al., 1992). This second fact indicates that the product of economic growth has been distributed more widely in Japan than in the United States.[3] Together, the first and second stylized facts challenge a common view that reducing inequality is incompatible with increasing economic growth.

The remaining stylized facts concern major dimensions of inequality: the role of education, age, employer size, and gender in earnings. The third stylized fact summarizes earnings ratios for groups by schooling levels. The relative pay rates of different educational groups are much more equal in Japan than in the United States. This fact could be interpreted as indicating a weaker incentive to accumulate human capital in Japan, but it is also consistent with Japan's lower level of overall inequality.

The fourth stylized fact states that age–earnings ratios (i.e., the relative pay of different age groups) are more unequal in Japan than in the United States. Two workers with similar education but of different age or seniority will be paid quite differently in Japan and relatively similarly in the United States. Later we will show that two workers doing similar work in the same company but of different ages will be paid quite differently. The greater importance of seniority as a determinant of pay in Japan makes the lower overall inequality in Japan all the more remarkable.

The fifth stylized fact concerns the role of employer size in pay differences. Japan is considered by many to have a sharply dualized labor market in which small employers, such as retailers or parts suppliers in the manufacturing sector, pay very low wages relative to large manufacturing exporters. Company size does play a major role in Japan's labor market structure. While the U.S. labor market is also segmented by company size, the effect of size on pay is greater in Japan.

The sixth stylized fact states that gender pay differentials are greater in Japan than in the United States. In the postwar era up to the mid-1970s, gender pay differences were narrowing in Japan while remaining unchanged in the United States. By 1975, female–male pay ratios for full-time workers stood at 56 percent in Japan and 59 percent in the United States. In the early 1980s, gender pay differences in the United States began to diminish while Japanese gender pay differences began to increase. The growing contrast between U.S. and Japanese gender inequality suggests that gender patterns do not correlate with the different inequality and growth experiences of the two economies.

The Argument of the Chapter

In this chapter, we argue that these six stylized facts are enduring, are not in contradiction with one another, and result from the historically contingent and specific institutions of each country rather than from general economic tendencies that apply to all advanced economies. The labor market institutions that generate lower inequality in Japan are those that also generate more rapid economic growth. In particular, incentives for employers to train and involve their workers in the production process over a long time period, and incentives for workers to work hard and to improve their skills and knowledge over their careers, are greater in Japan than in the United States.

Regular workers in large and medium-sized companies in Japan experience increased earnings as they age and gain experience with seniority. They constitute a primary labor market segment. As we shall see, the career pattern is weaker and pay is lower in the secondary labor market segment, which comprises small companies, part-time and temporary workers, and family businesses. Yet the employment and training institutions in Japan do generate continuous productivity and earnings growth among a broader proportion of workers and over longer proportions of their careers than is the case in the United States. As a result, Japanese institutions generate higher economic growth with less earnings inequality among its work force.

We discuss first the U.S. and Japanese institutions that govern the relation among pay, experience, and skills. We then analyze career paths in each country, using company-level, industry-level, and national data sets. Finally, we discuss the relation between inequality and growth and then review the evidence on intercountry inequality differences.

Pay Systems

A well-structured compensation system provides rewards that simultaneously motivate effort and productivity growth over time and satisfy norms of fairness. Effort and productivity growth can be motivated by career-structured incentives, structured fairness and reciprocity between employer and workers, or a combination of these two. When one compares the United States and Japan, it is important to examine differences in the concept and practice of fairness, the role of individual appraisals, and the relation of individual workers to the groups to which they belong. We shall suggest that while career incentives and concepts of fairness are seen as competitive with each other in the United States, they are seen as complementary in Japan.

Fairness and Individual Appraisals

Fairness is enhanced when rewards are connected to performance in a uniform manner for all individuals. Insofar as pay or promotion are connected to evaluations, fairness requires that supervisor ratings of employees are done carefully, without favoritism or gross differences between supervisors in ratings criteria.

In our field interviews, perceived unfairness and favoritism by supervisors constituted one of the most frequent complaints of U.S. workers, at levels far exceeding those voiced among Japanese workers. These differentials are partly cultural in origin, in the sense that social norms make U.S. workers feel more entitled to voice complaints about fairness than is the case among Japanese workers. But they are also structural in that worker evaluations are conducted much more carefully in Japan, and most frontline supervisors as well as many lower-level managers are recruited from the ranks of production workers. The personnel department plays a much more active role in a Japanese company than in an American company, especially in setting up and overseeing the evaluation process, job assignments, and promotions. Cultural norms in Japan do allow individual workers to informally voice their problems and grievances to their supervisors during after-hours socializing.

The U.S. approach to fairness varies between blue-collar and white-collar occupations. Blue collar fairness is more associated with equal outcomes in pay; white-collar fairness is more associated with equal opportunities, while merit appraisals form a much more important determinant of pay. Fairness is also enhanced when pay differences among jobs are related to widely accepted social norms. The differentials that are most often recognized as legitimate by both workers and management involve differences in skill or training, responsibility, effort, working conditions, and schedules. In Japan, seniority also provides a legitimate source of pay differentials for the same job as well as for promotions, while in the United States seniority is viewed as a legitimate source of pay differentials only for promotion.

An interesting question concerns the elasticity of effort with respect to pay in each country. Some Japanese academics suggested to us that small monetary incentives will generate rather large increases in motivation and effort because of more conformist social norms in Japan, the greater dependence of Japanese families upon a single earner's pay check, and the lower inequality in income among families. This suggestion seems plausible and would explain the coexistence in Japan of less inequality and greater growth. It has not, however, been the subject of any direct empirical tests.

Team Elements of Compensation

The compensation system can include both individual and group elements. The group elements can take the form of team-based or company-based elements of compensation (gain sharing and profit sharing). As we present below, the pay rates of team members are more compressed in the United States than in Japan, where individual earnings include components for performance as well as seniority. The U.S. and Japanese patterns conform to the "pay politics" model of Lazear (1989), in which pay is more compressed for highly opportunistic workers in order to reduce rewards to noncooperative behavior among workers and to elicit cooperation in teamwork. However, the assumption made by Lazear that performance pay is based on individual outcomes is not observed in Japan, where individual performance appraisal includes an evaluation of the worker's contributions to the team and to co-workers. In this way, performance-based pay, individual effort, and team effort are made compatible and reinforcing.

In the United States, teamwork seems to require pay compression in order to counterbalance employee suspicions about management conducting fair appraisals. However, flat pay schedules resulted in our hearing complaints at one plant that some teams ("the slugs") did not work enough. In Japan, where the appraisal system is seen as more objective and where free riding is discouraged (in part by long-term employment relations), the individual incentives encourage rather than discourage cooperation.

Pay Systems in Large U.S. Companies

JAM Pay Systems

Although most personnel managers claim to base their pay systems upon individual performance, in most large companies appraisals for nonmanagerial or non-professional workers are not important. In unionized companies, individual appraisals are infrequent, are often only cursorily performed, and usually focus only on whether each worker is meeting minimum production and attendance standards. Seniority is more important than merit for pay increases, and pay increments are relatively small. In nonunionized companies, individual appraisals play a larger role in determining pay increases, although they do so less often than personnel managers claim, and again with small differentials (Mills, 1984).

Appraisal systems are limited by the difficulty of measuring individual contributions objectively. Managers typically rely upon individual supervisors to make subjective judgments about each worker, leading often to excess leniency, low reliability, charges of favoritism, or feelings of resentment (with self-appraisals generally higher). Although such problems can be reduced by careful training of supervisors, special training to conduct appraisals is not very common.

Managers and professionals have a more performance-oriented pay system. Evaluations are more frequent, more formal, and affect promotion and pay increases. In many companies, some younger managers may be able to advance rapidly, and it is not uncommon for lower-level managers to be supervised by much younger and less experienced fast-trackers.

Pay systems in JAM companies have evolved very little in the past fifty years. In the early postwar period, personnel practices moved away from individual appraisals and toward attaching pay to the job, using formal job evaluation techniques, rather than to the worker.[4] In the late 1970s and early 1980s, the importance of job evaluations continued to grow, as they were a central issue in the comparable-worth or pay-equity controversies. Profit sharing and other gain-sharing plans were widely touted in the 1980s and have grown in some companies. But, as we present below, the proportion of current pay that is based upon such variable elements remains extremely small, averaging under 5 percent.

SET Pay Systems

According to our model, pay systems in SET companies should support each of the components of SET. A pay system that rewards longer tenure with the firm supports the practice of employment security by inducing workers to stay and by encouraging management to train workers as they gain experience and move up the pay tables. A pay system that rewards acquisition of knowledge and skills motivates employees to acquire additional training and to be involved in work tasks using their skills. A pay system that rewards individual performance encourages employees to be active in workplace improvements and induces managers to develop efficient and equitable appraisal systems. These considerations suggest that an ideal SET compensation system would contain all three of these pay elements. Nonetheless, the pay systems at the SET companies in the United States generally do not incorporate all three elements, and at many companies pay continues to be structured in a traditional manner.

The example of Together Manufacturing illustrates this gap between the organization of work and the pay system. At Together Manufacturing, new production hires receive pay increments for each of three years until reaching the standard rate, which does not vary with experience. Vacation days increase with tenure, which is not the practice in Japanese companies, and seniority plays a role in the selection of team leaders. Nonetheless, the age–pay relationship is flatter at Together Manufacturing than at traditional U.S. auto plants, where seniority plays a larger role in the movement up a job-classification scale tied to small pay increments as well as in assignment to the less-taxing jobs. It is striking that the pay system at Together Manufacturing (and at other Japanese transplants in the automobile industry in the United States) provides fewer rewards to tenure than do traditional U.S. management practices. In this respect, Japanese practices in the United States represent a move away from the Japanese management model.

Employee involvement at Together Manufacturing, while widespread among employees, is also only modestly rewarded. The only monetary incentive provided is a small awards program for the submission of individual suggestions, with the amount of the award tied to the dollar cost reduction resulting from the suggestion. There is no group-based element of compensation. Gain sharing in the form of a companywide profit-sharing formula, which has become standard among the Big Three, was not present until the early 1990s at Together Manufacturing, and its introduction was opposed by the local union leadership. Nonetheless, as Together Manufacturing's profitability position improved, discussion of gain sharing returned, and a modest (relative to the Big Three) program has been initiated.

The pay system at Together Manufacturing does provide some rewards through promotion, which requires additional training. Production workers can qualify for the team leader position, which provides a small pay increment, and some team leaders advance to group leader, which is a management position. Production workers can also qualify for the four-year training apprenticeship program, which provides a substantial pay increment as well as certification for skilled jobs in the external labor market.[5]

Incidence of Innovative Pay Systems

Our research in U.S. SET companies suggests that their pay systems are still in transition. Innovative pay methods are being introduced in some of these companies but on an experimental and incomplete basis.[6] Other accounts of companies attempting to make the transition to SET suggest a higher diffusion rate of some type of gain sharing. We summarize these studies in this section.

In the United States, several studies have found a low but increasing incidence of skill-based pay, pay for performance, and profit sharing. Kruse (1993) reports that profit sharing is found in about 40 percent of larger companies, but about half of these plans take the form of deferred compensation upon retirement.[7]

In another study, Osterman (1994) found that 30 percent of surveyed personnel managers in establishments of fifty employees or more report having some form of profit sharing for their nonmanagerial employees. Pay-for-knowledge systems are more likely in establishments that have work teams, job rotation, total quality management systems, or problem-solving QCs. But there are reasons to suspect that Osterman's findings overstate the incidence of innovative policies. Companies that have innovative workplace practices are more likely to be better run and to employ managers who better understand and appreciate the survey; these managers are therefore more likely to return a completed questionnaire.[8]

Osterman's survey did not collect data on the proportion of pay that profit-sharing plans provide or on whether these are current or deferred (until retirement) plans. A study that did obtain such data found that profit-sharing pay averages about 5 percent of pay among nonmanagerial employees in companies with profit-sharing plans.[9] Although such a proportion will be noticeable to employees, it does not constitute a major incentive element.

Keeping these caveats in mind, it still seems likely that a growing proportion of workers in medium and large companies are finding that their profit sharing formulas are determining some perceptible component of their pay. Whether the popularity of profit-sharing will continue to increase, remain at a stable level, or decline sharply, as it did after the Great Crash in 1929, remains to be seen.

Pay Systems in Large Japanese Companies

Postwar Evolution of the Pay System

Until the early twentieth century, Japanese manufacturers paid most of their blue-collar workers on an hourly basis. In subsequent decades, employers gradually increased the link between pay and short-run employee performance through a variety of piece-rate systems and close monitoring of effort and output (Gordon, 1985, Chaps. 8–10). Both blue-collar workers and their unions disliked this performance-based pay system but were too weak to change it.

After World War II, Japanese unions and their associated political parties were reborn as totally new social institutions endorsed by the U.S. occupational forces. Among the unions' first demands were that pay should be related mainly to needs, based upon minimal household living standards, rather than to individual worker productivity. The unions did recognize that such needs varied significantly over the life cycle. This recognition gave rise to age-based pay as well as dependent and housing allowances, introduced first in the electric power industry and then diffused to other industries. Labor's political and economic strength succeeded in overcoming management opposition, and age-based pay became standard policy in Japanese companies (Gordon, 1985; Ishida, 1990).

Intense union–management conflict over the pay system continued in the 1950s and 1960s, when employers sought both to introduce what they called job-based pay (*shokomu-kyu*) and to weaken the age–pay connection. Job-based pay was meant to rationalize pay structures to reflect greater comparability in similar jobs and greater differences with dissimilar jobs. In many ways, job-based pay in Japan was modeled upon similar efforts in the United States in the 1940s and 1950s, such as the Cooperative Wage Survey in the steel industry (Stieber, 1959). Japanese unions were strongly opposed to job-based pay and succeeded in blocking its use (Ishida, 1990). A compromise proposal, originally opposed by the militant wing of the Japanese labor movement (Sohyo) but supported by the moderate wing (Domei), eventually was adopted. The compromise wage system retained the age–pay linkage (*nenko*), added a base-pay component, and added a third component, known as ability pay (*shokuno-kyu*).

In the 1970s and 1980s, employers sought to spread and refine this ability pay.

Periodic performance appraisals, called *satei,* are used (along with experience) to determine the speed of promotion among the ability ranks, each of which has its own pay range. Blue-collar workers tended to accept ability pay, and the connection between individual workers' appraisals and their pay spread through Japanese companies. This modification met less opposition than job-based pay, indicating that many Japanese workers consider it fair to relate pay to merit. Some unions did and still do seek to protect the effects upon lower-paid workers and those who might be most harmed by merit pay.

In any case, the diffusion of merit pay as an actual practice is said to have become important only in the 1980s. But Japanese researchers have not yet been able to gauge its actual impact. For example, Koike (1994), who has done much research in this area, is able to draw upon only a small number of case studies.

The Components of Pay

As indicated above, pay in Japan consists of three main parts: base pay, age pay, and ability pay. Housing, family, commuting, and other allowances fill out scheduled pay, while overtime pay and semiannual bonuses fill out total pay. Workers' base pay is usually set by adding a regular annual increment (called *teisho*) to their starting salary and thus is tightly correlated with workers' seniority. Actual increments are marginally differentiated by the results of appraisals. Age pay can also be termed life-cycle-needs pay because it usually increases until age 55, when workers are no longer financing their children's education.

White-collar and blue-collar pay tables are integrated into a single table that erases the distinction between the two occupational categories. There is also no major gap between production workers and craft workers. New workers are placed at the bottom of the ability rank table and given simple assignments. As they rotate among different work positions, they expand and deepen their skills and are promoted to a higher ability rank. Thus, they move from an unskilled classification to a more skilled classification through a sequence of small gradations.

Appraisals are equally important for blue-collar and white-collar workers, figuring in both cases in their promotions and rates of skill development. Supervisors typically fill out an evaluation form that includes detailed categories. Those evaluations are usually reviewed by other section and department managers to maximize objectivity and uniformity across work groups.

Frequent performance evaluations and their use for determining pay, which is called merit pay in the United States, generally are absent from Japanese plants in the United States (Milkman, 1991; Abo, 1994). In one unionized plant that we visited, a merit pay system was introduced and accepted by the union. Evaluations initially were conducted by Japanese managers. When this task was turned over to U.S. managers, workers began to file complaints and the merit system was withdrawn.

The Importance of Each Pay Component

Years of seniority in a company continues to be the most important determinant of pay among male workers of similar education levels (Genda, 1994). The persistence of seniority's effect on pay has surprised many observers, who expected that the greater cost (relative to productivity) of older workers and the reduced morale of the lower-paid younger workers doing the same work was not consistent with a stable competitive equilibrium. In particular, some expected that slower overall economic growth and the aging of the work force in the 1980s and beyond would eventually result in the dismantling of the seniority system. The reported reliance on appraisals in the determination of pay in the 1980s was also expected to diminish the importance of seniority. Two studies did find flattening age–earnings profiles in the 1980s, supporting the reduced importance of seniority-based pay (Clark and Ogawa, 1992; Hashimoto and Raisian, 1992).

Other considerations point in the opposite direction. First, the aging of the work force, although rapid in the 1980s, began well before and is evident already in the 1960s. Second, economic growth has slowed several times since the 1970s, most notably after the 1973 oil crisis, and yet the seniority-based pay system adapted without showing any permanent erosion. The strength and the resilience of this system were displayed following the yen's appreciation after the 1985 G-7 Plaza Agreement and during the recession of the early 1990s.

Detailed empirical studies by Mosk and Nakata found that age–earnings profiles flattened from 1961 to 1975 as a result of the declining proportions of young workers, who were increasingly in demand, support this point of view (Mosk and Nakata, 1985; Nakata, 1987). They also found that age–earnings profiles steepened from 1976 to 1982, which they explain as a structural adjustment to the oil crisis. Slower growth reduced the demand for entry-age workers, thereby reducing their wages relative to older workers. The flattening observed during the remainder of the 1980s, when more rapid growth resumed and the supply of younger workers again fell, is seen in recent historical perspective as cyclical and not representing a longer-term shift.[10] These studies also found that the age–wage relationship is much more flexible in smaller firms than in large companies, which suggests that the buffer role of small firms protects not only large company profits but also the relative position of senior workers in large companies.

Career Paths in the United States and Japan

Company-level Data

Using data collected through field work at six large U.S. and Japanese companies, we document and analyze the career paths of nonmanagerial (or nonexempt) workers. We focus on two main issues: the steepness of age–earnings profiles and the role of appraisals and merit pay in pay differentials among workers of the same age.

Figures 4.1–4.3 present age–earnings profiles for production or clerical workers at three U.S. companies with SET systems: Together Manufacturing, Hi-Tech, and CommEx. These profiles were constructed by integrating job-based company pay data with information on the average time a representative worker spends at each pay level (see the Appendix at the end of this chapter for more details of how the career paths are constructed). As these figures indicate and as Table 4.1 summarizes, the career paths for workers provide a range of upward pay mobility over time. The wage–tenure profile is quite flat at Together Manufacturing, providing a 38 percent wage-growth factor during the three-year introductory (or "catch-up") period. The typical career path at Hi-Tech provides wage growth of 1.9 times during 15 years for production workers. Career paths at CommEx provide wage growth of 1.9 times in 13 years for technicians and of 2.4 times in 19 years for clerical workers (customer service representatives and administrators). However, the opportunities for clerical workers, mainly women, have diminished considerably at CommEx in the late 1990s since downsizing has closed off opportunities for advancement. The entry-level position is now a dead-end job with high turnover rather than the first step on a career ladder. Each of these companies used a post-and-bid system for promotions and transfers. "Fast-trackers" might be able to move up the path somewhat faster than "average" workers, but in general tenure tends to dominate as the determinant of pay increase.[11]

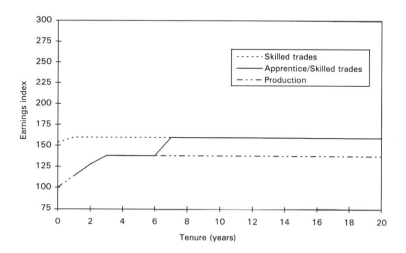

FIGURE 4.1. Together Manufacturing Standard Career Paths, 1994

Source: Interviews with management and union representatives and 1994 contract.

Note: Promotion to team leader provides a $0.60 per hour pay premium and is widely available. Promotion to group leader, first level of management, is very unusual.

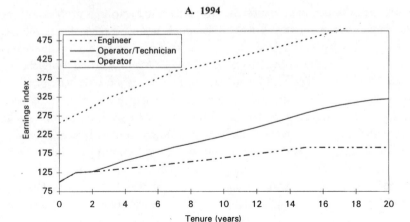

A. 1994

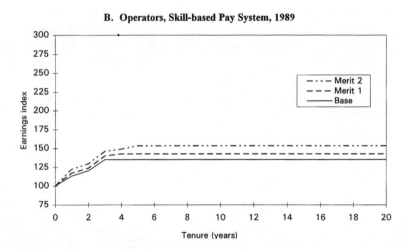

B. Operators, Skill-based Pay System, 1989

FIGURE 4.2. Hi-Tech Standard Career Paths

Sources: A: Company-provided data. B: Company memorandum, "Manufacturing Operator Skill-Based Pay Compensation Program."

Note: B: The different pay levels reflect skill certifications and performance evaluations based on attendance, flexibility, and contribution to problem solving.

At each company, opportunities exist for some workers to extend their job ladder even further. At CommEx, technical employees can become eligible for slightly higher-paid positions through additional training. At Together Manufacturing, selected operators can enter the company-sponsored four year apprenticeship program to learn a skilled trade. Crafts workers are on a flat earnings profile, which is approximately 20 percent higher than the profile for production workers. At Hi-Tech, operators have the opportunity to train to become technicians by undertak-

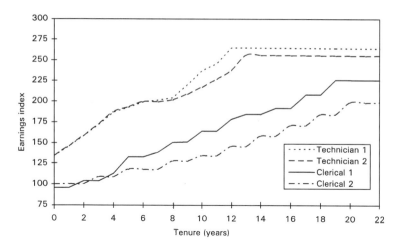

FIGURE 4.3. CommEx Standard Career Paths, 1992

Source: Computed from data in an unpublished survey of CommEx employees conducted by C. Brown, M. Reich, and D. Stern, interviews with personnel managers and union representatives, and 1992 contract.

ing a rigorous and time-consuming educational program on their own time. To do this, an operator has to complete three home study courses and earn an AA degree in electronics, as well as undertake planned and structured OJT. A select group of operators can earn the AA degree in four years or less by attending classes on-site after work hours. A highly motivated high school graduate can become a technician in eight years and double his or her wage. Employees who begin as operators but who have some college education can progress faster. However, most operators do not become technicians, and those who do usually take longer than eight years. Overall, approximately one-third of the operators become technicians and one-half of the technicians have been promoted from being operators. In 1994, operators were promoted to the position of technician or supervisor at a rate of 3 percent, and the promotion rate from the position of technician to supervisor or engineer was 4 percent.

Hi-Tech has introduced skill-based pay on an experimental basis in one of its new plants (Figure 4.2b). The earnings profile is only slightly steeper than the profile at Together Manufacturing; operators can typically increase their earnings by 35 percent in three years by learning all of the machine stations. Merit pay allows them to increase their pay as much as 45 percent (merit 1) or 55 percent (merit 2). Since the merit determinations are made annually, workers' pay can fluctuate up to 15 percent between the highest merit pay and base pay. Otherwise, the earnings profile is flat after four years. The manager in charge of compensation said that the company had not expected all workers to acquire all of the skills necessary to re-

TABLE 4.1. Job Ladders for Nonexempt Workers

Industry	Type of Job	Year	Typical Career				Potential Career[b]		
			Entry Wage (hourly)	Wage Growth Factor	Top Wage (hourly)	Minimum Years to Top Wage[a]	Wage Growth Factor	Top Wage (hourly)	Minimum Years to Top Wage
Hi-Tech	Operator/tech.	1994	$7	1.9	$13	15	3.2	$22	20
CommEx	Technician	1992	$10	1.9	$20	13	2.0	$21	24
CommEx	Clerical	1992	$7	2.4	$18	19	—	—	—
Together Mfg	Prod./skilled trades	1994	$13	1.4	$19	3	1.7	$22	7
CommSun	H.S., median	1991	¥8	2.2	¥18	20	—	—	—
Agile Auto	Male H.S.	1991	¥9	2.1	¥19	20	—	—	—
Star Electronics	Male H.S.	1991	¥9	2.0	¥17	20	—	—	—

Source: See Figures 4.1–4.7.

Note: Pay amounts have been rounded.

[a] These reflect the years involved in "steady progression," which usually represents the minimum years required and is faster than most employees' progress.

[b] Wage growth and minimum years to top wage are calculated from entry wage.

ceive the top skill pay in three years, but this is what occurred. So the earnings profile was steeper and flattened sooner than management wanted or expected. This plan is similar to those reported in a survey of 97 skill-based pay systems, where most employees could learn the maximum number of skill units in fewer than three years. However, the average employee mastered only 70 percent of the skill units in two years and plateaued before "topping out" (Jenkins et al., 1992).[12]

In contrast, Figures 4.4–4.6 present observed (or actual) age–earnings profiles for union workers at three large Japanese companies: Agile Auto, Star Electronics, and CommSun. Standard profiles are also presented for two companies. The standard career profiles were computed from the negotiated wage tables with assumptions concerning rates of progression from interviews with managers and union officials (see this chapter's Appendix). The calculations required for the Japanese profiles were much more complex than those for the American profiles since pay increases for individuals could occur through multiple channels with more indirect connections to the current jobs of individual workers.

None of the Japanese companies had a post-and-bid system, and job assignment by managers was the norm. All three Japanese firms have an enterprise union that is part of a companywide union that in turn belongs to a national (industry) federation. Wage structures and wage increases are bargained nationally for all union workers during Shunto (see Chapter 6). For this reason, the earnings profiles of union workers across industries are somewhat similar. All newly hired regular workers, both high school and university graduates, belong to the union until they reach managerial ranks, which begin at the U.S. equivalent of third-level manager. University graduates may reach management in ten years, typically by the time they reach ages 35 to 40. High school graduates may reach management in twenty-two years, and most have reached a management grade by age 50. Much of the career-based pay increases take place only when, and if, workers are promoted to managerial positions that are not in the union, generally after age 35. The earnings growth of managers is not shown in the charts.

Japanese HR policy discussions often suggest that performance (or ability, in Japanese parlance) has become more important, while seniority has lessened in importance, in determining individual pay. Our research on performance schemes in individual companies and their actual impact is reported in these figures. The results do not support a large role for performance pay. In fact, our first calculations of standard profiles, which were based on assumptions given by managers in interviews, resulted in progressions for high performers (or fast-trackers) that were much more rapid than observed. We adjusted our calculations after further consultation with Japanese managers. For highly rated workers, however, fast-tracking was more prevalent than in U.S. firms and can provide significant incentives, although only 5 to 10 percent of workers realize these rewards.

Male production workers at Agile Auto (Figure 4.4) typically are on a career lad-

A. Observed

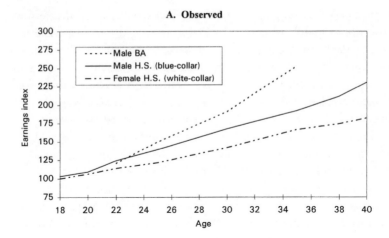

B. Standard Union

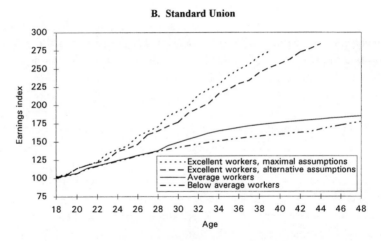

FIGURE 4.4. Agile Auto Career Paths, 1991

Sources: A: Calculated from survey data collected by the Confederation of Japan Automobile Workers' Unions and reported in their privately published document, *Wage-Work Condition Survey Materials,* volume 3, November 1991. B: Calculated from company pay tables provided by the Agile Auto workers union.

Note: A: Team leader and group leader positions are included in observed data; promotion to these positions is the norm. B: Excludes managerial pay, bonus, and overtime and includes allowances. For assumptions, see Appendix at the end of this chapter.

der that increases their earnings 2.1 times over 20 years (before leaving the union). Female clerical workers have a less-steep earnings profile, and their earnings potentially increase 1.7 times over 20 years in the atypical event that they do not leave the firm with the birth of the first child. Women are not used in regular positions on the assembly line.

Male production workers in Star Electronics (Figure 4.5) are on a career ladder that doubles their earnings in 20 years. Female production and clerical workers typically are on a career ladder that increases their earnings 1.5 times over 20 years.

The career paths for union workers at CommSun (Figure 4.6) show the observed variation in pay for high school and university graduates. High school graduates are on a career path that increases earnings 2.2 times for the average worker over 20 years. High performers' earnings increase 2.3 times and low performers' earn-

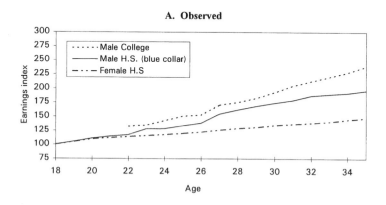

A. Observed

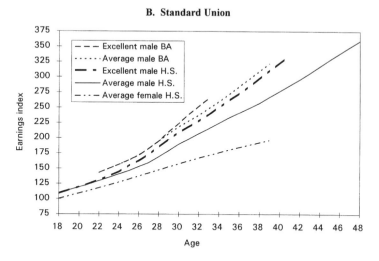

B. Standard Union

FIGURE 4.5. Star Electronics Career Paths, 1991

Sources: A: Calculated from survey data collected by Denki Roren (Confederation of Electrical Workers' Unions) and reported in their privately published document, *Chingin Jittai Chosa Hokoku,* volume 2, no. 1, November 1991. B: Calculated from company-provided data.

Note: B: Excludes managerial pay, bonus, and overtime and includes allowances. For assumptions, see Appendix at the end of this chapter.

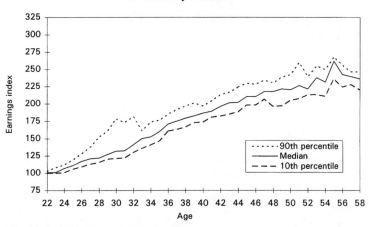

A. High School Graduates

B. University Graduates

FIGURE 4.6. CommSun Observed Career Paths, 1991

Source: Calculated from survey data collected by the Zendentsu (Telecommunication Workers'
Union) and reported in their privately published document, *Condition of Wages and Labor Power
Organization of Zendentsu Union Members: 1991 Report on the Survey of Wage Conditions* (Zen-koku
Denki Tsushin Rodo Kumrai), pp. 64, 95.

Note: Earnings equal base pay plus position pay. Data refer to workers who belong to the union (i.e.,
who have not achieved managerial status).

ings increase 2.0 times over 20 years. By age 50, the high school graduate is typically earning 2.7 times entry pay. Variation in wage growth reflects differences in promotion rates and performance pay. Notice that variation in pay by age increases around age 30, when some workers (the high flyers) begin to enter management, where their pay can increase more rapidly (not shown). However, the variance then remains fairly constant for those not becoming managers until workers approach retirement age in their late 50s.

Career ladders are uniformly better developed in Japan. However, differences appear across industries. Telecommunications companies provide developed career ladders in both Japan and the United States, although the ladders in Japan provide more wage growth over a longer period. Automobile companies in the United States have not developed career ladders; Japanese car makers have career ladders, but they are not as well developed as those for telecommunications workers. Hi-Tech has well-developed career ladders by American standards, and its career ladder for operators is only slightly shorter than the Japanese career ladder for operators. However, operators at the U.S. company face a much more developed career ladder than the Japanese ladder if they work to become a technician. Since operators in Japan are expected to develop technician's skills over their careers, the comparable wage growth for the skills is not as great in Japan as at Hi-Tech.

Industry-level Data

Industrywide data for these industries (automobile, telecommunications, and electrical industries for the United States in Figure 4.7 and for automobile and electrical industries for Japan in Figure 4.8) suggest the same general contrasts, but with smaller intercountry differences than in the company data. Age–earnings profiles are steeper among large companies in the Japanese automobile and electrical industries than in the same industries in the United States.[13] Educational differences, however, are somewhat smaller. Differences between industries are much smaller in Japan than in the United States, a point to which we return below. Differences by company size are much greater in Japan, where supplier tier is more important than industry in defining labor market structure.

National-level Data

Age–earnings profiles for workers in Japan and the United States show that national earnings profiles are steeper in Japan (Figure 4.9). As we have argued, the greater importance of age in pay reflects Japan's SET system. Some observers mistakenly relate age-based pay only to Japan's "lifetime employment system" and suggest that this system is becoming increasingly costly to the Japanese economy. Lifetime employment is thought to be inconsistent with a competitive economy

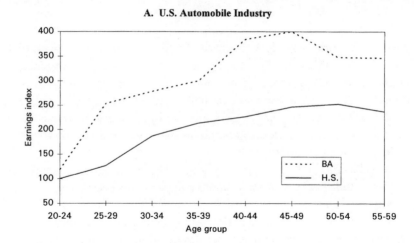

A. U.S. Automobile Industry

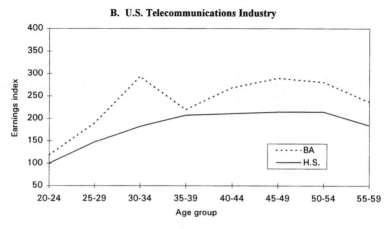

B. U.S. Telecommunications Industry

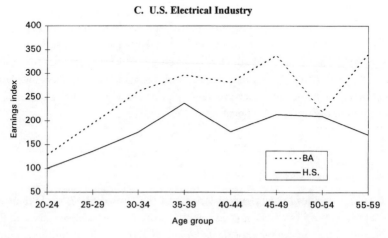

C. U.S. Electrical Industry

FIGURE 4.7. Earnings by Age and Education, United States, 1989–1991

Source: Computed by the authors from the Current Population Surveys, March 1989, 1990, 1991.

Note: Positive earners only; earnings averaged over 1989–1991 to enhance cell sizes; SIC code: A, 351; B, 441; C, 341.

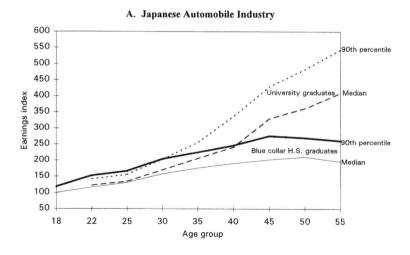

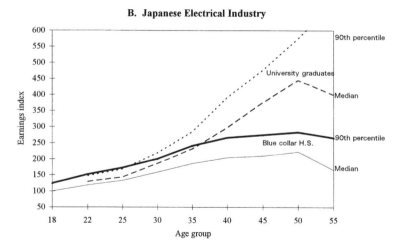

FIGURE 4.8. Earnings by Age and Education, Japan, 1988

Source: Nakata (1991a). The underlying data are from *Basic Survey of Wage Structure*, Japan Ministry of Labor.

Note: Data are for establishments with ten or more regular workers.

because competition should produce higher earnings for more educated groups and should relate pay to productivity rather than to age. The lifetime employment system in Japan therefore is regarded as being in a state of disequilibrium or unstable equilibrium and is not likely to endure.

Human capital theory and institutional considerations generate a different conclusion. Human capital theory predicts that steeper age–earnings profiles are sus-

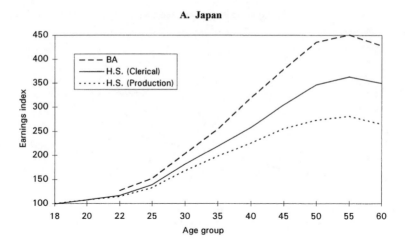

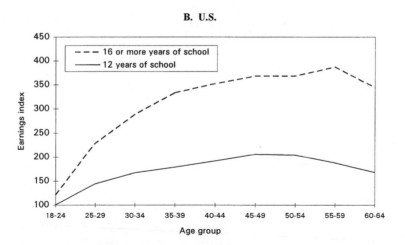

FIGURE 4.9. Earnings by Age and Education, 1990

Sources: A: Computed by the authors from *Basic Survey of Wage Structure,* Japan Ministry of Labor.
B: Computed by the authors from the Current Population Survey, March 1990.

Note: A: Regular male workers, scheduled earnings. B: Male private wage and salary workers, annual
earnings.

tainable under conditions of long-term employment relations. Long-term employment relations lead to greater company and employee investment in worker
training, which raises productivity and permits higher pay for longer-term workers (Mincer and Higuchi, 1988). This effect explains the greater correlation between age and earnings in Japan than in the United States.

Our institutional analysis suggests that the causal mechanism between training and age–earnings profiles also works in the opposite direction. The steeper profiles in Japan arose in the early postwar era from union demands to connect pay to income needs over the lifecycle. Although these steeper profiles were initially established over the opposition of Japanese employers, they have had the effect of providing an incentive for employers to ensure that worker skills increase with age. Consequently, employers in Japan have been concerned that the skill paths of Japanese workers over their careers are arranged through a more structured set of institutions than is the case in the United States.

As has already been presented, pay in U.S. blue-collar jobs does increase with age, but the profiles are flatter than those of production workers in Japan or white collar workers in the United States. In the United States, the institutional role of seniority developed with the evolution of union-management relations from the 1930s to the 1950s. Since the rise of the CIO in the late 1930s, U.S. unions mainly have opposed piece rates or other incentive pay systems that undermine income security. Unions have favored tying pay increases to seniority but have also looked down upon large wage differentials among employees working in similar jobs. As a result, unions have favored relatively flat age–earnings profiles, with seniority having a larger effect upon job assignment, scheduling, and layoffs than on pay. At the same time, U.S. unions have supported moderately higher pay for skilled craft workers, who do very different jobs. This sharp discontinuity in pay, work, and status among blue-collar workers does not exist in Japan, where career ladders for production workers incorporate both semiskilled and skilled jobs.

Professional and managerial white-collar workers in the United States face steeper profiles than blue collar or clerical workers. Promotions can be particularly rapid for exceptional performers, as most companies have opportunities for fast-track advancement. Interfirm mobility, whether actual or potential, provides a major stimulus to such rapid promotion.

Earnings Inequality

The Relation between Growth and Inequality

Some economists argue that economic growth and changes in inequality are positively related because growth can be both a cause and an effect of inequality. By increasing incentives to save, to work, and to invest in education and technical change, greater inequality can cause an increase in growth. Higher inequality can also be the result of rapid growth, as company profits and managerial compensation increase faster than labor earnings.

Other economists argue that compressed earnings differences are more conducive to economic growth. Policies of fairness and inclusion, for example, can reduce workers' resistance to technological change, thereby permitting more rapid productivity growth. Similar policies can enhance coordinated union receptivity to wage restraint, thereby dampening inflationary pressures through means other than periodic recessions (Persson and Tabellini, 1994).

The first of the above views places more emphasis on profits, savings rates, and work effort as the principal causes of higher growth and higher inequality. This view predicts that higher growth is associated with a higher level of inequality. The second view places more emphasis on the role of institutions and predicts a negative relation between growth and inequality. While these two views might seem mutually exclusive, a third view proposes that they are complementary rather than rival hypotheses. This eclectic view posits an inverted U-shaped relationship between earnings inequality and economic growth. Rapid growth is more compatible with high or low levels of inequality than it is with medium levels of inequality (Weisskopf, 1987; Calmfors and Driffil, 1988; Calmfors, 1993; Soskice, 1990).

The eclectic approach suggests that national inequality levels are affected by a country's institutional labor market structure. The institutional differences often found to be significant in this literature include the extent of unionization, the degree of centralization of wage bargaining, the ratio of the legislated minimum wage to the average wage, the structure of school-to-work transition systems, and the level of social welfare benefits (Freeman, 1994, intro.; Blau and Kahn, 1996).

Overall Comparisons

International comparisons of earnings inequality can be made by examining inequality levels at a single point in time and comparative inequality trends over time. The United States not only has higher measured levels of inequality than other countries. It also had the highest rate of growth in inequality in the 1980s (OECD, 1993a).

The finding that the overall inequality level is greater in the United States than in Japan (Table 4.2) puzzles many human capital-oriented economists, since the usual demographic and educational variables do not predict these differences. In fact, the age distribution of workers and the relative proportions of university graduates to high school graduates are roughly similar in both countries. The lower inequality in Japan is also surprising to institutionalists, as it runs against the steeper age–earnings profiles. It also surprises observers who recognize that the annual earnings of females relative to males are lower in Japan than in the United States.

Part of the greater inequality in the United States can be attributed to differences between the structures of labor supply in these countries.[14] Yet intercountry differences in inequality remain high even when measured among just full-time male workers (Table 4.2) or among just high school or college graduates (Davis, 1992).[15]

Our next comparison examines inequality trends in the United States and other countries in the 1980s. The current level of earnings inequality in the United States is high not only relative to other countries but also relative to our own his-

TABLE 4.2. Earnings Inequality in the United States and Japan

U.S.	Decile Ratio	1981	1990
Males	D9/D5	2.44	2.57
	D1/D5	0.44	0.42
Females	D9/D5	2.19	2.19
	D1/D5	0.55	0.47

Japan	Decile Ratio	1979	1990
Males	D9/D5	1.63	1.73
	D1/D5	0.63	0.61
Females	D9/D5	1.54	1.63
	D1/D5	0.70	0.70

Sources: U.S.: Calculated by the authors from data from Current Population Reports, P-60 series, U.S. Bureau of the Census (1983b), Table 59; U.S. Bureau of the Census (1991), Table 31. Japan: OECD (1993), Table 5.2. The underlying data are from the *Basic Surveys of Wage Structure,* Japan Ministry of Labor.

Note: Dj = earnings level at jth decile. U.S.: Annual earnings of year-round full-time workers. Japan: Monthly *scheduled* earnings (including housing and family allowances but excluding overtime pay and bonuses) of *regular* workers aged 18–59, excluding workers in government, agriculture, and establishments with fewer than 10 workers.

tory. Although the dispersion of earnings fell during the 1960s, it has been rising since the early 1970s. By the late 1980s, it was higher than at any other time since the beginning of the postwar era, when modern measurement techniques and data sources were first introduced. Moreover, inequality continued to increase in the 1990s. The increase in inequality exhibits a secular trend that remains after cyclical factors have been controlled.

As Levy and Murnane (1992) have emphasized, much of the growth of inequality in the United States in the 1980s occurred *within* age-education-gender groups, implying that neither supply shifts nor demand shifts are mainly responsible for the rise in inequality. An alternative view that highlights the institutional changes in the structure of U.S. labor markets since the early 1970s does account for these patterns (Gordon et al., 1982; Davidson and Reich, 1988; Mishel and Bernstein, 1994).

Our final international comparison focuses on inequality trends in OECD countries during the 1980s. Although a number of industrialized countries experienced measurable increases in earnings inequality in the 1980s, only the United States and the United Kingdom experienced major increases. The United States had the largest increase (OECD, 1993a). In some countries, such as France, earnings inequality did not increase in the 1980s, while Japan and Germany had very modest increases.

Initially, economists attempted to explain the greater increases in the United States as resulting from a greater growth in the demand for college-educated labor relative to the growth in supply (e.g., Katz and Ravenga, 1989). This shift was thought to result from the effects of technological change upon skill demands, such as the growing use of computer skills in work places (Krueger, 1993). But further examination indicated the variety of inequality trends across countries, again suggesting that institutional differences might be more likely to account for many of these patterns (see, e.g., Katz et al., 1995; Mishel and Bernstein, 1994).

In sum, international comparisons of earnings trends, earnings inequality levels, and earnings inequality trends indicate relationships among these variables that run counter to the predictions of traditional economic analysis. Average earnings levels have been rising faster in Japan than in the United States at the same time that inequality has been lower in Japan. These patterns indicate that, insofar as labor earnings are concerned, the trade-off between growth and equality is sloped positively, not negatively, as is often asserted. In particular, there is plenty of room for the hypothesis that Japanese employment and training institutions have produced both higher growth and less inequality than the counterpart U.S. institutions. These comparisons suggest that there are other means of increasing savings, investment and growth than through increasing inequality in earnings.

Components of Earnings Inequality

We delve further here into the components of earnings inequality that were introduced in the stylized facts presented at the beginning of this chapter. In addition to the import of education, gender, and employer size differences, we briefly examine interindustry pay differences, the pay of managers and CEOs relative to production workers, and the position of part-time workers. These disaggregations suggest the significance of each of these variables for inequality in each country.

Education Differences

Age–earnings profiles for high school and for university graduates are presented in Figure 4.9. In both countries, university graduates have higher pay and steeper profiles than do high school graduates. However, the difference between these two educational groups is not as great in Japan as in the United States. Nakata and Mosk (1987), who calculated the net present value of lifetime earnings of Japanese workers, found that high school graduates' lifetime earnings were less than university graduates' earnings in the early 1960s but were catching up rapidly through the late 1970s. Moreover, the gap between the two groups declined from a ratio of 1.26 in 1961–1965, to 1.17 in 1966–1970, to 1.13 in 1971–1975, to 1.11 in 1976–1980, even as the proportion of university graduates expanded rapidly. In the 1980s, the educational pay differential rose very slightly in Japan while the pay of university graduates relative to high school graduates rose sharply in the United States (Table 4.3).

As several studies have found, educational pay premia respond in both Japan and

TABLE 4.3. Earnings Ratios, University to High School Graduates,
United States and Japan, 1973 to 1992

Year	U.S.[a]		Japan[b]	
	M	F	M	F
1973			1.31	1.40
1975	1.55	1.49		
1979	1.57	1.47	1.25	1.32
1989	1.73	1.64	1.28	1.36
1992	1.89	1.83	1.28	1.38

Sources: U.S.: Current Population Reports, P-60 series, U.S. Bureau of the Census (1977–1993).
Japan: Basic Survey of Wage Structure, Japan Ministry of Labor (1974–1993).
[a] Annual earnings of year-round full-time workers.
[b] Monthly cash earnings of regular workers in firms of ten employees or more.

the United States to market pressures (Nakata and Mosk, 1987; Katz and Ravenga, 1989). In Japan, however, labor market institutions such as the inclusion of both high school and university graduates in the enterprise union and the use of a unified pay schedule for all workers constrain movements in educational pay premia. Consequently, supply and demand shifts generate smaller responses in educational pay differentials.

Firm-size Pay Differentials

In the United States, large companies pay higher wages than smaller companies. Companies with fewer than 25 employees paid an average of 72 percent of the hourly wage paid in companies of 1,000 employees or more.[16] The ratio is .79 for companies with 25–99 employees and .90 for companies with 100–999 employees. Statistical analysis (Table 4.4) shows pay differentials persist even when holding other variables constant, including measurable worker characteristics, such as gender, race, age, and education, as well as job and company characteristics, such as industry, occupation, and union status.[17] Brown and Medoff (1989) sought to explain these pay differences as reflecting economies of scale, but an alternative explanation (Gordon et al., 1982) suggests that the persistence of firm-size differentials, even after the growth of international and domestic competition in the 1980s, results from the segmentation of U.S. labor markets. Large companies are also more likely to maintain a HR system that supports higher pay.[18]

In the Japanese labor market, segmentation by firm size is much more pronounced than in the United States. Pay in very small companies (10–25 employees) in 1988 was 25.3 percent below the average for all companies, while pay in very large companies (5,000 employees or more) was 32.1 percent above the average (Tachibanaki, 1993, Table 2).[19] The impact of firm size on pay is larger for women

TABLE 4.4. Earnings Regressions, Controlling for Firm Size, United States, 1990

Constant	.813	.738	.704	.666	.975	.952
	(30.75)	(27.79)	(4.84)	(4.62)	(5.62)	(5.55)
Highest grade of school	.089	.085	.081	.078	.052	.049
	(53.41)	(51.47)	(48.60)	(46.88)	(29.12)	(28.02)
Experience	.031	.030	.026	.026	.024	.024
	(25.89)	(25.26)	(22.70)	(22.59)	(22.18)	(22.02)
Experience^2	−.001	−.001	−.000	−.000	−.000	−.000
	(−21.32)	(−20.54)	(−18.27)	(−18.10)	(−18.05)	(−17.80)
Part-time	−.340	−.327	−.286	−.284	−.262	−.259
	(−6.43)	(−6.32)	(−5.72)	(−5.74)	(−5.56)	(−5.58)
Married	.121	.118	.010	.099	.076	.075
	(12.45)	(12.39)	(10.85)	(10.90)	(8.75)	(8.79)
Black	−.145	−.168	−.148	−.164	−.084	−.100
	(−8.93)	(−10.54)	(−9.66)	(−10.81)	(−5.77)	(−6.96)
Female	−.278	−.276	−.236	−.2237	−.228	−.227
	(−31.24)	(−31.54)	(−25.69)	(−26.12)	(−24.23)	(−24.43)
Union member	.130	.091	.080	.058	.091	.070
	(3.31)	(2.36)	(2.145)	(1.57)	(2.59)	(2.01)
Resides in an MSA	.004	.008	.010	.011	.003	.005
	(.301)	(.618)	(.800)	(.940)	(.298)	(.430)
Employer size						
25–99	—	.100	—	.066	—	.071
		(7.24)		(4.89)		(5.62)
100–499	—	.161	—	.103	—	.104
		(11.68)		(7.60)		(8.12)
500–1,000	—	.210	—	.151	—	.148
		(10.61)		(782)		(8.16)
1,000+	—	.238	—	.191	—	.185
		(20.99)		(16.58)		(16.98)
19 Industry dummies	No	No	Yes	Yes	Yes	Yes
13 Occupation dummies	No	No	No	No	Yes	Yes
R^2	.311	.338	.385	.400	.457	.471

Source: Completed from Current Population Survey, March 1991 Demographic File.

Note: Dependent variable is log wages. Sample size is 11, 877. t-statistics in parenthesis.

than for men, and the disparity increases with age. In large firms, young women (25–29 years old) earn 78 percent as much as men, but women in small firms (10–99 employees) earn only 63 percent as much as men in large firms. Prime-age women (35–39 years old) in large firms earn 66 percent as much as men, and women in small firms earn 43 percent as much as men in large firms.[20]

According to Tachibanaki, the persistence of firm-size wage differentials surprised many Japanese economists. Although firm-size pay differentials grew wider from 1950 to the early 1960s, the expectation had been that subsequent rapid economic growth would create a growing demand for labor that would reduce size differentials and eliminate this "dualism" of the Japanese labor market. From 1965 to

1973, such differentials did decrease. In manufacturing, the ratio of average monthly earnings of employees in small companies (30–99 employees) to those in large companies (1,000 employees or more) rose from 59.1 percent in 1965 to a peak of 71.8 percent in 1973 (Sakurabayashi, 1982, p. 77).

But after 1973 the narrowing trend reversed, and dualism began to increase again. According to Sakurabayashi (1982), earnings of workers in small companies relative to those in large companies fell gradually during the 1970s to 66.3 percent in 1979. As Table 4.5 shows, this downward trend continued through the 1980s but reversed in the early 1990s. These findings are confirmed by evidence presented in Tachibanaki (1993, Table 2), which indicates that the wage in small companies (30–99 employees) fell from 15.8 percent below the average for all companies in 1978 to 20.3 percent below the average in 1988. In this same period, the wage premium in very large companies (5,000 employees or more) rose from 28.7 percent in 1978 to 32.1 percent in 1988. From 1970 to 1990, the size–wage effect grew steadily, whether measured as relative earnings of all employees in the size class or after controlling for employer-size differences in employee composition by gender, education, age, and tenure.

Interindustry Pay Differences

Among large companies, interindustry wage differentials are broader in the United States than in Japan, where pay levels and policies are remarkably similar in most large companies. In the United States, the pay ratio for salaried managers to assemblers varies across industries. The ratio was 2.3 in motor vehicles, 3.1 in electrical machinery, 2.8 for manufacturing, and 2.3 for all industries in 1979.[21] These differences suggest that interindustry wage differentials are socially rather than technologically determined and provide additional evidence of segmented labor markets in the United States.

In Japan, pay policies of individual companies tend to follow a small number of leaders as well as the advice of the Japan Productivity Center and the well-organized employers' associations such as Nikkeiren. Some union leaders that we interviewed claimed that their unions have had some impact upon wage structures in their individual companies, but the effects were small. In contrast, U.S. company

TABLE 4.5. Wage Ratios by Firm Size, Japan, 1968–1992

Number of employees	1968	1970	1975	1980	1985	1990	1992
10–99	84.0	86.8	82.9	81.2	78.8	79.3	81.3
100–999	86.7	89.8	89.5	86.3	85.4	84.6	85.5
1,000+	100.0	100.0	100.0	100.0	100.0	100.0	100.0

Source: *Basic Survey of Wage Structure*, Japan Ministry of Labor (1969–1993).
Note: Wages are scheduled monthly earnings, *males* only.

wage policies vary considerably and in some instances are strongly influenced by unions and by barriers to competition in product markets. Modern rent-sharing models of wage determination in the United States reflect these influences (Dickens and Katz, 1987).

Some earlier studies (for example, OECD, 1989a) found greater interindustry wage differentials in Japan than in the United States. To some extent, the findings depend upon the level of aggregation. The OECD study examined only interindustry differentials within manufacturing. Our own calculations across one-digit industries (Table 4.6) also show large dispersions.[22] These differentials have

TABLE 4.6. Wage Dispersion among One-Digit Industries, United States and Japan (Percent Deviation from Weighted Mean Wage)

	U.S.		Japan	
			No Controls	
	No Controls	Human Capital and Demographic Controls	30+ Workers	5–29 Workers
	1984	1984	1988	1988
Mining	40.6	22.2	−8.0	−11.2
Construction	46.6	10.8	−6.9	−11.5
Manufacturing	11.0	9.1	14.7	−23.8
Transportation and communication	34.3	14.5	0.8	4.2
Wholesale and retail trade	−19.6	−11.1	−24.0	−23.4
Finance and insurance	−7.9	5.5	27.0	21.9
Real estate[a]			3.0	9.9
Services	−7.6	−7.8	−3.4	−9.1
Public utilities[b]			26.2	43.0
Average absolute deviation from weighted mean wage	23.9	9.4	12.7	17.6
	1974	1974	1978	1978
Mining	23.8	17.9	−0.1	−15.9
Construction	60.3	19.5	−12.3	−12.4
Manufacturing	4.8	5.5	−14.0	−22.3
Transportation and communication	29.0	11.1	4.5	5.0
Wholesale and retail trade	−17.6	−12.8	−13.9	−17.2
Finance and insurance	−9.3	4.7	15.4	11.8
Real estate[a]			−1.6	15.4
Services	−10.7	−7.0	NA	NA
Public utilities[b]			21.9	35.6
Average absolute deviation from weighted mean wage	22.2	11.2	10.5	17.0

Sources: Computed by the authors from *Employment and Earnings,* U.S. Department of Labor (various years); *Japan Statistical Yearbook,* Japan Statistics Bureau (1989), Table 3-27, pp. 92–93; (1979), Table 282, pp. 396–399; Krueger and Summers (1988); and Tachibanaki and Ohta(1994).

[a] Finance and insurance and real estate aggregated for the United States.

[b] Transportation and communication and public utilities aggregated for the United States.

been rising in both countries since the early 1970s (Table 4.6; Davidson and Reich, 1988; Tsuru, 1992), but the increase has been much greater in the United States. Davidson and Reich (1988) interpret the U.S. trends as evidence of increasing segmentation in U.S. labor markets during this period.

Managerial and CEO Pay

Whereas the earnings profiles for Japan's production workers are steeper than those for production workers in the United States, the pay of middle-level managers and of chief executive officers relative to production workers is lower in Japan than in the United States. As we observed above, U.S. salaried managers averaged 2.3 times the pay of production workers. In contrast, division managers earned approximately 1.6 times the pay of production workers in the Japanese automobile industry in 1988 (Table 4.7).[23] These patterns reflect the smaller pay differentials between blue- and white-collar workers in Japan.

The pay of CEOs relative to that of production workers provides an even greater contrast between Japan and the United States. While production worker pay data are relatively accurate, in both countries the estimates of CEO compensation can vary substantially. A 1989 Towers Perrin study of Japanese companies with annual sales of about $100 million found a ratio of 9.4 to 1, very close to the 9 to 1 ratio expected by several Japanese economists we interviewed.[24] For very large Japanese companies, estimates of the ratio range from about 17 (according to Crystal, 1991) to 25 (according to Blair, 1994).[25] Chief executive officers of the very largest Japanese companies often are also board members of several of their subsidiaries and related companies. Members of this elite subset of Japanese CEOs thereby draw additional salaries, which may explain the range of estimates.

Estimates of CEO pay for the United States are somewhat more precise, but it is clear that CEOs are highly paid. In 1974, the ratio of the pay for the CEOs of the largest 200 companies to that of the average production worker was about 40 to 1. This ratio was already much higher than the comparable figure for Japan. After 1980, the pay ratio began to increase very rapidly as substantial incentives, such as stock options, were added to CEO compensation packages, while the average work-

TABLE 4.7. Manager/Production Worker Pay Ratios, Japanese Automobile Industry

Age	1978		1988	
	Supervisor	Division Manager	Supervisor	Division Manager
35	1.28	1.51	1.19	1.59
45	1.25	1.91	1.19	1.61
55	1.23	1.46	1.17	1.86

Source: Computed by the authors from the *Basic Survey of Wage Structure,* Japan Ministry of Labor (1979, 1989).

Note: Annual earnings of regular male workers. Supervisors are defined as *shokucho* and division managers as *kacho.*

er's pay stagnated. By 1992, the ratio had risen to 157, and media accounts of rising CEO pay generated widespread resentment among workers who were being asked to do more for less pay.

The differences between Japan and the United States are still present but not so extreme in medium-sized companies. According to a survey by the Towers Perrin compensation consultants firm, 1991 compensation for CEOs of U.S. companies with $250 million in sales averaged about $600,000, or twice as high as the CEO of a similarly sized Japanese company (cited in Milgrom and Roberts, 1992, p. 426).

These CEO compensation comparisons may be biased because they omit important perks received by Japanese executives, such as access to expensive golf club memberships and meals in expensive restaurants. Although it is true that the data exclude noncash executive benefits, such as corporate club memberships, these perks are common in both Japan and the United States, though perhaps at very different relative prices. More important, the data do include bonuses, golden parachutes, and stock options, which are rare in Japan but extremely common and generous in the United States and of far greater monetary value than noncash perks.[26] We can conclude that the U.S.–Japanese differences are real and have evident consequences for perceptions of unfairness and for overall inequality.

Gender Differences

Relative to many other OECD countries, and certainly to the United States, Japan has a stable two-parent family structure and a high level of gender segregation in the labor market. Women often are consigned to a buffer stock role, and their interests are underrepresented in the polity. Many observers therefore suggest that Japan has long had greater gender pay differences than the United States. This turns out to be the case.

In the United States, the ratio of female pay to male pay for year-round full-time workers decreased from about 63 percent in the early 1950s to just under 60 percent in the late 1970s. This inequality persisted, despite steadily increasing labor force participation among women as a whole, including even greater increases among women with children, because most women workers remained confined in the lower-paying occupations. Even in the 1970s, after the advent of federal antidiscrimination laws and enforcement activities and the beginning of female entry into higher-paying occupations, gender segregation in jobs and low levels of labor market experience continued to constrain female pay. By the early 1980s, gender patterns of inequality began to show signs of transformation. The female-to-male median earnings ratio increased to 65 percent by the mid-1980s and reached 71 percent in 1992, indicating that the unequal position of women in the labor market has diminished (Figure 4.10).

The mechanisms that increased relative pay for women in the higher-paying occupations differ from those at work in the lower-paying ones. At the upper end, im-

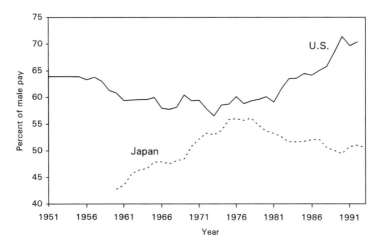

FIGURE 4.10. Female/Male Pay Ratios, United States and Japan, 1951–1993

Source: Current Population Reports, P-60 series, U.S. Bureau of the Census (various years); *Japan Statistical Yearbook,* Monthly Labor Survey data, Japan Management and Coordination Agency.

Note: U.S. data based on median annual earnings for year-round, full-time workers. Japan data based on average monthly cash earnings of regular employees in establishments with thirty or more regular employees.

provements in occupational access and gains in experience have been primary. College-educated women now are much more likely to enter professional career tracks, and they constitute sizable proportions of the younger cohorts in the professions, far beyond token levels. Among this group, improvements in women's relative pay are attributable to the closing of the gender gap in average experience levels.

At the lower end of the labor market, shifts in the relative pay of female-dominated and male-dominated jobs have been the primary mechanism. Among high school graduates, the equalizing trends since the early 1980s are attributable to decreasing pay levels among male workers, combined with constant pay levels among female workers.

In Japan, pay for women relative to men improved during the 1960s and early 1970s, while female labor force participation rates also increased. But since the mid-1970s, female pay has declined somewhat to under 51 percent of pay for men (Figure 4.10), and female labor force participation rates have grown very slowly. This timing is consistent with the general pay compression in Japan until 1975 and the subsequent stability of the wage structure, suggesting that relative pay for women has followed rather than led the evolution of Japan's wage structure.[27]

The difficulties facing Japanese women are illustrated by the continuing reluctance of Japanese companies to promote women to managerial levels. Most managerial positions are still filled by men. Among large companies (1,000 or more employees) in 1990, 0.05 percent of women held the title of department head, compared to 2.74 percent of men, and 1.16 percent of women in these companies were section or group leaders, compared to 15.17 percent of the men.[28] In the labor force as a whole, 0.98 percent of women were managers or administrators, compared to 6.66 percent of men.[29] Gender segregation is also strong in highly paid blue-collar occupations, with men disproportionately represented in technician and other high-paying job titles.[30]

For Japanese women, the trade-off between having children and accumulating experience and promotions also remains stark. In contrast to most women in the United States, many Japanese women leave the labor force during their prime childbearing ages (26 to 34), indicating a greater trade-off between careers and having children (Figure 4.11).

Improvements for Japanese women may yet occur, but they will require more than equal-pay legislation, which was enacted in Japan only in 1986. If the U.S. experience is any guide, the key elements will involve reducing Japan's gender-based pattern of occupational segregation and revising the current trade-off for women between childbearing and the ability to follow a continuously rising career path.

Summary and Major Findings

The pay systems in the United States and Japan are both highly segmented, but the divisions occur along different lines in the two countries. In the United States, JAM and SET pay systems for production and clerical workers are usually highly compressed, with small wage differentials determined mainly by seniority, within a context of interfirm mobility and interindustry wage differentials. Job ladders for blue-collar workers are relatively short, and while most companies have evaluation systems, appraisals are tied only loosely to pay. Blue-collar and clerical workers in large nonunion companies tend to have somewhat broader differentials than in union companies, but they still typically face relatively flat age–earnings profiles. College-educated workers are in professional and managerial occupations, with different pay tracks and steeper age–earnings profiles from those of production and craft workers. Gender differences in pay and promotion, while still important, have been diminishing.

The pay system in Japan is segmented along the dimensions of age, employer size, gender, and, to a lesser degree, education. The components of pay in large Japanese companies are life cycle (or age, with housing and family allowances), job-grade, and performance pay. Skill and performance are appraised frequently and are tied to pay and promotion. Nonmanagerial workers have career ladders with steep age–earnings profiles. There is no U.S.-style division between craft and production workers. High school graduates (blue-collar and white-collar workers) and university graduates (white-collar workers) are on the same published pay sched-

A. U.S.

B. Japan

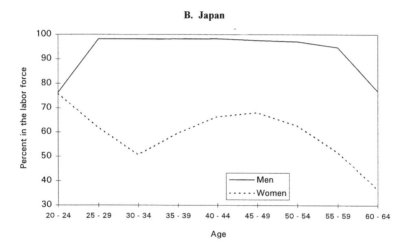

FIGURE 4.11. Labor Force Participation Rates by Age and Gender, 1992

Sources: A: Current Population Reports, P-60 sereies, U.S. Bureau of the Census (1993); B: "White Paper on Labor," Japan Ministry of Labor (1992).

ules, but university graduates move up much more rapidly and enter management sooner.

Individual incentives encourage skill development and performance for blue-collar workers in Japan. Koike and Inoki (1990) have suggested that the merit pay component of Japanese pay systems has grown since the 1970s and that, as a result, age-based pay has diminished in importance. This view is supported by several studies that found that age–earnings profiles were flattening in Japan in the 1980s. Our findings provide only partial support for Koike's hypothesis. We argue that the long career ladders reflect management's response to a system of lifetime employment with age-based pay by ensuring worker's productivity and increasing their responsibilities as they gain experience. The SET pay system in Japan rewards and supports security, employee involvement, and training in a system that produces less overall inequality than exists in the United States.

APPENDIX: CALCULATION OF STANDARD CAREER PATHS

U.S. Companies

Together Manufacturing

Data sources. Hourly pay data are taken from the 1991 and 1994 United Auto Worker contracts with Together Manufacturing. The contracts, along with discussions with Together Manufacturing's community relations department, provided the understanding of the career progressions.

Career ladder estimations. The Together Manufacturing union contract specifies two categories of workers: general production and skilled trades (general maintenance and tool and die). The paths illustrated in Figure 4.1 show typical wage progressions for various promotional paths, all based on a forty-hour work week. Entry-level step increases occur for production workers during the first thirty-six months of employment at a rate of six increases at just under $1 each. Workers beginning in skilled trades receive one entry-level step increase of over 17 percent after ninety days. Apart from across-the-board increases, production or skilled trade workers can increase their wages by $0.60 per hour with a promotion to team leader (after four to eight years for production and skilled trade workers, respectively). Beyond this, further increases in pay come from overtime, COLAs, a factorywide bonus related to quality and productivity targets, and new contracts.

Workers who wish to become team leaders usually are able to do so after two to three years with the firm, although this time period can vary considerably. About twenty to thirty general production workers per year enter the apprenticeship program, which lasts four years; completion of this training results in promotion to skilled trade status.

The 1994 contract lowered entry wages for production workers compared to the 1991 contract but extended the entry-level ladder from three increases of approximately $0.90 each over the first eighteen months to six increases of around $0.95 each over the initial three years. Skilled trade wages increased 5 percent over those in the 1991 contract.

Hi-Tech

Data sources. The Hi-Tech career paths are based on documentation provided to us by Hi-Tech. The internal documents reviewed included charts of typical career progressions, durations of employees at each job grade and at each tenure level, and hourly pay by job category. Figure 4.2a shows typical career pays for operators, operator/technicians, and engineers.

The data for Figure 4.2b are based on documents from a new Hi-Tech plant experimenting with a skill-based pay system. These documents were explained to us through interviews with company officials.

Career ladder estimations. Based on the data discussed above, the starting grade for each job category in Figure 4.2a was established and the associated starting pay was set at the minimum level for that grade. Then the progression of grades for the occupation was determined, along with an estimation of the number of years necessary to achieve average and/or top wages in that grade. With these points fixed, the data was then smoothed between the subsequent years. Earnings have been calculated with the assumption of a forty-hour work week, and no additional pay such as overtime, bonuses, or incentive pay has been included.

Operators begin at the minimum hourly pay for the entry-level pay grade, achieving the average pay for that grade after one year of tenure. With two complete years and department certification, operators move to the next grade, with their pay increasing to the minimum of that grade. Operators remain there for the remainder of the twenty years, making the top pay in the grade after fifteen years and receiving no real wage increases thereafter.

With additional education and training, operators can become technicians. Following two years at the entry-level operator grade and three more years at the operator grade, operator/technicians move into the technician career path as a tech associate, becoming a technician after three years. They then spend three years at the initial tech level and five years each at the next two technician grades, achieving above the mid-level pay of the top tech grade with over twenty years of company tenure.

Engineers typically progress to the senior engineer level in three years. After four years they move into a staff engineer position, where they remain for eight years before becoming a specialist. Specialists achieve the mid-range pay for their job title in five years.

The paths depicted for Hi-Tech in Figure 4.2b represent compensation levels for manufacturing operators and result from both skill certifications and merit performance evaluations. Skill certification typically involves competency to operate a particular machine. Performance evaluations are based upon attendance, flexibility, and contribution to problem solving. Flexibility refers to a worker's response to change in work assignment and willingness to work overtime. Employees receive a grade for each review category, and the three grades are averaged. The resulting score puts the worker at certification level, at merit level 1, or at merit level 2. The majority of workers received scores at the certification level, with only a small proportion expected to receive the highest score. Each evaluation level has a wage path associated with it. Evaluations are scheduled every six months.

CommEx

Data sources. For an understanding of the career paths in CommEx, we analyzed the CommEx–CWA union contract and interviewed personnel managers and union officials. In addition, in 1991 we conducted a survey of CommEx employees, which documented the job ladders used to identify job families.

Career-ladder estimations. CommEx has three broad job families: technical, customer service, and administrative employees. Our interviews with personnel managers and union officials indicate that workers experience considerable mobility within a job family and little mobility across job families. For each family, we identified the following career paths (ordered from entry level to highest ranking within each category), based upon the results of our employee survey.

Technical: engineering administrator, facilities technician, systems technician/communication technician. Within this job family we identified two separate paths, Technician 1 and Technician 2, distinguished mainly by the highest job level achieved by different workers in each path.

Customer service: operator, customer associate, maintenance administrator, service representative (Clerical 1).

Administrative: reports associate, data specialist, operations administrator, data administrator, computer operator, staff associate (Clerical 2).

Using responses from our employee survey, we identified the average age at each job title from the CommEx 1992 union contract. Pay within a job title also varies with tenure in that position: earnings can rise a step every six months, up to a specified maximum within that job title.

Japanese Companies

Agile Auto and Star Electronics

Data sources. The standard career ladders at Agile Auto and Star Electronics were calculated from the pay charts provided by the companies.

Career-ladder estimations. Interviews with company and union officials gave us information regarding at which point employees (by gender and education) began on a pay chart, how quickly they moved up the chart in terms of years at each job grade, and when they were expected to reach management (and thus were no longer on the union pay chart). The speed of promotion depended on tenure, on performance ratings, and on the company performance scale.

At Star Electronics, female workers remain at the same grade, which has four steps. Agile Auto does not have regular female workers.

CommSun

The standard career ladders at CommSun could not be calculated because we were unable to obtain the pay chart.

NOTES

1. U.S. President 1995, Table B-47 and Chart 5–2; Japan Management and Coordination Agency, 1995. The data in these official sources are not fully comparable. The earnings measure for the United States refers to hourly earnings in the nonfarm business sector, while the

Japanese measure refers to monthly earnings of regular employees in companies with thirty or more employees. The productivity index for the United States refers to the nonfarm business sector, while the Japanese index is restricted to mining, manufacturing, and public utilities.

2. Between 1991 and 1994, pay stagnated in the United States while productivity increased 8 percent. Both total real earnings and productivity declined slightly in Japan during the recession.

3. The difference in inequality levels between the two countries is growing. In the 1980s, earnings inequality grew slowly in Japan and rapidly in the United States (OECD, 1993).

4. Stieber (1959) describes this evolution in the steel industry. Formal job evaluation systems were favored by the union as a means of improving fairness among workers and reducing arbitrary supervisor discretion over pay.

5. Only two of our SET companies maintained a pay-for-knowledge program (see Chapter 3).

6. The slow rate of diffusion of these pay forms may have resulted from the phase of the business cycle at the time that we were conducting our field work. A recession was just beginning and profits had already fallen, as they usually do in advance of a business cycle peak. A period of falling or negative profits is not the time to introduce profit-sharing formulas.

7. Kruse (1993) also reports that profit sharing is associated with a one-time increase in productivity of 4 to 5 percent and is not correlated with other organizational practices.

8. It is difficult to estimate the extent of such managerial self-selection into the sample. Some of Osterman's establishments are corporate headquarters, which have policies that often do not extend to other work sites in the company. Since Osterman's survey did not poll workers, we cannot compare managers' stated responses to actual practices on the shop floor. Unfortunately, it is not possible to test the validity of these data.

9. The survey was conducted by Towers, Perrin and was reported in Pearlstein (1994).

10. Mosk and Nakata's computation of senior–junior wage ratios involves taking a weighted average of wages across educational groupings. A more detailed inquiry requires separate examination of trends in age–earnings profiles for major educational groups. Nakata (1987) does this, using decennial data. He shows that age–earnings ratios flattened continuously between 1960 and 1980 for all educational groupings.

11. Two of these three companies have instituted modest gain-sharing programs to reward worker effort. In both cases, the programs were plantwide or divisionwide, reflecting the reduction in individual pay incentives that often accompanies implementation of "team-oriented" HR systems in the United States.

12. The typical plan has ten skill units, and each takes twenty weeks' learning time. The average employee masters only 68 percent of the skill units in fewer than two years. Employees stop acquiring skills because of their own decision or because their supervisor did not want to train more people on certain machines. Three-fourths of these plans link skill acquisition to pay increases. Entry pay was approximately $8, and the typical employee's earnings was 40 percent higher, with the top earnings potential 70 percent higher.

13. Japanese age–earnings profiles flatten somewhat during periods of high growth and demographic decline in the number of new labor market entrants. Both of these factors are present in the late 1980s and early 1990s. There is, however, no secular flattening trend. Age–earnings profiles in the United States steepened during the 1980s, as earnings of youth fell sharply.

14. As is argued by, for example, Davis (1992); and Katz et al. (1995).

15. Sakamoto and Chen (1993) reported similar patterns for the late 1970s. Using the matched March–May 1979 Current Population Survey for the United States and the 1975 Social Stratification and Mobility Survey for Japan, they calculated overall inequality among males aged 25–64 in both countries. They found that the variance of log earnings is .56 in the United States and .39 in Japan, a 42 percent difference. Among employees of large companies (those that have 1,000 or more employees), the variance of log earnings is .23 in the United States and .12 in Japan. The corresponding figures for medium-sized companies (500–999 employees) are .32 and .15. Their sample included the earnings of the self-employed as well as family workers and government employees. The Japanese data included bonuses in the earnings measure. Excluding self-employed earnings substantially increases the overall difference in measured inequality between the two countries.

16. Calculated from the Current Population Survey, 1991 March Demographic File.

17. Brown and Medoff (1989) report similar findings in an earlier study that used 1979 Current Population Survey data.

18. However, industry differences are more prominent in pay segmentation in the United States, as we discuss below.

19. Firm size is correlated positively with age, education, and male gender. But both gross and net effects of firm size are greater in Japan than in the United States. Using the switching regression technique introduced by Dickens and Lang (1992), Ishikawa and Dejima (1993) also provide evidence of labor market dualism in Japan.

20. Wages are scheduled monthly earnings only. Japan Ministry of Labor, *Basic Survey of Wage Structure*, 1989.

21. Ratio of annual average earnings of employed males in each occupation (Bureau of the Census, 1983, Table 2).

22. Our calculations of wage dispersion across two-digit manufacturing industries in the United States and Japan show even greater dispersion within manufacturing than across all industries.

23. The U.S. data refer to mean earnings of salaried managers and administrators, while the Japanese data refer to the second and third levels of management.

24. Louis (1993). According to data from the Federation of Japanese Managers Associations (cited by Louis), the ratio of CEO pay to starting pay for a new university graduate hire stood at 100.6 in 1927, 11.9 in 1963, 9.0 in 1973, and 7.5 in 1980.

25. Comparable estimates for France and Germany are about 25 (Crystal, 1991).

26. A recent study by Abowd and Bognanno (1995) uses relative price data in each country and arrives at similar conclusions regarding the pay differences and the comparability of the data.

27. Blau and Kahn (1995) found a similar pattern in a study of ten other industrialized countries.

28. These figures were computed from Japan Ministry of Labor, *Basic Survey of Wage Structure*, 1991, vols. 1 and 3.

29. Computed from the 1990 population census (Japan Management and Coordination Agency, 1992, Table 8).

30. See Brinton and Ngo (1993) for a discussion of occupational segregation by gender in each country.

Employers and Unions

Now we turn to consider some aspects of the wage-setting process, which is in part highly decentralized and in part generally centralized in Japan and highly decentralized in the United States. In Japan, wage setting is finalized at the level of the firm, either under collective bargaining between autonomous enterprise-based unions and firms or unilaterally by management but with guidance and coordination emanating from an annual economywide process known as Shunto. In this chapter, after noting how certain characteristics of wage performance in the economy at large tend to interact with the SET system of labor management within the enterprise, we examine the wage-determining behavior of large Japanese firms, the structure and objectives of trade unionism, and the bargaining power of Japanese enterprise unions.

SET and Economic Outcomes

In Chapter 4, we pointed out how the firm's internal wage structures have either supported or conformed to essential features of its SET system. In Japan tolerance of large individual differences in pay in the work place (differences that result from steep age–earnings profiles) has made it possible to combine career incentive properties of SET with effective teamwork in small groups. Moreover, by increasing experienced employees' fear of dismissal and reluctance to quit (Koshiro, 1983c), steep profiles strengthen the incentives for their employers to invest in employee training as well as their ability to motivate their workers (see Chapter 4). At the same time, other characteristics of the firm's internal wage system are decidedly egalitarian—for example, the absence of conventional incentive pay systems and the narrow (by international standards) differences between managerial and blue-collar pay. Such egalitarian features in part depend on the existence of the senior-ity-based inequalities of the lifetime incentive system. These inequalities have been reduced as age-earnings profiles have been flattening over time,[1] but the reduction in inequalities has not caused SET systems to lose efficiency in terms of employee capability and performance.

Certain distinctive characteristics of Japanese wage behavior have also been consistent with the efficient operation of SET systems of labor management within the big-firm sector, and these characteristics link SET systems to the overall performance of the economy. In this connection, let us first take note of four facts:

Fact 1. Real hourly earnings in the manufacturing sector have grown rather more rapidly in Japan than in the United States and other major industrialized countries. This is shown in Figure 5.1 for the long postwar period, 1960–1993. (It also holds for the subperiods 1960–1973 and 1979–1989, but not for the period between the two oil price shocks, when Japan fell behind Italy, France, and Germany in real wage growth.)

Fact 2. Relative to productivity, however, real wages in manufacturing grew less rapidly in Japan than in Germany or France (Figure 5.1). Japan's pre-eminence in productivity growth over the long period is also apparent. (After 1968, however, Japan's absolute growth in productivity declined,

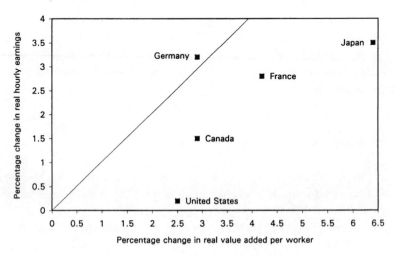

FIGURE 5.1. Changes in Real Earnings and Real Value Added Per Worker in Manufacturing, 1960–1993

Source: OECD (1995a).

especially between 1973 and 1979; except for the pre–oil shock subperiod 1968–1973, real wages followed suit.)[2]

Fact 3. While hourly wage *levels* (in terms of purchasing power parity) in Japanese manufacturing had caught up with or surpassed those in the major European economies by the late 1970s and in the United States by the 1990s (Table 5.1), the working year remains much longer in Japan than in the United States and Europe. However, work hours have steadily declined. By the early 1990s, the work day in the United States and Japan was the same length, but Japanese workers still had fewer days off (see Chapter 2).

Fact 4. Unemployment has been markedly lower in Japan than in the United States and other major countries since the 1950s, and so has consumer price inflation since the end of the 1970s (Table 5.2).

Now let us turn to a discussion of a set of artifacts or outcomes involving the cyclical responsiveness of employment, unemployment, hours of work, and wages.

1. Japan's low levels of unemployment have been associated with markedly low cyclical variability of employment and unemployment (Elmeskov and Pichelman, 1993).

2. The comparative rigidity of employment relative to output in Japan (resulting in procyclical swings in productivity) has not been offset by a higher elasticity of hours with respect to output (Elmeskov and Pichelman, 1993).

3. On the other hand, various econometric studies have found both real and money wages to be markedly responsive by international standards to such variation in unemployment as has occurred in Japan (Elmeskov and Pichelman, 1993; Tachibanaki, 1987; Coe, 1985; OECD, 1989a).[3]

4. Greater wage flexibility in Japan than in the United States does not appear to have been associated with less variability in profits, at least in the past decades. Indeed, for the twelve-year period 1981–1992, the standard deviation of the ratio of profits to wage bills was 0.02 in Japan and 0.01 in the United States (Bank of Japan, 1992 Table 57(2), p. 119; 1994a, Table 59(2), p. 127).

TABLE 5.1. Hourly Compensation Costs for Manufacturing Production Workers in Six OECD Countries, 1975–1993

Country	1975	1985	1990	1993
United States	$6.36	$13.01	$14.91	$16.73
Canada	5.96	10.94	15.83	16.33
Japan	3.00	6.34	12.80	19.01
France	4.52	7.52	15.23	16.23
Germany	6.35	9.60	21.96	25.70
United Kingdom	3.37	6.27	12.71	12.76

Source: Data is from U.S. Department of Labor (1995b).

Note: Compensation costs are converted to U.S. dollars using the annual average exchange rate.

TABLE 5.2. Indices of Economic Performance

	1960–1968	1968–1973	1973–1979	1979–1990	1989–1993[a]	1960–1993
	Average Annual Change in CPI: Mid Year to Mid Year					
Japan	5.7	7.1	9.9	2.6	2.3	5.2
U.S.	2.0	5.0	8.5	5.5	3.9	4.9
Germany	2.7	4.6	4.7	2.9	3.6	3.5
France	3.6	6.1	10.7	6.9	2.8	6.3
Canada	2.4	4.6	9.2	6.3	3.4	5.3
	Average Annual Unemployment Rate: Mid Year to Mid Year					
Japan	1.3	1.2	1.9	2.5	2.2	1.9
U.S.	5.0	4.6	6.7	7.0	6.5	6.0
Germany	0.8	0.8	3.5	7.1	7.3	3.8
France	1.5	2.6	4.5	9.3	10.0	5.5
Canada	4.8	5.4	7.2	9.3	10.2	7.3
	Average Annual Real Hourly Wage Growth, Manufacturing: Mid Year to Mid Year					
Japan	5.2	9.7	1.7	1.6	0.1	3.5
U.S.	1.5	1.3	0.0	−1.0	−1.0	0.2
Germany	5.0	5.8	2.4	1.4	2.0	3.2
France	4.0	5.3	3.7	0.9	1.0	2.8
Canada	2.3	3.6	2.2	−0.2	0.3	1.5

Source: OECD (1992a; 1995a).

[a] Average unemployment rates measured for the period 1990–1993.

These characteristics of overall performance in the manufacturing sector of the economy are consistent with the emphasis on security, EI, and training and with the related system of compensation within the firm. Systems following the SET model contribute to the higher productivity growth, which often has tended to outpace the growth of real wages in the manufacturing sector. Moreover, pay systems based on seniority and opportunities for advancement serve as incentives to employee effort and as sources of internally generated savings available for further growth in output capacity and firm growth as long as the firm's labor force is growing.[4] In addition, such pay systems can help employers restrain wages relative to productivity growth when their employees depend more on seniority increments and promotion than on across-the-board increases for advancement in pay.

The SET model is also consistent with the persistence of long hours of work. The implicit security guarantees under SET furnish incentives to an employer to increase hours per worker, especially overtime at premium rates,[5] instead of employing a larger work force in securing a required number of worker hours; doing this reduces the expected cost of the guarantee. In addition, workers tend to favor current income, via more paid work, including overtime at premium pay, and less time off. In interviews, auto workers told us that they factored their overtime hours into their family budgets, since they had come to expect overtime. When international comparisons of yearly hours of work are combined with comparisons of hourly wage levels, it is apparent that Japan's companies incur low unit labor costs and high levels of international competitiveness.

Employment security and career-oriented pay systems provide a source of flexibility in both wages and profits during cyclical recession (our third and fourth outcomes). More important, security offered by career employment in the firms can constitute a strong incentive to Japanese employees to accept reduction in the growth of their regular wages and actual reduction in the bonus during recessions[6] and hence to share the costs of fixed employment with their employers. The employer share is reflected in that part of the cyclical reduction in profits resulting from the cost of retaining redundant employees on the payroll.[7]

Thus, different features of SET favor both downward flexibility and upward restraint in wages as well as growth in output and real wages. These outcomes, however, also reflect the market power and policies of employers, the bargaining propensities and power of the unions with which they deal, and the national institution for synchronous wage determination known as Shunto.

The Power and Prudence of Large Japanese Employers

In many cases, Japan's major firms have been characterized as oligopolistic competitors in their product markets; and they have also exhibited some market power within their labor markets. Building from a power base provided by their market positions and consistent with the Japanese values of security and continuity, large Japanese companies have been able over time to shape their employment systems to increase their control over employees while at the same time sharing the fruits of the companies' success with the workers through rising wages and employment security. Indicators of large firms' labor market power and the demarcation of market segments include the intense competition for jobs in large firms, the low labor turnover in large firms, and the higher interfirm mobility rates among smaller companies (see Chapter 2).

Confronted with labor turbulence in the late 1940s and early 1950s followed by extremely rapid growth in the 1960s and early 1970s, large employers were able to respond with a set of policies and programs that effectively addressed the renewal of prewar demands for equality of status across occupations, including employment security for blue-collar workers. They also maintained high wages relative to smaller employers while promoting high rates of growth of productivity relative to real wages, minimizing turnover, and coping with labor shortages. Those policies have both reflected and added to the relative insulation from competitive forces that have characterized the firm's labor supply. However, such insulation has not resulted in the imprisonment and exploitation of workers in a low-wage dungeon, the fate that monopsony theory was originally devised to explain in the nineteenth century, but rather to place them in a gilded cage—immobilized and hard working, to be sure, but secure, relatively well paid, and with every prospect of orderly advancement until (often early) retirement from the firm.

Paternalism presupposes market power; and policies followed by large firms in various areas of personnel management have been consistent with at least an intent to delineate and control their respective labor markets. Thus, locational policies have in some instances reflected an intent to reserve supplies of labor for the firm's own use. Included among them was a postwar revival of the practice of locating new plants in rural areas, where firms hire employees who commute between plant and farm (Dore, 1973, p. 306). In prewar times, this practice had resulted in the restriction of geographic labor markets in what Levine (1958, p. 21) described as "manorial channels, whereby workers in search of employment . . . were confined to specific routes, usually between a given farm area and a given factory or enterprise." After the war, the practice was resumed with help from the government's Shinsantoshi program, which supported the establishment of infrastructure in rural communities in an effort to reduce the migration of workers to Tokyo and other metropolitan areas. Mosk (1995) observed that smaller subcontracting firms have tended to be located in the same areas as their large customers and credits lower search costs as the reason for labor either to stay within firms or to move between firms in the same region. Perhaps more important, many families prefer to live near their family grave sites in order to honor their ancestors on national holidays. Reference is still made in the press to "factory castle towns" (Sakakibara, 1993, pp. 16, 26). It should be noted, however, that manufacturing activity remains concentrated in large metropolitan areas. Nevertheless, the postwar expansion of capacity and employment in areas where firms can easily find new workers and possess greater control over their labor supplies enhances their ability to expand without unduly increasing labor's bargaining power.

Moreover, the development of SET employment systems at large companies resulted in internal labor markets that bound the worker to the firm. By agreeing to include age, seniority, or family need among the determinants of pay and by instituting long career ladders associated with continual training and promotion, the large employers moved further to bind their employees to the firm. Japanese labor organizations had historically opposed conventional wage incentive plans, in which current pay is tightly tied to current performance, as a denial of equal status with salaried staff (Gordon, 1985). But recognition of seniority and career progression amount to a stretched-out incentive system with deferred compensation that the worker must forfeit in the event of early departure from the firm.

Policies designed to internalize the labor market to the firm have also included policies intended to restrict access to them by other employers, including the firm's smaller suppliers in the same locality or its big competitors in the same product markets. Any market advantage held by the larger firm in continuing commercial or even financial relationships with smaller contractors can enhance its ability to maintain a high relative wage level, which would help to insulate its own work force and also assure it preferred access to sources of new labor. Dore (1973) has suggested that employees and their enterprise-based unions in large firms owe their wage premiums at least in part to the unorganized status of employees of small suppliers. If the latter were to become organized and force the suppliers to pay higher wages, they would have to charge their big customers higher prices, which would reduce the ability of the latter to pay high wages to their own employees. This also explains an alleged lack of interest on the part of the enterprise-based unions in organizing workers in these smaller firms. Overall, a large firm's market power over its suppliers reinforces its market power in the labor market.

Labor market competition with product market competitors, who have comparable ability to set wages, poses a potentially more serious problem for the large firms; and it is a problem that could be exacerbated by the intense competition that has prevailed within such product markets. Since a handful of large firms share the market power, they would find it both feasible and advisable to take one another's policies and actions into account when formulating their own and to arrive at informal understandings designed to minimize competition in particular spheres of activity. The exchange and transmission of information is the major function of industry employer associations. The latter do not engage in industrywide bargaining, but under the centralized Shunto process, they do serve to link local settlements within industries and to prevent leapfrogging in wage changes. Generally, informal agreement constitutes the "mechanism by which big businesses check their respective labor costs with each other . . . to ensure that they are reflected in the negotiations over revision of product prices" (Nitta, 1990, p. 2).

As a complement to their restraining influence on wages, such "gentlemen's agreements" have also sought to prevent the poaching of workers. Galenson and Odaka (1976, p. 616) cite an OECD report of 1971 that attributed a paucity of labor mobility among big firms to an "arrangement [that] seems to have been rather effectively policed by employer understandings not to poach regular employees of another firm or hire such former employees." To the extent that the practice of hiring experienced workers from competitors becomes generalized throughout the industry, immediate savings in training costs would be offset by a competitive bidding-up of wages of experienced workers. Hence, no-poaching understandings among the member firms in a concentrated industry could closely complement their informational exchanges, which have been designed (inter alia) to deter the leapfrogging of wages while the companies maintain employee efficiency. The latter advantage might help to explain why no-poaching agreements apparently proved more durable in Japan than in other countries where seniority has been less significant as a determinant of the firm's internal wage structure.

Managers in large Japanese enterprises have tended to deploy their market power with a degree of paternalistic prudence, which reflects both a genuine regard for the welfare of their employees and an enlightened self-interest in maintaining the efficiency of the work force and the long-run viability of the enterprise. Enlightened self-interest has prompted the adoption of paying relatively high wages (efficiency wage policies). Thus, Koshiro (1977) reported that managerial determination to avoid a repetition of the labor unrest that had occurred in the postwar years exerted a moderating influence on corporate wage policies in the aftermath of the first oil price shock in the 1970s. And, according to an observer on the left, "management itself . . . reacts sensitively to worker discontent and copes with problems before they become serious" (Tokunaga, 1983, p. 326). Thus, while the degree of wage flexibility exhibited in Japan has been regarded as relatively high by international standards, it may be limited by an appreciable element of self-restraint on the part of management.

Enterprise-based Unions: Weak or Willing?

Can wage behavior that generally conforms to employer preferences and policies be reconciled with the prevalence of unionism and collective bargaining in the sectors dominated by large-scale enterprise? The answer can be yes if those enterprise-based unions are characterized by bargaining weakness. The answer can also be yes if these unions have a preference for policies that both conform to the requirements of economic efficiency and are responsive to (or do not contravene) the wishes of their members.

A union is regarded (in economic theory) as acting efficiently, or "rationally," if the wage policy it pursues is designed to maintain the employment of its current members, allowing money wages—or increases in money wages—to be reduced significantly to avoid layoffs or dismissals during recessions and raising them high enough to preclude the hiring of additional workers (known as "outsiders") during expansions. Wage levels or wage changes are regarded as "flexible" to the extent that they can vary (inversely) in response to changes in output or employment; otherwise, when they are relatively inflexible, they are "rigid" and conducive to unemployment during recessions.

Hence, two contrasting stereotypes of union wage behavior emerge at the opposite ends of the wage flexibility–rigidity continuum: a "rational" stereotype at one extreme and what might be termed a Keynesian stereotype at the other. However, the characteristic policy approach pursued by a particular union (or by a representative union in a national union movement) might be characterized as hybrid if it conforms more closely to one stereotype during downswings in demand and to the opposite stereotype during expansions. When viewed in this narrow perspective, U.S. unions and Japanese unions can be considered examples of two contrasting hybrid models.

Are Japan's Enterprise-based Unions Rational?

The wage behavior of American unions has been characterized as more responsive to such Keynesian variables as relative and real wages and past growth in wages and also to the expected level of employer resistance than to the current and expected state of demand and supply. Employment considerations have, at least recently, been regarded as less influential in determining wage policy, partly because of characteristic shortsightedness concerning the long-run substitution or output effects of wage increases. They have generally rejected wage deflation as a device either to preclude or reduce unemployment. Higher employment levels have often been sought through attempts to impose restrictive practices that, to the extent they have obliged employers to employ more labor than required at the going wage, involve raising costs rather than lowering them. Unions have agreed to settlements below the industry average when judged to be necessary to the continued viability of firms in precarious economic health, but such treatment was usually regarded as "exceptional" and indeed could be withheld in instances where it could threaten the industrywide wage level with competitive erosion. During the 1980s, however, the incidence of "concession bargaining"—which resulted in freezes or even absolute reductions in nominal wages—became widespread. It was associated with sharply declining levels of unionization and strike activity, heightened employer hostility, and wage settlements lower than expected on the basis of historical (statistical) relationships. But Mitchell (1994) found no evidence that settlements became significantly more responsive to cyclical changes in business conditions.

During expansions, American unions have typically found it possible to negotiate acceptably higher levels of pay for their current (insider) membership at acceptably low costs of striking[8] without choking off firm growth and precluding increased employment of outsiders (which incidentally increases dues revenue). But neither have they been notably disposed to forgo attainable increases in pay in the interest of greater firm growth, profitability, and employment security in the long term. Hence, while wage policies of U.S. unions have conformed more closely to the Keynesian, rigid-wage stereotype than to the rational stereotype during periods of declining demand, they have been closer to the insider rationality stereotype during periods of economic expansion.

In contrast, the wage policies of Japanese unions have been responsive to downswings in activity. And, according to Shimada (1983, p. 183), it is the rationality of Japanese unions that "tends to make [them] accept flexible wages in return for maintaining stable employment." This explanation suggests that the employer's prior commitment to rigid employment has elicited the type of flexible wage behavior that helps to keep employment stable.

The contrast with the American stereotype can be extended. Rather than conforming to the requirements of a static insider–outsider model and pushing up wages at the expense of firm growth, Japanese unions have been credited with following wage policies conducive to economic expansion and growth (as well as to the maintenance of employment at high levels during cyclical downswings). Willingness to accept moderation in wage growth has been reflected in the adoption of the institutions of lifetime and continuous employment and age-determined wages. Passing up part of a potential wage increase and permitting the company to grow and expand its work force can be regarded as partial payment for job insurance (along with downward flexibility of negotiated wage increases during recessions) by an enterprise union with members deeply averse to risking the loss of relatively high-wage careers with their firm. And, as noted earlier, forgoing current gains in favor of later rewards can be regarded as an act of saving and investment in the company by the individual worker, just as the "underpayment" of younger employees can be viewed by them as an investment in their future careers. Koshiro put the point in its historic context:

> As a result of several severe experiences of early militant labor disputes in the private industries, union officials as well as rank and file members of enterprise unions have become convinced that the best way to improve their wages and working conditions is to increase productivity and grow with the respective enterprises which usually promise them permanent employment until the retirement years. In other words, unions do not wish to kill a golden egg-bearing goose to improve the immediate conditions of employment. (1976, p. 6)

An even more benign view of union policy toward the growth of the firm, taken by Aoki (1984, 1988) and Koike (1988), can dispense with the assumption of strong risk aversion. Koike observes that opportunities for advancement and the accumulation of skills on the part of the existing work force are increased by the growth of firms, although this holds only to the extent that firm growth includes growth in employment of new hires (as opposed to substitution at the margin of capital, hours of work, midcareer transfers, or foreign workers in overseas subsidiaries).

According to Aoki, the firm's regular employees not only have a stake in the growth of the firm and its work force but also exert, through their enterprise union, sufficient bargaining power to force growth beyond the scale and output level at which total profit is maximized, at least in the short run, in order to gain increased opportunity for individual advancement. Although, as we have observed, a firm's employees are quite immobile, "the body of employees may withhold its effort to accumulate and efficiently utilize the stock of knowledge" (Aoki, 1988, p. 155). Whether acting as "benevolent arbiter," "neutral referee," or even agent of the shareholders, management, in this model, must make growth decisions that ratify the enterprise union's bargaining power—and its members' preference for forgoing immediate, across the board wage increases in favor of greater long-term "investment" in the company. In fact, one prominent economist has even claimed that, "above all, the management is to be characterized as the representative of the employee group. This is sometimes unique to Japanese firms with practically no parallel in other countries" (Komiya, 1987, p. 41; see also Sakakibara, 1993, pp. 13, 128). According to this view, therefore, enterprise unions should be classified as union representatives.

This approach emphasizes the role played by the stable work force of regular employees as "stakeholders" in the Japanese firm, although to blame its excessive growth on a company union seems far-fetched. A management that has sufficient power in its own right to function as an arbitrator between labor and capital in the company also possesses sufficient autonomy to make growth decisions for reasons other than the desire to do distributional justice. Management might respond to subsidized capital or to "administrative guidance" in the national interest. And if growth proceeds from such sources, the employees would be rewarded in the same way and at the same costs in terms of sharing with outsiders, deferred compensation, and "learning effort" (Aoki, 1988, p. 156), as if management had been propelled by union bargaining power.

Alternatively, a union intent on pushing the static insider position to its extreme would prefer a general wage increase to an "investment" wage policy (i.e., a "front-loaded" contract to a "rear-loaded" contract), even if the former does not support the long-run growth of the firm. Such a policy would tend to flatten, rather than steepen, age–earnings profiles; it would not tend to increase the experienced worker's chances of advancement to higher-paid positions; and it could result in lower total career earnings than a policy of relative abstinence. But a front-loaded policy could nevertheless result in higher present values of career earnings (if, for example, it raised labor's share in the income of the firm more than it stunted its growth). And it would lower the worker's cost in effort expended and leisure forgone (Ulman and Nakata, 1994). However, while a union with strong bargaining power might "rationally" pursue a wage policy that is not (per se) conducive to the growth of the firm, it might nevertheless support an investment wage policy in exchange for guarantees of security and career advancement for its (insider) members.

Enterprise Unions: Powerful or Persuasive?

According to some econometric evidence, enterprise unionism in Japan has not passed the U.S. economists' standard test for union bargaining power—that is, the ability to secure higher wage rates than are found in nonunion but otherwise comparable establishments. In a study based on a survey of 689 firms employing more than 100 workers, Tachibanaki and Noda (1992) estimated a (firm) wage equation that includes a union dummy variable and other control variables—firm size (number of employees), average experience of employees, sales per employee, firm working hours, and dummies for manufacturing for three regions. They found the coefficient of the union dummy to be not significant for both male and female workers and negatively signed for male workers. Similarly, Tsuru and Rebitzer (1995, p. 466) found that "union status has no statistically significant effect on male earnings."

This type of procedure, however, fails to take account of the possible indirect effects of unions on wages as well as their possible impact on nonwage conditions of work. For example, enterprise unions can protect firm-size differentials simply by refraining from organizing or negotiating on behalf of employees in small contracting firms, as noted above. Moreover, an enterprise-based union might be able to improve the well-being of its members without raising their *relative* wage if nonunion firms raise the wages of their own employees in response (or anticipation). Tachibanaki and Noda (1982) attribute their finding of no significant positive union–nonunion wage differential to a spillover of wage increases from unions to nonunion sectors in the annual wage settlement rounds under the Shunto procedure.

An enterprise union might improve nonwage conditions for employees even if it does not independently affect its wage rate. Here we note once again the priority assigned by Japanese unionized workers to their employers' commitment to continuous career-long employment in the firm and, since it imposes risks and costs on the employers, their surrender of some potential wage gains as a quid pro quo. At the same time, unions have acted to enforce security commitments and have on occasion struck against dismissals (Koike, 1988, p. 171; Dore, 1986, p. 88). They have sought to improve the terms of their implicit contract by attempting to raise the age of mandatory retirement (Koshiro, 1983a, p. 247). And they have opposed employer preference for substituting performance-based pay for seniority wages.

Unions have also tried to reduce hours of work, including overtime, and to raise premium rates for overtime; whereas managers have typically preferred to respond to labor shortages by increasing hours and work loads rather than by increased hiring (Dore, 1973, 1986; Koike, 1988; Koshiro, 1983a, 1983b, and 1983c; Shirai, 1983; Kawanishi, 1992, p. 231). Furthermore, unions have been active (in both politics and collective bargaining) in securing improved conditions and supplementary compensation in the areas of industrial health and safety (Koshiro, 1983c, pp. 72–74). Finally, they have been consulted and/or informed extensively by management on a wide range of issues, including not only transfers and promotions and working conditions but also such nonbargaining topics as the firm's investment and development plans and its financial condition (Koike, 1983, pp. 47–48; 1988, pp. 121–122, 252–257; Koshiro, 1983a, p. 245). Union–management consultation in the latter areas can qualify as a nonpecuniary benefit on the widely shared assumption that the Japanese worker prizes the (large) firm that employs him not only as the source of a better job and career than he could obtain elsewhere but, beyond that, as a "center of primary attachment" and a source of psychic welfare.

However, there are some indications that union bargaining power in the realm of nonwage conditions has been limited, even when supported by government policy. In the first place, while the strongest econometric evidence of union impact lies in the areas of standard working hours and vacations (Tachibanaki and Noda, 1992), Japanese industry continues (as noted above) to post longer hours and fewer days off than are experienced in the other advanced industrial countries. Nor have reductions in hours necessarily meant increases in work force, as unions intended. Instead, according to Kawanishi (1992, pp. 48–51, 208–212), firms have adjusted by increased work loads (higher standard times) and overtime, which, while yielding more pay, were often judged to be excessive. Unions have long attempted to increase the legal minimum overtime premium to 50 percent (from an actual level of only 25%), but as Koshiro (1994, p. 7) observed, they have been unable to overcome employer resistance. Similarly, union and government efforts to increase the mandatory age of retirement have encountered the same type of stubborn and protracted resistance; and (as noted above) progress in this area has been slow and, by international standards, incomplete.

While enterprise unions have actively moved to uphold the tradition of employment security and to resist dismissal of their members, employers are primarily restrained by the courts and the legal doctrine of "abuse of the right to dismiss" (Koshiro, 1983a, p. 245); the right to dismiss may, however, permit the selection of less efficient and higher-paid workers for dismissal (Hanami, 1991, pp. 33–41). The enterprise union appears to have been effective mainly as a whistle-blower, protesting any alleged violation of an implied contract to which large-scale employers have continued to subscribe. Unionism might have been effective in that deterrent role, although, in the late 1940s and early 1950s, management had demonstrated a capacity first to defeat militant unions in major strikes against layoffs and individual dismissals (and other issues as well) and subsequently to encourage the organization of "second unions," which supplanted the troublemakers (Tokunaga, 1983, p. 315; Womack et al., 1991, p. 54). Nevertheless, it is a plausible hypothesis that modern enterprise unions could not have taken root without at least tacit support from the employees who joined them (although often under union shop arrangements); and so they can serve as a constant reminder to employers that reneging on unwritten guarantees of employment security can entail a penalty price associated with employee discontent.

In other words, while enterprise unions may have lacked strike muscle, they have acquired a voice that large-scale employers might heed. For, as we have seen, the market power of the big firms has provided them with some leeway in setting their wage and employment policies. Thus, they can avoid minimizing labor costs in the short run, when to do so would jeopardize the employees' goodwill, their involvement in and attachment to the firm, and hence their productivity. Econometric evidence that the pure "voice" of unionism played a part in holding down separation rates (and thereby enhancing labor productivity) was found by Tomita (1992).

Moreover, the consultative, nonadversarial, and pacific nature of industrial relations in unionized Japanese firms has contributed to lower inventory costs. The celebrated just-in-time delivery system is premised on dependably peaceful industrial relations because it leaves the production process highly vulnerable to any random (or even threatened) stoppage of work (just as it requires uninterrupted transport from supply point to consumption point). Employers elsewhere (mostly in the United States and Germany) who have copied the Japanese lean inventory system without replicating the Japanese style of industrial relations have discovered how more generally disruptive isolated strikes in parts-producing facilities have become. (A strike at two General Motors brake part plants by a local union of the United Auto Workers in March 1996 promptly resulted in the shutdown of twenty-one of the company's twenty-nine North American assembly plants and thirty other parts plants.)

Of course, there are limits to the influence wielded by nonadversarial enterprise-based unions. When the cost of settlement exceeds the cost imposed by loss of worker morale and efficiency, the employer is likely to find the union voice unpersuasive; for example, in 1996 an ailing automobile manufacturer decided to stop production for a few days each month (as an alternative to dismissals), despite union warnings that stoppages would be bad for morale (*Economist*, July 13, 1996, pp. 66–67). Moreover, joint consultation appears to have become a partial substitute for collective bargaining with enterprise unions. In Japan, as in the United States and Germany, employees are not supposed to strike over issues that lie outside the scope of wages, hours, and working conditions—the normal domain of collective bargaining. In the United States, unions have often circumvented this restriction by pressing hard for "mandatory" (or strikeable) demands so that employers have been willing to give way on issues over which strikes may not legally be called (because they are not deemed to be sufficiently related to wages, hours, or other conditions of work). In Japan, on the other hand, Koshiro (1983a, p. 249) has reported that "many employers may prefer to resolve as many issues as possible by the joint consultation process." And consultation concerning issues such as the company's investment or development plans or competitive position is in most cases a matter of information sharing; it is not an instrument of worker participation in management (Koike, 1988, p. 252). On the contrary, management in effect has been charged with participation in unionism, notably through the frequent election of union officers drawn from the ranks of career managerial employees, and Shirai (1983, p. 141) found that enterprise unions are both "susceptible to employer interference and pressure" and "relatively weak in their bargaining power against employers."

Now, consultation under such circumstances does not imply exploitation: union representatives with a career stake in company management have been freely elected by the employees because it is believed that company-oriented officers can effectively represent company-oriented members. This is the essence of the rebuttal to the charge by Japanese leftists and some American observers that enterprise-based unions are company-dominated.[9] However, consultation does imply that management retains its discretionary authority (its "rights"). It can thus be regarded as an institutional implementation of the discretionary power of the large-scale employer. Management is not bound by negotiated rules of seniority, which Koike (1988, p. 239) regards as "giving the [American] unions a most powerful voice."

In failing (or not attempting) to secure binding constraints on managerial discretion in such areas as employee promotion and transfers, the enterprise unions have done little or nothing to prevent intense competition among employees in their quest for favorable performance evaluations from supervisors (Koike, 1988, pp. 144, 151, 251; 1983, pp. 43–45; Endo, 1994, p. 77). For the same reason, workers frequently elect not to take paid vacation time, thereby reducing the practical effectiveness of union efforts to negotiate increased vacation time (OECD, 1989b, pp. 53–54). As recently as 1992, Rengo, the Japanese Trade Union Confederation, complained that, although the Labor Standards Law "morally" prohibits employers from penalizing leave-takers, leave-taking can result in employees being registered as absentees, which may entail the loss of allowances for full attendance, and poor performance evaluations, which in turn result in reductions in bonuses. A survey of working time (*Japan Labor Bulletin,* October 1991, p. 3) found that "Japanese workers spent more time than their counterparts of other nations hanging around offices before and after work . . . indicating that they are more committed to corporate society." Perhaps this behavior is in part competitive loitering. The failure of enterprise unions to abate competition among employees (their members) has contributed to the maintenance of characteristically high levels of effort in the work place—both in the form of high effort expended per hour and in the form of long working hours per year (in forgone vacations and holidays)—despite some evidence of fewer work hours in union firms than in nonunion firms and despite union efforts in the areas of employment security and health and safety. Our reading of the union record in these nonwage fields (combined with our impression of the growth strategy followed by big firms in international product markets) leads us to concur with Shimada's (1992, p. 8) assessment:

> One of the problems of the Japanese system is that strongly motivated workers who are keenly aware of their own responsibilities in the production system may run the risk of working and learning endlessly. Labor unions who are cooperating closely with the management in securing employment opportunities for their members primarily by means of trying to expand market share often fail to put a limit on the overworking of workers.

In general, a Japanese enterprise can operate safely on the assumption that its counterpart union will be well behaved when the latter, as Kawanishi (1992, p. 147) has written about one of them, "operates on the basic assumption that there is an imbalance in its power relationship with management, and that it will best serve its members by cooperating with management in raising productivity." Both of these assumptions square with the view that union bargaining weakness has been imposed by a low degree of militancy on the part of workers who have been reluctant to support union policies or tactics that might impair the market position or prospects of the enterprise. A different interpretation, however, was offered by a group of left-wing unionists who, in the late 1940s and early 1950s, attributed not only union weakness but also worker passivity and risk aversion to decentralization of union and bargaining structures.

Bargaining Power and Structure

Ironically, the bargaining weakness of the enterprise unions has been reflected in their strong institutional position within the union movement—in their independence of and even influence over the *tan-sans,* or industrial union federations, with which they are affiliated. Enterprise unions retain the authority to strike, bargain, and finance themselves (Kawanishi, 1992, pp. 12–13). The tan-sans possess no strike authority, and they are not represented in negotiations with the companies in most industries. And while their officers play an important role in assembling and disseminating information and economic analyses to the enterprise unions, they themselves may come from the leadership ranks of enterprise unions based in major firms (Nakamura, 1991, p. 6). Therefore, the bargaining power of the enterprise union vis-à-vis the firm was originally compounded solely out of its own resources, which vary inversely with the level of employee satisfaction and loyalty to the firm and directly with employee propensity to resort to concerted action in the form of strikes or slowdowns.

In other advanced industrial countries, industrywide unions have possessed greater authority to bargain with and strike against either employer associations or (more characteristic in the United States) individual firms in major industries. In the United States, such national unions came to acquire the striking, financial, and bargaining capabilities denied the tan-sans in Japan, partly in order to contain competitive pressures within industrywide product markets and/or national labor markets. To this end, they have been assigned seven historic missions:

1. To reduce wage differentials (mainly geographic) in order to protect jobs in high-wage firms and to secure wage "equity" in low-wage firms
2. To protect industry wage levels from competitive erosion and "whipsawing" in bad times, when each individual local union might be tempted to make "concessions" because it is confronted with a highly elastic demand curve in its own jurisdiction
3. In certain industries (e.g., construction), to cope with geographically mobile labor forces that threaten to overrun closed shop arrangements in local market jurisdictions
4. To organize nonunion establishments within their respective jurisdictions (which their success in wage bargaining ironically could help to generate)

5. Through either industrywide bargaining or "pattern bargaining" with individual firms in sequence, to maximize the probability that a given pay increase negotiated for any given firm would also be negotiated with its competitors and also (although only in the case of pattern bargaining) to allow the national union to strike one employer while its competitors remained in operation. (It should also be noted that uniting in an association has held out certain advantages for employers—whether to resist bargaining [as in certain U.S. industries prior to the 1930s and the passage of the Wagner Act], to present a united resistance to union demands under collective bargaining, or to "take wages out of competition.")
6. To prevent multiplant firms from "whipsawing" local unions by shifting production between plants through bargaining on a companywide basis
7. To help determine working conditions on the shop floor through participation with their local unions in "supplementary" agreements with individual employers and in the appellate stages of negotiated grievances procedures. (Ulman, 1955; Reder and Ulman, 1993, pp. 13–44)

Collective bargaining with national unions proved efficient in securing advances in pay and benefits to workers in large-scale industries and elsewhere in the U.S. economy. It was found to have passed the relative wage (union–nonunion) test and it also narrowed geographic differentials. But the national unions' bargaining power tended to exceed "their organizing power" (as Sumner Slichter, 1941, p. 341, put it); they too often failed to organize lower-wage nonunion firms, whose competitiveness was often exacerbated by the unions' own bargaining success. Nor could national unions (by definition) cope with lower-wage competition from abroad, which began to emerge strongly in the 1970s (Reder and Ulman, 1993).

In Japan's case, organizing weakness has been blamed in part on the "enterprise egoism" of enterprise unions that have been accused of enhancing the economic position of their members by neglecting to organize nonunion subcontractors and not admitting temporary or part-time fellow employees to membership (Kawanishi, 1992, p. 25; see also note 6). But American national unions have presided over an even more dismal organizing record despite the wider perspectives that more centralized organizations presumably possess.

On the other hand, American experience might seem to suggest that the bargaining power of unions in Japan could have been greater if the tan-sans had been empowered to bargain and call strikes. However, the market conditions and worker and employer attitudes that had helped originally to empower national unions in the United States—and later to weaken them—have not prevailed so strongly in postwar Japan. Thus (at least until the 1990s), the viability of autonomous enterprise-based unions in Japan has been underwritten by comparatively high growth rates, which helped to minimize industry wage differentials, and also by security-conscious and company-oriented workers who could look to increased promotional opportunities as their major source of individual wage growth.

But while the large-scale employers in Japan have not resisted enterprise union-ism, they have opposed industrywide bargaining and dealing with "outsiders," no-tably radical labor leaders and tan-sans representatives. They had formed industry associations in response to the establishment of industrywide bargaining arrange-ments in the late 1940s, as demanded by militant left-wing union groups in many industries; but then, aided by the banning of a threatened industrywide strike in 1947 by the occupation authorities, they succeeded in disestablishing industrywide bargaining along with radical-supported enterprise unions that had gained con-trol of plant-level labor relations in a number of establishments. The industry em-ployer associations remained, but without bargaining functions, as formal collec-tive bargaining was confined to the company level and employers in large-scale industries found it preferable to coordinate wage-determination activities on an informal basis (Dore, 1973, p. 172; Kawanishi, 1992, pp. 77–78, 82–83; Koshiro, 1983a, pp. 212–214; Shirai, 1983, p. 123; Solomon B. Levine, 1958, pp. 27, 47; 1984, pp. 336, 341). In contrast, the American system of pattern bargaining confronts the isolated employer with an industrywide national union.

Nor did the employers require united defense against isolated strikes by the new generation of enterprise unions. The latter, while potentially capable of such action in an environment of growth, were generally too company-oriented to uncork the punch they might have packed. Galenson and Odaka (1976, p. 637, n. 95) recounts an episode in which Walter Reuther (the outstanding leader of the United Auto-mobile Workers) asked a group of enterprise union leaders why they didn't follow the UAW example and let their JAW (Confederation of Japan Automobile Work-ers' Unions) select one company as a strike target for setting an industrywide pat-tern. The reply of the Japanese unionists was that the workers in any company cho-sen as a target would be unwilling for their employer to suffer loss of market share during an isolated strike. American unionists could assume that, in most cases, the same possibility would prevent the target employer from taking a strike in the first place! For under pattern bargaining the lead firm knows that any settlement to which it agrees will be pressed on its competitors by the same strongly centralized and well-heeled national union with which it conducted its own negotiations.

The enterprise union's fear of isolation could have been removed by substitut-ing industrywide bargaining for sequential pattern bargaining. That course of ac-tion, however, would have required confronting oligopolistic employers, industry by industry; and few individual tan-sans would have volunteered (or have been allowed to do so by their constituent enterprise unions) for those jobs. Instead, a call for action on a broader front came from Sohyo, the left-wing socialist-affili-ated general union federation. In 1954, Óta Kaoru, Sohyo's deputy chairman, called for a concerted wage push by the major industrial federations, noting that even cowards can hold hands and move forward together in the dark. Thus was inaugurated the Annual Spring Labor Offensive (or Shunto) (Kawanishi, 1992, pp. 172–173).

Summary

Japan's distinctive set of employer policies has been complemented by a distinctive set of union–management relations. Together they have been conducive to relatively high growth in productivity, to growth but restraint and flexibility in real and money wages, to maintenance of employment in the firm but also long hours of work—and hence to the comparatively high rates of savings, investment, and output growth and to the low rates of inflation and unemployment that have prevailed in the economy as a whole since the beginning of the 1960s.

Japan's employer policies and labor relations have reflected the discretionary authority and the bargaining strength that have accrued to large-scale oligopolistic firms with market power in labor markets and also with respect to smaller supplier firms. Policies such as lifetime employment and age-based pay, which were adopted in response to worker unrest in the early postwar period, as well as recruitment, training, and employee involvement have helped the enterprise to internalize its local labor markets, insulate its employees from external market influences, and bind them to the firm. These management policies have thus reinforced the market power of larger firms.

Similarly, seniority-based internal wage structures, together with the relatively high wage levels characteristic of large corporations, tend to discourage quitting, even when labor markets are tight. These wage premiums have received some protection by the market power enjoyed by large companies vis-à-vis their traditional smaller suppliers and outlets, which can indirectly limit the ability of the latter to raise their own relative wages. Downward wage flexibility during slumps in demand, when employers are constrained from laying off their regular employees, is limited, however. In short, the gains to Japanese employers from monopsonistic control over their local labor markets accrue in the form of high productivity rather than low wages; their employees inhabit gilded cages.

Yet employer policy and power have been able to impose upper as well as lower limits on wages and to administer shortages of labor. In addition, large firms in concentrated industries have bolstered their market power by entering into durable "gentlemen's agreements" to prevent poaching of experienced (midcareer) workers and by using employer associations to exchange information on prevailing wages and other labor market conditions. But a major role of employer associations in other countries—to strengthen the employer side by offering a united defense against demands by centralized unions in industrywide bargaining—has not been performed by Japanese associations because the big companies possessed enough bargaining power to eliminate industrywide bargaining in the late 1940s.

Japanese unions have characteristically pursued policies that reflect greater willingness to accept smaller negotiated wage increases in order to maintain employment during recessions and greater restraint in the interest of enterprise growth during expansions than have their U.S. counterparts. Furthermore, they have supported age-based wage systems rather than job-based pay as a major channel of individual economic advancement. And, consistent with their enterprise orientation, Japan's enterprise-based unions have sought to implement their policies through peaceful persuasion rather than adversarial confrontation with their employers. Their voice did not go unheeded, especially when enterprise unions advised that failure to adopt, modify, or abandon the policy under discussion would be likely to adversely affect employee morale and hence productivity.

In contrast to econometric analyses of union impact on relative wages in the United States, a Japanese study found no significant evidence of union impact in Japan; however, Japanese unionism has operated to protect firm-size wage differentials in favor of large unionized companies. There is evidence that unions have made some difference in reducing hours of work; and they have attempted to increase low premium rates for overtime and to raise the mandatory age of retirement (and thus lifetime earnings for employees). They have been determined in their resistance to dismissals and in their protection of implicit guarantees of employment security, although they did not establish formal grievance machinery of the type that in the United States constitutes a curtailment of "management rights."

For unions that have placed employment security, individual advancement over the long term, and cooperative and peaceful industrial relations high on their list of priorities, lack of accomplishment through cost-raising measures is almost beside the point. To many unionists reared in the American traditions of immediacy and aggressive adversarialism, however, enterprise unionism smacks of the type of employer-controlled organization outlawed by the Wagner Act of 1935, although the popularity of the U.S. stereotype has declined sharply over the postwar period.

In the early 1950s, militant left-wing union leaders in Japan also attacked enterprise unions as company dominated. What others supported as rational and cooperative behavior they condemned as cowardice induced by an inferior bargaining position. Weakness was revealed after the big firms (with the support of the authorities) canceled a brief postwar revival of industrywide bargaining, leaving Japan without the centralized institutions on which both unionists and employers in the United States and all other industrialized countries relied to "take wages out of competition." But Japan's militant unionist produced a corrective to structural fragmentation in the form of synchronized bargaining on a broad national scale, which, they reckoned, would remove one rational reason for the passivity of employment-conscious enterprise unions. They called it Shunto, or the Annual Spring Labor Offensive.

NOTES

1. Nakata (1987) documented that the ratio of peak earnings to starting earnings for male regular workers with a high school diploma in manufacturing industries declined from 7.3 in 1961, 4.0 in 1970, to 3.8 in 1980.

2. Changes in manufacturing real wages bore the same relationship to changes in real GDP growth per capita as to changes in manufacturing value added per wage earner.

3. According to an OECD report (1989a, pp. 42–44), the semielasticity of money wages with respect to the unemployment rate that was found to exist in Japan (−1.89) has been greater than in any other OECD country except Sweden (−2.17), where the average unemployment rate was equally low (1.9%). The elasticity in the United States (−0.61) has also been high by European standards, although obviously much lower than in Japan. The responsiveness of real wages to changes in unemployment has also been much higher in Japan than in the United States and has been exceeded in the OECD countries only in Sweden and Switzerland (Elmeskov and Pichelman, 1993).

4. Nakata has demonstrated that, based on a two-labor input model, for a fast-growing firm with a large share of junior workers among its employees, deferred compensation is an economical compensation scheme that allows the firm to save out of the wage bill for further growth.

5. The condition that overtime premiums be sufficiently low relative to costs of turnover is satisfied in Japan, where overtime costs are high and turnover costs are low by international standards (Koshiro, 1994, pp. 7–8).

6. Semiannual bonuses, like overtime payments, have varied procyclically, and these two categories make up about a third of average earnings in Japan. Nevertheless, most of the flexibility in earnings has been accounted for by the changes in regular pay that are negotiated annually under the Shunto procedures (Aoki, 1988; Mizuno, 1987–1988).

7. Moreover, a procyclical reduction in productivity—due to declining output while employment remains invariant—could tend to prevent prices from decelerating as rapidly as money wages. In this respect, policies guaranteeing continuance of (regular) employment within the enterprise could make for real as well as nominal wage flexibility. Nominal flexibility, however, could result in an initial decline in unit labor costs, which could help the firm to maintain the level of employment (Tachibanaki, 1987, p. 658).

8. Theoretical models of union behavior (including Blanchard and Summers, 1986) that arbitrarily assign exclusive control over wagesetting to unions ignore the degree of employer resistance of which the union must take account when setting a wage target.

9. Thus, Shirai (1983, p. 141), after some stern criticism, adds: "The experience of more than 30 years of enterprise unionism in postwar Japan leads the author to conclude, perhaps somewhat reluctantly, that within the socioeconomic and cultural context of Japanese industrial society, the enterprise union seems to employed workers to be the most acceptable and effective form of union organization."

6

National Wage Determination in Japan

Shunto as a Union Bargaining Instrument

Although Shunto has come to be regarded as an outstanding example of social contract policy (Taira and Levine, 1985), it was originally designed to increase union bargaining power in order to raise Japanese wages to European levels and to end "discriminatory" wage inequalities resulting from wage setting at the company level (Takanashi et al., 1989, pp. 5, 6). Shunto has operated not through centralized bargaining but through an annual synchronized process of pattern setting and pattern following.

Under Shunto, formal collective bargaining remains confined to the individual companies and their respective enterprise-based unions, but it has been relegated to the end of a lengthy and pervasive process of consensus building (typically extending from autumn through early spring). The process begins with negotiations within a group of key industries that set the pattern for wage increases in the year ahead. Pattern setting has come to be strongly influenced by current economic analyses, which are supplied by the central federations of unions[1] and employers (Nikkeiren), government (notably, the Economic Planning Agency), and private sources, which are extensively discussed in the news media. Information is transmitted through industry and regional and local affiliates of the central federations on both sides. The national unions, or tan-sans, meet regularly, not only with the "central struggle committee" and the "strategy committee" of the union confederation but also with employer associations in their respective industries and with delegates from enterprise unions in their industrial jurisdictions (as exemplified in Table 6.1). Influence flows with information, for tan-sans and local central bodies pipe up-to-the-minute news of the world outside into the internal labor market of the firm—especially news that a competitor or neighbor has just settled on the Shunto pattern. Thus, the information network (Shimada, 1983, p. 96) character-

TABLE 6.1. Partial Shunto Schedule of JAW (Japan Auto Workers), Involving All-Toyota Union

1992: Meetings		
October	17	Automobile Employers Association (semi-annual consultation)
	18	All-Toyota Union's Central Executive Committee (discussion of the 1993 Shunto basic policy)
November	9	JAW Central Executive Committee (discussion of Shunto demand framework)
	19	Rengo Central Committee member (adoption of the 1993 Shunto basic policy; JAW is a Rengo Central Committee member)
December	3	All-Toyota Union's Central Executive Committee (adoption of the 1993 Shunto basic policy)
	16	JAW Central Executive Committee (the 1993 Shunto target is chosen)
	18	All-Toyota Union's Central Executive Committee (the 1993 Shunto overall schedule set), IMF-JC Strategy Committee
1993: Meetings		
January	12	Rengo Central Committee (the 1993 Shunto strategy adopted)
	20	JAW Central Executive Committee (the 1993 Shunto strategy adopted)
	25	IMF-JC Strategy Committee (March 24 chosen for the target settlement)
February	3	Automobile Employers Association (semi-annual consultation)
	17	JAW Strategy Committee
	24	Enterprise unions at major auto firms (negotiation session) IMF-JC Strategy Committee
March	3	Enterprise unions at major auto firms (negotiation session)
	5	JAW Strategy Committee
	9	IMF-JC Strategy Committee
	10	Enterprise unions at major auto firms (negotiation session)
	12	JAW Strategy Committee
	15	IMF-JC Strategy Committee
	17	Enterprise unions at major auto firms (negotiation session)
	18	JAW Strategy Committee
	19	IMF-JC Strategy Committee
	20	JAW Strategy Committee
	24	Enterprise unions at major auto firms (final negotiation—management replies and settlements) (major settlements in steel, electric manufacturing, shipbuilding, and heavy equipment)
1993: Outcomes and Meetings		
April	6–8	Most auto dealer firms reply and settle
	9	JAW Strategy Committee
	21	IMF-JC Strategy Committee
May	13	Of 147 JAW unions, 145 are settled
	24	Of 2,752 IMF-JC unions, 2,398 are settled
June	3	Rengo Central Committee (1993) (Shunto Settlement Report adopted)

Source: Interviews with JAW officers.

istic of the Shunto process has generated a strong basis for pattern following: an employer would be reluctant (ceteris paribus) to settle for more than the pattern, and his employees for less. It was an essential part of the original union strategy to make workers focus more strongly on their relative (interfirm) wages and thus to counter the efforts of large-scale firms to insulate their own labor markets.

Patterns could be set at the highest feasible level by holding lead negotiations in major firms and industries that were strongly organized and currently prosperous. Under conditions of rapid growth and labor shortage in the late 1950s and 1960s, pattern setters were increasingly drawn from major firms in the private and open sectors of the economy, at first from private railways and steel, then from shipbuilding, autos, and (since the 1970s) electrical equipment and electronics. In years of "growth recession," however, the lead was originally shared with unions and employers in economically sheltered industries, notably in the public sector where unions were militant and under the influence of left-wing leadership, and focused on the right to strike in the public sector (Yamaguchi, 1983, pp. 306–309). Their propensity to strike was invariably opposed by government agencies, which ultimately succeeded in subjecting public enterprises and national corporations to government-sponsored arbitration and in enforcing the principle that the pay of civil servants should follow, rather than lead, pay changes in the private sector. Public sector militancy was also opposed by moderate Domei leadership in private sector unions. Nevertheless, until the early 1970s, unions in the private sector sought to benefit from public sector militancy in securing high Shunto settlements (Taira and Levine, 1985, pp. 263, 269). Indeed, an analysis by Koshiro (1983a,b, pp. 219–220, 232–236, 287) suggested that public employee stoppages had a substantial impact on average wage increases between 1961 and 1975, including a "threat effect" on the private sector as employers sought to encourage moderate Domei-led enterprise unionism.

The employers, having been previously engaged in successful efforts to depose industrywide bargaining that had been established in the early postwar years, were initially opposed to Shunto. Nikkeiren, their confederation, at first wanted to abandon the new objective of uniform settlements and the payment of age-based wage income in favor of greater reliance on wages based on job content and wage changes that could vary among enterprises and the individual workers within them. The employers were also opposed to Shunto's militant left-wing leadership. But in 1957 they had to acknowledge that, by coordinated action, the Shunto unions had set a new course that the employers could not reverse (Takanashi et al., 1989, p. 6).

In fact, the employers adapted promptly and efficiently to the Shunto format. Nikkeiren, surrendering its advocacy of long-term, enterprise-specific wage agreements, came out in favor of annual agreements not to exceed the increases in real GNP per employee, including individual increments (Solomon B. Levine, 1984, p. 343; Takanashi et al., 1989, p. 6). This productivity guidepost was designed to counter a union demand that each year's increase be guaranteed to exceed the previous year's ("plus alpha") and hence to avert wage acceleration.

The loci of employer bargaining power survived, however, although Shunto downgraded the role of formal enterprise bargaining and enhanced the importance not only of the tan-sans and the central labor federations but also of the industry and regional employer associations and the central organization (Nikkeiren) with which they were affiliated. Nikkeiren, however, continued to be dominated by the major firms in the private sector. Moreover, the ability of the large companies to concert their wage policies (as noted in Chapter 5) and bargaining tactics both within and now across industry boundaries was improved by the Shunto process itself and also by the increase in industrial concentration that occurred in the 1960s. The company's ability to maintain superior bargaining power at the industry level under Shunto was demonstrated by the "Big Five" companies in the steel industry when they defeated the national union, the Tekkororen, in a series of eleven strikes over the years 1957–1959. As a result, the employers were able to establish "one-shot" or "take-it-or-leave-it" bargaining (a practice borrowed from General Electric in the United States), and the union's leadership passed into more moderate hands (Kawanishi, 1992, pp. 80–81; Takanashi et al., 1989, p. 19).[2]

Finally, various major firms stood to gain by the organization of "second unions" in their plants with which they could deal in place of the old Sohyo-led enterprise unions and that exemplified what a study group of Shunto termed "a growing tendency [by Japanese workers] to accept economic unionism" (Takanashi et al., 1989, p. 6). This tendency was manifested in a series of company-level settlements whereby annual increments in pay were balanced by union agreements to cooperate with management in raising productivity.

Money wage increases (see Figure 6.1) climbed to double-digit figures in the 1960s and early 1970s and exceeded increases in productivity. Moreover, wages tended to accelerate between 1967–1968 and 1974, a development that, according to Shimada (1983, pp. 184–185), was characterized by "the almost routinized practice of starting wage negotiations above the level of what has been achieved in the previous round," thereby imparting "downward inflexibility in the amount of wage increases (not even the absolute level of wages)." Consumer prices also accelerated in the later subperiod, from an average rate of increase of 6 percent between 1960 and 1973 to almost 10 percent between 1968 and 1979. Finally, Shunto wage patterns became characterized by a "standardization of wage increases in both absolute and percentage terms" and by "decreasing wage differentials by size of firm" (Koshiro, 1983a, pp. 222, 224).

Thus, the union rule of no backward step for wage increases and the union objective of greater wage equality under Shunto fared better in practice than did the Nikkeiren productivity principle. But when Nikkeiren called for the adoption of an official, albeit "voluntary," income policy in 1968, a special commission of econo-

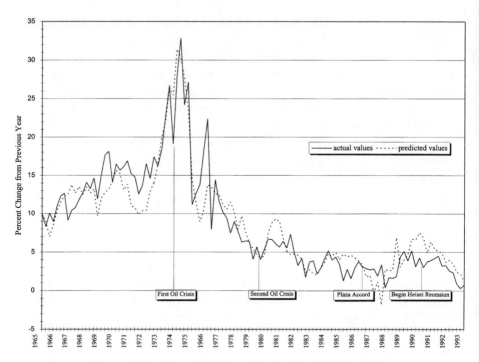

FIGURE 6.1. Japanese Wage Growth, 1965 to 1993, Actual and Predicted Values

Source: Appendix, Equation 6.1.

mists convened by the Economic Planning Agency declined to go beyond endorsing the productivity principle and deploying the trade-off between inflation and unemployment as an explanatory device. In fact, wage-change estimating equations that assign explanatory roles to unemployment levels and productivity change variables were interpreted as lending some support to the hypothesis that a combination of extremely rapid economic growth, labor shortages, and low unemployment was sufficient to explain the high rates of wage and price inflation that occurred during the first two decades of Shunto. (As an example, see OECD, 1990, Annex equation, p. 105, and Equation 6.1 in this chapter's Appendix.)

Of course, some "demand push" could also have been exerted during this period, to the extent that monetary policy was sufficiently easy to accommodate such "institutional" developments (noted above) as the spillover from public sector disputes and settlements, union moves to design ever greater wage increases, and a variant of efficiency wage policies adopted by large-scale employers in support of moderate unionists. Equation 6.1 in the Appendix to this chapter, which (like various other equations) utilizes the ratio of job openings to vacancies, instead of unemployment, among its right-hand variables, allows some room for an institutional push on wages in that the net sum and frequency of the residuals are strongly positive for the decade beginning in the mid-1960s (i.e., actual increases in money wages exceeded, on balance, those predicted on the basis of increases in the cost of living, aggregate demand, and labor shortage).

Evidence of Shunto's effectiveness in imposing a greater degree of uniformity and equality on wage changes has been inferred by Tsuru (1992) from the existence of negative time-trend variables in equations estimating annual measures of wage dispersion after controlling for variations in the (inverse) unemployment rate (or from the ratio of job openings to applicants). And evidence that pattern following under Shunto made its own contribution to the Shunto wage increases that occurred in the late 1960s and early 1970s has been inferred (again by Tsuru, 1992) on the basis of a negatively signed and lagged "spillover variable"—as measured by the difference between the base wages in the "key" and other industries—in a wage-change estimating equation.

Hence, while enterprise unions individually have exerted no significant impact on relative wages (as reported in Chapter 5), pattern setting on an economywide scale, with the participation of the tans-sans and the central bodies to which they belonged, helped to impart an upward movement to the general level of nominal wages in Shunto's early period. Óta's remedy for firm-based cowardice seemed to be producing its intended effects. Nevertheless, the commission reasoned that the *enterprise* unions enjoyed a reputation for sensitivity to the economic conditions of their respective firms and would not have countenanced any demands that would jeopardize their economic welfare (Koshiro, 1983a, p. 228). This judgment evidently rested on the assumption that the enterprise unions retained sufficient autonomy and authority under Shunto to exert a restraining influence on the pattern setting that occurred in the early stages of the process. Shunto would therefore have to respect the employment consciousness of the enterprise unions and their members.

Another reason given by the commission for declining to endorse a full-blooded income policy was the absence of a deficit in the balance of payments, which implied that the firms in the export sector indeed retained the "ability to pay" Shunto increases. Through 1968, this was eminently the case. Figure 5.1 shows that, while real wages in manufacturing were rising more rapidly in Japan than in the European countries, Canada, and the United States, Japan's relative gain in manufacturing productivity was at least as great. (In the United States, the increases in both magnitudes were markedly lower.)

In 1968–1973, however, Japan lost some of its relative advantage in this respect. Its own productivity growth slowed down, while money wages accelerated. Shunto increases, which averaged 11.3 percent in the first half of the 1960s, stepped up to 14.2 percent in the second half, 16.1 percent in 1971–1972, and 20.1 percent in 1973. Thus, even prior to the oil price shock at the end of 1973, it appeared that money wage behavior had been growing unstable under Shunto—although, relative to productivity growth, it was less unstable than in Germany and France. Indeed, in the early 1970s, the annual labor offensives were marked by large protest demonstrations and an increase in the number of work stoppages as Sohyo's demands for reaching "European standards" more rapidly, for reforms of the tax structure, and for environmental improvement seemed to be attracting considerable popular support (as well as a touch of European-style militancy).

Wage Restraint under Shunto

Two Oil Shocks Compared

In Japan, as elsewhere, the first oil price shock marked a watershed in postwar economic history, ushering in an era of slower economic growth and, as in most other places, of higher unemployment as well. A "People's Shunto" reacted to the shock to the price of energy inputs with a 32.9 percent rise in the price of labor inputs in the 250 major companies, which crowned (if that is the word) the gathering process of acceleration referred to above. It reflected union determination to claw back not only the rise in the cost of living but also the loss of overtime earnings resulting from the oil shock to the economy. It exceeded increases in both the cost of living and wholesale prices (Koshiro, 1976, p. 5). The real wage increase (2%) was low by previous standards; but, since the shock to output resulted in a short-term decline in productivity, the wage response entailed some further price increases. And so the People's Shunto also featured demands for indexation to protect against further inflation, threats to call another, special Shunto a few months later, and a general strike to support ongoing strikes by public sector transportation unions for their right to strike. Big business and its close allies in the ruling Liberal Democratic Party caved in out of deference to imminent national elections (Koshiro, 1976, p. 8; Ono, 1976, p. 7; Taira and Levine, 1985, p. 261).

The contrast offered by the response to the second oil crisis in 1979–1980 was dramatic. Although the induced rise in raw materials prices was actually greater in the second episode, wage and price increases were only about one-third as great; real wages fell "for the first time in postwar history" (Shimada, 1983, p. 178) and by almost as much as they had risen after the first shock; labor productivity in manufacturing was able to continue rising by as much as it had declined in 1973–1974; and the unemployment rate, which had vaulted from 1.4 percent to a new plateau of 2 percent in the first episode (for the first time since the 1950s), barely moved in 1979–1980. The reductions in both real and product wages that occurred in the second episode were signs that this time wages had accommodated rather than resisted the price rise in energy inputs—and that labor had agreed to pay its share of the "OPEC tax" (Taira and Levine, 1985, p. 250).

In the interim, the Japanese economy, while operating at higher rates of inflation and unemployment and lower rates of growth than in the 1960s and early

1970s, had fared better than the other major countries listed in Table 5.2, except the Federal Republic of Germany. Japan's relatively high inflation rate was balanced by a markedly lower rate of unemployment and a comparable rate of economic growth. Moreover, in comparison with other industrialized countries, manufacturing productivity grew at a much more rapid rate in Japan in 1973–1979—as the structure of output shifted away from energy-intensive to technology-intensive products (OECD, 1980, pp. 52–53)—while real hourly earnings in manufacturing increased much more slowly (except in the United States). This contrasts with the situation in 1968–1973, when Japan had enjoyed a commanding lead in the wage category as well as in productivity growth. Moreover, Japan's real wage restraint in manufacturing in the former period was reflected in a sharp decline in labor's share of national income (from 1977 through 1981). During the same subperiod, labor's share increased (from approximately the same level) in the United States and the United Kingdom and (from a higher starting level) in France, while it declined more gently from a still higher level in the Federal Republic of Germany.

Wage Restraint and Demand Restraint

The record of wage behavior in the 1970s has been widely regarded as a tribute to the adaptability and flexibility of the Japanese system of labor relations. It was also associated with the assumption by government of a more important (de facto) role in wage determination and by a change in leadership of the union movement. In the face of the dramatic developments of 1974, the Ministry of Finance included wage restraint among the instruments of "total demand restraint" with which it intended to pursue the objectives of price stability and full employment (OECD, 1975, p. 36). The goal of price stability reflected the government's fear of loss of international competitiveness, although Japan's competitors had also been confronted by the oil shock and the large increases in unit labor costs experienced in Japan were making only a small contribution to the increase in wholesale prices (Ono, 1976, p. 8). It was evidently the government's purpose to restrain wage costs to offset the rise in energy costs and as a quid pro quo for the maintenance of employment at high levels.

Full Employment, Lifetime Employment, and Wage Restraint

In Japan, official adoption of the goal of full employment bespoke support for commitments made by individual employers to their own regular employees for "lifetime employment without layoff" (Chapter 2). It is also true that private systems of employment security have operated indirectly to ease the trade-off between the macroeconomic price and employment objectives.

These private systems of employment security contain certain built-in mechanisms of wage flexibility: first, they offer the firm an incentive to maintain long hours of work as an alternative to a larger ("insured") work force; second, they offer it an opportunity to temporarily reduce those long hours of work by reducing overtime at premium pay during periods of slack. But we have also noted that the process of reducing pay levels by cutting overtime is not as "automatic" or discretionary as it appears: savings on overtime pay must not be canceled by compensatory increases in base pay negotiated by the unions. This is a form of bargaining restraint that the Sohyo unionists had explicitly resisted in 1974 but that was implicitly forthcoming after the second oil crisis at the end of the decade.

This suggests that bargaining militancy had begun to give way to restraint after the first oil crisis in the 1970s, an inference that has received some confirmation from econometric analyses of aggregate wage behavior. Shimada (1983, p. 182) interpreted negative residuals in the years following 1974 in wage-change equations as indicative of "wage moderation by way of the changed mode of wage determination." Our own regression analysis yielded predominantly negative residuals for the subperiod 1975–1993. This is consistent with the story of a period of militancy followed by a structural break in the data and a contrasting regime of restraint. The results of a wage-estimating study (OECD, 1990, p. 105) (on which our regression has been substantially patterned) are, prima facie, more ambiguous. This analysis, which includes separate estimating equations for the subperiods 1964–1984 and 1973–1989 (as well as for 1964–1989), finds that the coefficient on an unemployment variable for the shorter and more recent subperiod to be considerably smaller than the coefficient for the entire period. This result is interpreted, however, as evidence not of greater downward rigidity of money wages in Japan but rather of "a tendency towards a declining effect of tight labor market conditions on wage increases" (ibid., p. 20). It could have been produced by shifts from regular increases (in scheduled earnings) to bonuses and by increasing the proportion of part-time workers at relatively low wages to total employment—changes that tended "to reduce the increase in the fixed components of labor costs" (ibid.). But it could also reflect the willingness of employees and their enterprise-based unions to accommodate the growth of their respective firms (as discussed in the previous chapter), especially after rapid growth was no longer taken for granted and after the export sector had acquired increased importance in the national economy. It would also be consistent with the ability of the larger firms to administer labor shortages without moving at once to eliminate them by promptly raising wages to market-clearing levels. Finally, it would be consistent with a frequent objective of overall wage policy, which is to restrain the responsiveness of wages and prices to the expansion of demand.

In any event, Table 5.2 reveals two pertinent facts: first, that in the 1980s Japan experienced the steepest decline in inflation from the 1970s—and even the 1960s— to the lowest level found in the group of comparison countries and, second, that its rate of unemployment, while rising to higher levels, remained far below the rates of the other countries. Moreover, Figure 6.1 shows that, following their explosion in the early 1970s, money-wage increases slowed down sharply. Indeed wage growth declined much more than did the growth in productivity. As a result, while Japanese industry retained its lead in productivity growth, it moved from first to last place (in the 1980s) in the ranking by nominal wage increase and hence in the ranking by change in unit labor costs. These facts are also consistent with the hypothesis of increased wage restraint and suggest that, under the influence of certain changes in the roles played by government and the unions, Shunto could be transformed into an instrument of cost restraint and macroeconomic stability and growth.

Government Interest and Involvement

The first change to occur consisted of official support of wage restraint as a part of the package of "total demand restraint" during the crisis Shunto period in 1974. As it had in the late 1960s, the Economic Planning Agency appointed a special commission to look into the matter, and this time the new committee could point to evidence that the increase in import prices had been making a much greater contribution than had rising unit labor costs to the sharp increases in wholesale prices that were occurring and also could conclude (once again) that demand pressures continued to be the main determinants of wage and price inflation. As before, it was widely believed that the responsiveness of wages and prices to changes in demand pressure reflected the inherent flexibility of the industrial relations system. An extremely rapid fall-off in price inflation after the first quarter certainly seemed to justify this confidence. However, since unit labor costs continued to rise (reflecting short-term reductions in productivity), it seemed that the cost increases were being absorbed by reductions in profits (OECD, 1975, pp. 20–25). Thus, while demand restraint could be counted on to reduce inflation, direct wage restraint could shift part of the cost of adjustment from profits to wages. In addition, while it was believed that the slowdown in growth rates was not likely to prove a temporary phenomenon, it was also believed that wage acceleration (having occurred under past conditions of higher growth in productivity) could conceivably return. This made it seem desirable to retain a continuing wage restraint capability in order to minimize the trade-off between inflation and unemployment in the future.

The upshot was, however, that the new committee, like its predecessor, rejected proposals for a mandatory income policy on the grounds that the current spate of inflation represented a necessary one-shot adjustment to the higher price levels caused by the oil crisis, that the balance of payments was no longer in deficit, and that the enterprise unions could be counted on to respond to their employers' lower profits and to slack labor markets with appropriately reduced wage demands (Koshiro, 1976, p. 8).

Nevertheless, government officials did call for wage restraint as a complement to a tight monetary policy; and, when the unions were obliged to accept an increase of less than half the previous year's—and lower than Nikkeiren's ceiling—they attributed their "defeat" to what Shimada (1983, p. 190, n. 8) described as "strong pressure from complex sources outside conventional negotiation units." More overtly, the post-1974 era was characterized by official exhortation and tripartite consultative meetings, backed by economic analyses and education, especially during frequent meetings of Sanrokon, the Industry and Labor Conference that had been formed in 1970 to consider important economic and social problems (Taira and Levine, 1985, pp. 259–265). With the emergence of a trilateral influence on wage determination, the Shunto system could be duly qualified as a "social contract" (Koshiro, 1976; Shimada, 1983; Taira and Levine, 1985). However, the formal bilateral process and machinery of Shunto remained intact; and the unions did not enter into "explicit" agreements with the government in 1975 (Koshiro, 1976, p. 5). Thus, the policy depended only on voluntary compliance along the lines favored by the academic committee, the union side, and some leading politicians who had been calling for what Ono (1974, p. 8) characterized as "a soft, Japanese-style policy."

Information Sharing

How could compliance with wage and employment norms under a nonmandatory policy be secured in the absence of centralized bargaining structures? Shimada (1983, pp. 196, 197) credited Japan's superior performance after the mid-1970s to a "complex system of information channels [that] has facilitated information exchanges and sharing among organized labor, employers, the government and the public" and that thereby provided the "functional equivalence" of the roles attributed to centralized structures in other countries. This strikes us as a valuable and valid insight, but not as the whole story. For one thing, the essential Shunto procedures had been developed as a booster to union bargaining power prior to the 1970s, when, as suggested above, the intensive dissemination of information to workers in the plants could serve to widen their "orbits of coercive comparison" and thus weaken a significant source of employer market power. After the oil crisis, the Shunto system was further developed; but Sanrokon, which was credited with playing an important role in the informational process, had originated back in 1970. The role of the government certainly appeared to increase in the 1970s, but that role was not confined to information sharing. Thus, in the absence of explicit controls, governmental jawboning does not preclude a bit of strategic arm-twisting (a.k.a. "administrative guidance").

Goal Sharing and Slower Growth

"Information sharing" was paired with "goal sharing" in Shimada's analysis. During Shunto's first two decades, the major parties had different priorities: union leadership under Sohyo was driven by the goal of winning wage parity with the Europeans as quickly as possible; Nikkeiren was intent on maximizing the competitiveness of the large firms in the export sector; and the Domei-affiliated unions in that sector were willing to adopt a general productivity guideline for money wage increases after Nikkeiren had proposed such a criterion. As long as growth remained high, both of the first two objectives could be reasonably well accommodated—with Japan leading the industrial world in both real wage and productivity growth (in manufacturing)—although increasingly at the expense of domestic price inflation. In the aftermath of the first oil price shock, however, these two objectives clearly became incompatible. Óta, the Sohyo union leader, refused to yield: "We should not give up the posture of attempting to gain wage increases over the previous year, even if economic growth slowed down or decreased to zero" (Koshiro, 1976, p. 9). The president of the steelworkers (Tekkororen), however claimed that it would not be possible to win a greater increase in 1975 and, indeed, that it was necessary to arrive at "a new form of planned wage increases in keeping with the [reduced] rate of economic growth" (ibid.).

Moderate Union Leadership

The latter view prevailed in Shunto pattern setting. Leadership on the union side was firmly held by moderates in the export sector after the economically sheltered unions in the public sector had failed to share the general sense of national emergency and indeed had made it a practical impossibility (in the Shunto setting) for the others to exercise restraint. After an eight-day rail strike in 1975, the government launched a determined program of work force reduction and privatization, and it proceeded to ensure that the settlements in government services, the national industries, and the regulated private industries would follow the Shunto patterns that were set in the major private sector industries. (As a result, while the Domei-affiliated unions in the private sector had found it advisable to follow the militant Sohyo group into Shunto in the late 1950s, the weakened public sector unions felt obliged to join Rengo, the Japanese Private Sector Trade Union Confederation, following formation of the latter in 1987.) (See Ono, 1974, p. 7; Shimada, 1983, pp. 191–192, n. 10; Taira and Levine, 1985, pp. 267–268; Nitta, 1988, p. 6; Takanashi et al., 1989, p. 15.)

Risk-aversion and Lifetime Employment: Some Limitations

With the change in union leadership, goal-sharing became achievable under Shunto, not only because the industrywide unions and central federations accepted the lower growth in productivity as a constraint on wage determination but also because, in so doing, they were more representative of the policies and practices of their enterprise-based affiliates than their more militant predecessors had been. We have noted above that even before the OPEC shock, enterprise unions had often promised to help their employers to increase productivity as a quid pro quo for wage increases (a practice known in Great Britain at the time as "productivity bargaining"). Now, however, many companies were offering their employees employment security in lieu of wage increases—or conditioning employment security for the individual on acceptance of a wage freeze by the enterprise union.[3] This reflected the heightened cost to employers of continuing to bear their quasi-fixed employment costs when productivity was actually declining (Shimada, 1983, p. 180, Table 2). It also reflected, according to Ono (1976, p. 7) that "this was . . . a basic element of the 1976 'employment security or wage increase' position."

To the extent that the government's full employment objective could be implemented at the level of the firm in this fashion, its policy of demand contraction could be met with minimal increase in unemployment, while a subsequent recovery in demand could be accommodated initially more by increased productivity at existing levels of employment than by increased employment and greater increases in money and real wages. As noted earlier, a firm-implemented employment policy offers workers (and therefore their enterprise unions) a strong inducement to accept wage restraint: the prospect not only of retaining their current jobs but also of moving on to better jobs in the same company, especially when those jobs command high wages relative to feasible alternatives, as is likely to be the case in those large-scale firms that offer "lifetime employment" to their "regular" employees. Conventional macroeconomic policies that are designed only to reduce unemployment in the aggregate, on the other hand, may actually offer some perverse incentives to individuals and enterprise unions to try to secure relative and real wage increases for themselves by exceeding the general wage norm and thus enjoying a free ride.

The Japanese policy, however, has been subject to a limitation of a different sort while sharing two other problems with the conventional approach. The limitation consists simply in the incomplete coverage of the lifetime employment guarantee (although it has been extended to employees of many smaller firms on a de facto basis and also to many nonregular employees in large, covered firms). Uncovered employees in the private sector would lack the sort of inducement to accept wage restraint that is provided by the enterprise guarantee. However, major firms, whose employees are provided with such an inducement, possess decisive influence over Shunto pattern setting. And they are thereby in a strong position to influence the authorities to adopt policies conducive to the maintenance of high levels of employment that would enable them to maintain satisfactory levels of capacity utilization—of labor as well as plant and equipment. The authorities, sharing these objectives but with their own strong bias against inflation and fiscal deficits, have sought to satisfy employers by following policies that rely as little on demand reflation and as much on restraint of costs as possible. Hence their concern with Shunto as an adjunct to macroeconomic policy.

In the second place, while a combination of enterprise-oriented employment policies and the Shunto process of wage determination might have contributed to a relatively high degree of downward wage-change flexibility, experience has also suggested that there are limits to worker tolerance. When Komiya argued for the lowest possible rate of wage increases, Koshiro (1977, p. 6) replied that, "in Japan, where the dominant forces in labor still have faith in Marxist theory, even anti-leftist labor leaders in Domei and IMF-JC, . . . who take practical lines, could not maintain their positions if wage hikes were restrained below a certain limit." Such a limit was set equal to the prevailing rate of increase in consumer prices by the leading unions (Ono, 1976, pp. 5–8). Major employers (as well as others) who have always assigned high priority to the maintenance of good employee morale would seek to forestall adverse efficiency wage effects and could accept a policy of real wage protection. The authorities also sought and could accept a policy of real wage protection. They sought to minimize money wage increases by engaging in some direct price restraint during the period of total demand restraint in the 1970s; and indeed the near-unity and highly significant coefficients on the price change variables in Equation 6.1 in the Appendix to this chapter lend some support to the suggestion that wage setting under Shunto subsequently continued to respect a principle of real wage protection into the 1990s. Nevertheless, the reduction in real wages that did occur in the aftermath of the second oil price shock showed that such real wage protection was not unqualified and that lapses occurring in response to adverse changes in such other wage determinants as productivity and terms of trade could be acceptable to a risk-averse work force and the enterprise unions.

Yet two subsidy measures adopted by the government during the decline in employment in the 1970s can be viewed in part as attempts to compensate for the limitations of workers' aversion to risk under adverse circumstances. First came the employment insurance law of 1975 (see Chapter 2). However, a firm's eligibility for employment assistance grants was effectively conditioned on prior reduction of overtime worked. Thus, firms were offered incentives not to substitute dismissal for temporary layoffs and not to substitute layoffs for reductions in overtime—and the associated reductions in hourly earnings. According to Dore (1986, p. 126), the new system was nicely designed "to operate with the grain" of the lifetime employment system (see also Koshiro, 1983a, p. 246; OECD, 1975, p. 47).

While the wage subsidy was designed to help maintain employment, a second subsidy measure was explicitly designed to make wages more downwardly flexible. In 1976, the steel workers' union accepted a reduction in their negotiated wage increase in exchange for an additional reduction in income tax. This effectively set the Shunto norm for the year (despite protests from the unions in auto manufacturing and shipbuilding, whose employees had been harvesting high export-generated profits). It was a bit of political exchange that further qualified Japan as a member of the neocorporatist club; Koshiro (1977, p. 7) reported that "the idea for restraining wage hikes in exchange for a tax cut was taken from Britain's new social contract, formulated in June of 1976." Indeed, increased government involvement, whether overt or tacit, in the determination and propagation of central wage norms, combined with the continued subordination of Sohyo, ultimately made it feasible for "top leaders of labor and management . . . to have regular dialogues on policy issues *during the wage negotiations*" (Shimada, 1988, p. 7; emphasis added). Areas of potential trade-off included price restraint, tax reform, improved minimum wages, shorter hours, even deregulation of markets (ibid.; Nitta, 1990, p. 8).

Surrogates for Centralized Institutions and Some Evidence concerning Their Effectiveness

If Japan's success in maintaining unemployment at outstandingly low levels reflects in some degree relatively high levels of wage-change flexibility, what could account for its success in also maintaining low rates of inflation since the end of the 1970s? Theoretically, employers who agree to maintain employment in their firms during any period of slack demand must be able to pay lower wages, relative to employee effort expended or to productivity, as compensation for assuming the extra risk involved (Akerlof and Miazaki, 1980, p. 321). But when labor demand exceeds supply at full capacity utilization, competing employers are able to bid wages above their "contractual" level and employees are able to quit for higher wages elsewhere (Shapiro and Stiglitz, 1984, p. 6). Indeed, any worker who refrains from doing so risks suffering a loss in his or her relative and real wage (and any employer risks competitive disadvantage resulting from labor shortage); and if a few break or depart from the terms of an "implicit contract," the rest come under pressure to follow. Neither information-sharing, nor goal-sharing, nor worker risk aversion, nor any or all of them in combination constitutes a sufficient condition for the observance of such implicit contracts under conditions approaching full employment and labor shortage. Hence, many economists have regarded implicit contracts as normally unenforceable under competitive conditions.

And, hence, political scientists have frequently included government controls or centralized bargaining institutions (or both) among the essential attributes of an effective neocorporatist regime (e.g., Schmitter and Lehmbruch, 1979). The potential efficiency of a union or of an employer institution at industry or wider levels as an instrument of wage restraint depends in part on the extent of its influence and authority over its affiliates at the level of the firm. In addition, the efficiency of a centralized employer institution varies directly with its bargaining power vis-à-vis the union, because employers are normally ranged on the side of restraint (except when competitive firms experience labor shortage).

In Japan, the absence of institutions with formal bargaining functions at the industry level or higher has been widely noted, but it is potentially offset by the market power of the large firms, together with the extensive consultative, informational, and educational activities of the tan-sans and the International Metalworkers, Japan Council (IMF-JC) on the union side, and, finally, by a strong pre-disposition to consensus and to the unwritten commitment within the community at large. Employer monopsony power in labor and product markets and oligopolistic coordination of employers to discourage poaching and to exchange cost and price information could help to hold the line when shortages of labor reappear on a significant scale. And communication and coordination among members of a small group of major companies in the economy have helped to set Shunto patterns in the first place.

Pattern-strengthening tendencies by employers have been reinforced by pattern-strengthening tendencies on the labor side. Monopsonistic resistance to raising wages under conditions of labor shortage has been paralleled by the economic disincentive offered by the nenko wage system to quitting a firm in "midcareer" for a higher starting wage elsewhere. Gentlemen's agreements against poaching have a looser counterpart in the form of a noneconomic deterrence to quitting imposed by the extraeconomic loyalty of a career worker to the firm or work group. And the pervasiveness of both kinds of disincentive would allow all individuals to expect that their decisions not to quit would be typical rather than exceptional and therefore would not entail a loss in their relative or real wages.

At the industry level, the effectiveness of a tan-san in heightening the relative external wage consciousness of individual employees and their enterprise-based unions could make for pattern following in the context of Shunto synchropay. At a more centralized level within the manufacturing sector of the economy, the formation of IMF-JC in the metals group was intended to increase the ability of member national unions in (currently) less profitable industries to follow the pattern effectively set by others (Shimada, 1983, p. 191).

In fact, the deceleration of wage increases that began in the mid-1970s was associated with increased wage dispersion. And just as the responsiveness of average wage changes to variations in unemployment (or other measures of labor market tightness) declined, so too did the responsiveness of the dispersion around those wage changes (OECD, 1990, p. 105; Tsuru, 1992). Moreover, econometric evidence of wage spillover (or pattern following) became much weaker during the later period; and coefficients of variation and other measures of dispersion lost their downward trends.

To Sohyo unionists (and more dispassionate observers as well), increased wage dispersion marked the end of Shunto as an institution to promote greater wage equality and its transformation into an institution that reflected employer dominance in an era of slower economic growth. Mutuality of economic interests among employers and their potential for concertation would ensure greater uniformity in wage changes at industry levels than beyond them; whereas the egalitarianism envisioned by the radical unionists had been potentially economywide in scope and encompassed extended pattern following and information sharing under Shunto. However, the subordination, on the union side, of the union's central Joint Struggle Committee to the moderate-dominated IMF-JC in the 1970s implied the suppression of an all-inclusive institution by one less inclusive.

Yet, as is suggested by the existence of widespread labor shortages in the latter half of the 1980s, the centralizing influence of Shunto has been sufficient to prevent departures from the norm from becoming "excessive and destabilizing" (as had been threatened in the late 1960s and early 1970s). More centralized systems elsewhere, on the other hand, have proved both more rigid and more brittle than the soft Japanese model; and often their effectiveness has been limited by their inability to cope with the pressures exerted by traumatic or cumulative economic change. Increased and variable dispersion among settlements under Shunto may therefore be viewed as on the whole contributing to that institution's effectiveness in restraining movements of the average level of wages over the long haul while accommodating structural changes in the economy.

Structural changes in the post-1974 period have included the decline of the steel and shipbuilding industries and relative growth in the information, communications, finance, real estate, construction, wholesale and retail trade, and transport sectors (Shimada, 1988, p. 5; Tsuru, 1992, p. 8). Table 6.2 shows that, in the 1980s, money wages rose much more slowly in steel and shipbuilding than in the more dynamic trade and transport sectors. Yet steel and shipbuilding have remained in the group of key pattern-setting industries in Shunto, while trade and other dynamic sectors, as well as the public sector, have been omitted. Thus, while the average wage increases in all private firms were closer to the increases received in the fast-growth industries than they were to the wage increases in the laggard groups, the latter have been in a better position to influence the Shunto patterns than the former. This, of course, tended both to restrain the average rate of wage growth and to increase the dispersion about the average—the reverse of the outcomes that Shunto's founding fathers on the left had sought to accomplish by assigning the most dynamic and prosperous private sectors as well as the public sector leading positions in the wage-determining process. The subsequent realignment, together with the dominant and continuing influence of the automotive and electronics

TABLE 6.2. Mean Shunto Wage Increase by Specific Industry

Industry	1981–1982	1983–1988	1989–1991
Slow-growth industries			
Steel	6.70%	2.77%	3.95%
Shipbuilding	6.89	2.84	4.93
Fast-growth industries			
Wholesale/retail	8.59	4.99	6.61
Transport	7.46	4.63	5.69
Private firm average	7.35	4.41	5.59

Source: Japan Ministry of Labor (1992b).

groups (together with IMF-JC), however, reflects the importance of Shunto to the maintenance of Japan's international competitiveness in an era of slower growth.

Wage Restraint, Export Growth, and Noninflationary Full Employment

It will be recalled that the policies of total demand and wage restraint that were launched after the first oil shock had been partly motivated by fear lest the economy's international competitiveness be impaired. In fact, the country subsequently entered an era of export-led recoveries (OECD, 1982, pp. 25, 26; 1983, p. 8; 1986b, pp. 43–46; 1991, pp. 55–56; Takanashi et al., 1989, pp. 8, 16) and growth, accompanied by trade surpluses and currency appreciation, in which Shunto played a supporting role as an instrument of wage restraint. Productivity-constrained wage increases could help to achieve the authorities' dual domestic objectives of price stability and full employment through maintenance or expansion of exports. Wage increases within the bound set by economywide increases in productivity (GNP or GDP per employee) could help to minimize increases in unit labor costs and prices and to maximize international competitiveness. Moreover, if Shunto wage increases were exceeded by productivity increases in the open sectors of the economy—because the latter tended to exceed the economywide average—they could help to generate greater operating surpluses in export enterprises and thus to finance their expansion.

Countries such as Japan and Germany, which have tended to gear their monetary-fiscal policies, along with "soft" wage policies, to the objective of domestic price stability, could enjoy an advantage over countries in which wage movements have been less subject to constraint, that have relied more on reflation of domestic demand, and that have also evinced greater tolerance of inflation. In this connection, it is interesting to compare the price-stability model of wage behavior with the formally elaborated Aukrust or "EFO" models that were designed to guide wage policies in Norway and Sweden in the 1960s and 1970s (Aukrust, 1970; Edgren, Faxén, and Odhner, 1973). Under the latter (which assumes fixed exchange rates), model uniform money wage increases are supposed to equal the rate of growth of productivity in the open sector plus the rate of growth of world prices. In view of lower productivity growth in the sheltered sector, some domestic inflation must be allowed, but (assuming that in fact it does not touch off excessive wage increases), the level of unit labor costs in the open sector is maintained. And, if the country's competitors follow (or disregard) the same wage rule, its level of international competitiveness can also be maintained, and so can a high level of employment. But if, as under a price stability model, wage increases in a competing country are set equal to lower (e.g. economywide) increases in productivity than actually prevail in the open sector, unit labor costs in that country could be reduced and potential profit margins would be greater in the open sector and permit greater investment in and expansion of export industries. Alternatively, of course, if that country's rates of productivity growth happen to exceed those of its competitors, its competitive position could be improved even if its nominal wage inflation should exceed (within limits) the target consistent with domestic price stability.

In Japan, nominal wages have been responsive to short-term changes in econo-mywide productivity. Thus, Japan could combine the lowest rates of inflation in both consumer and producer prices of any major OECD country in the 1980s with both the second highest external surplus of goods and services relative to GDP (Germany's was the highest) and with the lowest average rate of unemployment (OECD, 1992a).

On the other hand, if restrained wage setting under Shunto contributed to Japan's persistent trade surpluses, the latter in turn tended to induce currency ap-preciation, which would raise Japanese wage costs in dollar terms (OECD, 1993a, p. 65). Theoretically, exchange-rate flexibility could cancel out an episode of wage restraint. But it could also touch off further restraint. That seems to have happened in Japan in the 1980s. Japanese export firms have characteristically declined to completely "pass through" yen appreciations in the form of higher selling prices, thereby sacrificing short-term profit margins in order to maintain market share. (Figure 6.2 shows the movement in export car prices and wholesale car prices.) But their ability to do so has been conditioned on sufficiently flexible wage costs, which have combined with appreciation-induced reductions in the prices of imported in-puts to minimize adjustment costs to the firm. Thus, although Japanese wages (per worker) did rise from 60 percent of the American level in 1985 to equality five years later, they would have actually been higher than U.S. wages if the yen apprecia-tion had been fully taken into account, according to an OECD analysis (ibid.,

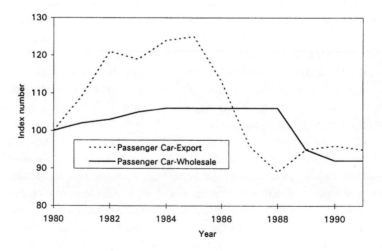

FIGURE 6.2. Movements in Yen Price Indices for Autos, Japan, 1980–1991

Source: Bank of Japan (1987, 1994b).

pp. 63–65). "In effect, wage flexibility helped Japan to maintain its competitive edge during the second half of the 1980s, as far as wage costs are concerned" (ibid., p. 62). (The yen actually depreciated in real terms after 1987.)

The responsiveness of nominal wages to changes in the value of the currency is reflected in the negative coefficient of the terms-of-trade (TOT) variable in Equation 6.1, the value of which approaches unity. In the OECD (1989a) regressions for the post-OPEC subperiod 1973–1989, this coefficient increased sharply in (absolute) value over its value for the earlier period (1964–1984), in contrast to a decline in the coefficient of an unemployment variable. Thus, it would appear that as money wages became less responsive to variations in domestic demand in the modern Shunto period, they grew more responsive to changes in external demand—in particular to structural increases in the exchange rate of the yen.

In order to relieve the pressure on profits resulting from appreciation without laying off employees covered by lifetime employment guarantees, wage restraint under Shunto has been paralleled by efforts by individual firms to increase productivity. And so the long run became the short run as currency appreciations, instead of eliminating trade surpluses created by prior productivity growth and wage restraint, generated fresh incentives and opportunities for further productivity growth and wage restraint.[4]

Problems and Critics of Externally Oriented Policies

Export-oriented policy has not been without costs, however; nor has it failed to attract critics as well as defenders. There have been costs associated with persistent external surpluses (which were only in part economic in nature) and with domestic labor shortages as well. A strongly appreciating currency tended to keep domestic price inflation low, but by reducing prices of energy and other imported inputs, it also helped to swell profits and liquidity, which fueled a destabilizing boom in land prices and in investment in the late 1980s. The "bubble" resulted in labor shortages (especially in the financial sector), which encouraged the hiring of mid-career workers and thus placed career employment systems under some strain (OECD, 1993a, p. 116, n. 6).

After the bubble burst in 1991, pressure from the supply side of the labor market eased; but it was replaced by downward pressures originating in product and capital markets and from abroad as output, capacity utilization, corporate profitability, and liquidity declined while the currency appreciated significantly. Wages proved flexible in response, with the level of overtime earnings and the rates of increase in nominal and real earnings declining sharply (OECD, 1993a). During this major contraction, nominal wage increases fell below their predicted values (Figure 6.1). Wage flexibility contributed to the persistence of a trade surplus as export firms were able once again to absorb part of the yen's appreciation—a practice that predictably resulted in charges of dumping by foreign competitors and their governments (notably the United States). In reply, one Japanese firm (Nissan Motor Company) explained, "If we pass on that [appreciation] as it happens, we'd just push ourselves out [of the U.S. market]. Our company's fundamental policy is to maintain the basic principles of lifetime employment [in Japan]" (*Wall Street Journal*, May 20, 1994, p. A2). The reply may have been ingenuous, but it was hardly persuasive to foreigners in places where unemployment rates had been two or three times higher than levels considered high by Japanese standards.

Inside Japan itself, trade-union critics of export-oriented policy take a different tack. While lifetime employees and their enterprise unions might have found it acceptable to exercise wage restraint in the interest of maintaining or improving the competitiveness of their respective enterprises, union spokesmen in organizations external to the firm—in the tan-sans, the IMF-JC, and the central federation, Rengo—grew impatient with a two-decades-old slowdown in the growth of real wages, both in their own terms and relative to productivity. In the first three years of the 1980s, labor's share recovered half of the sharp loss it had experienced in the last three years of the 1970s; but it declined again between 1983 and 1990—at a time when the shares in the United States, Germany, and France were increasing. Lower rates of inflation and smaller increases in unemployment (albeit to much lower levels) meant that "misery" increased much more slowly in Japan than abroad; but the national unions and their confederations maintained that the price paid for relatively full employment and price stability in terms of real wage stagnation was unnecessarily high.

As participants in the Shunto process of centralized wage setting, these union institutions have been in the business of raising base rates (and securing cost-of-living increases) rather than waiting on growth-dependent career "increments." Indeed, a Rengo proposal to "rectify the sagging wage curve for workers in their 30's and 40's" (JTUC Rengo, 1992, pp. 12, 19) by encouraging disproportionately large increases in entry rates—which would be calculated to restrain the hiring of high school "fresh-outs" as well as to flatten age–earnings profiles—suggested a preference by the tan-sans for what we have characterized (in Chapter 5) as front-loaded career wage contracts over a second-best wage progression based on seniority. Moreover, while the tan-sans have been more willing than their militant Sohyo predecessors to acknowledge the existence of a negative relationship between labor costs and employment levels and to accept productivity growth as a constraint on wage determination, they have not been reluctant to point to the income effect of wage changes, which can proceed not only from distributional consequences of wage increases but also from adoption by the authorities of sufficiently accommodating monetary and fiscal policies.

Thus, even when Domei-led unions joined the employers and the authorities in subscribing to a policy of productivity-based wage increases, they were interested in the wage norm as a minimum as well as a maximum, as a booster of purchasing power as well as a guard against excessive cost increases. And when the government called for increases in money wages to be reduced pari passu with price increases as the latter dramatically decelerated in 1974–1975, the unions agreed, but on the understanding that purchasing power (in the form of real wages) be maintained (Ono, 1976, p. 7). Later (in 1976) they attributed a decline in aggregate consumption to the failure of wages to rise as rapidly as the cost of living and demanded a larger wage increase "as a means for a recovery in personal consumption" (Koshiro, 1977, p. 6).

Moreover, as subscribers to the productivity principle, the moderate unionists could raise the question, Which productivity series should be used as the guide for wage changes—the series registering the growth of productivity in the economy as a whole or the series registering the more rapid growth rate in the manufacturing sectors alone? That question was implicitly raised in 1976, when, as we have noted, the unions in auto and electrical manufacturing challenged the political exchange of a reduction in income taxes for a reduction in the Shunto wage increase on the grounds that the wage increase was not large enough to reflect the higher profits registered by their own employers (who were in the export sector) (Koshiro, 1977, p. 7). Their challenge was unsuccessful, but in 1984 a union research foundation proposed what was essentially a Scandinavian formula. It was urged, according to Dore (1986, p. 102), that the Shunto wage increase equal the increase in *manufacturing* productivity "even at the expense of a bit of inflation. That way internal demand would be boosted, export cost advantages reduced, and the dependence of the economy not just on exports but on export *expansion* in a hostilely protectionist world, would be reduced."

In 1987, following the appreciation of the yen in the wake of the Plaza Accord (1985), and again in 1992, after the collapse of an investment and speculative boom, the union movement repeated the argument for a reflation of domestic consumer demand via higher wage increases as a superior alternative to export expansion via a decline in wages relative to productivity (a.k.a. the "endurance line").

Not surprisingly, the authorities and the employers have dissented. Although the authorities have agreed ever since the early 1970s (OECD, 1973, p. 5) that export surpluses ought to be reduced and that policies looking toward export-led recovery and growth have run their course, they have maintained that domestically generated expansion, no less than export-led expansion, requires wage restraint. The preferred way out, they claim, is by dismantling regulations and other barriers to entry in overly protected sectors of the domestic economy; but for deregulation to be effective (they argue), price flexibility—and therefore wage flexibility—would still be required. But in the absence of such structural reform (which has thus far proved highly elusive), their case for wage and price flexibility would have to depend on its effectiveness in stimulating consumption by raising the real value of wealth and in increasing investment by raising the real value of money. Falling prices, however, increase the real value of debt as well as assets; and since the bubble economy saddled Japan with much heavier burdens of indebtedness, wage flexibility could fail to impart a significant stimulus to output and employment. An argument to that effect appeared (surprisingly) in the *Economist* (November 27, 1993, p. 78), which asserted that "in Western Europe . . . where wages are sticky downwards, falling prices would deliver real wage gains and so support consumer demand. In Japan, by contrast, wages respond quickly even to reductions in prices, through smaller bonuses and reduced overtime."

The Heisei recession—the deepest in the postwar period—and the uncertain and protected recovery that followed in the first half of the 1990s did not yield much evidence of the restorative powers of downward wage and price flexibility. Shunto wage increases were smaller than expected on the basis of even the depressed economic conditions prevailing at the time, and the settlements of 1994 and 1995 set record lows (OECD, 1995b, p. 10). Total earnings disinflated even more steeply than Shunto during 1991–1993, reflecting absolute reductions of overtime and bonus payments. Real earnings also disinflated steeply and actually deflated in 1993 before recovering. Thus, real wages continued to rise during the contraction, but at a sharply declining rate; and the same was true of the separate components of real wages, nominal wages, and consumer prices. Prices of consumer goods (as opposed to services) together with the GDP deflator did decline in 1994, as did levels of wholesale prices and (since 1985) output prices in manufacturing.

Because some prices actually deflated while money wages only disinflated, Japanese experience at the beginning of the recovery (in 1994–1995) conformed more closely to the *Economist*'s European, or sticky wage, model than to its flexibility model: the immediate effect was to limit the extent of price deflation. The ultimate effect was not to support consumer demand (per the model) but to weaken it because while the price declines per se were credited with a stimulating effect, they were limited by the relatively "rigid" behavior of money wages (OECD, 1995b, pp. 3, 18). Downward pressure on money-wage increases (including Shunto settlements), on the other hand, was held to have reduced consumption by lowering incomes during the recession (OECD, 1994b, p. 11) and to retard their growth after recovery began (OECD, 1995b, pp. 10–12).

Nor did wage restraint result in sustained export-led recovery in the 1990s, although it did permit unit labor costs to fall in the face of a sharp drop in short-term productivity in manufacturing, where output prices continued a decline that had begun in 1985 (OECD, 1995b, pp. 18–24). In the export sector, declining prices (in yen) reflated "pricing to market" as firms sought to counter a sharp appreciation of the yen that began in 1990 by reducing their profit margins and their wage and other forms of unit labor costs (OECD, 1993b, p. 23; 1994b, pp. 27–29; 1995b, pp. 22, 35).

These measures helped Japanese exports to increase more rapidly in response to upswings in world demand and ultimately to make a contribution to a recovery in domestic demand in 1994; but they were not sufficient to arrest a loss of international competitiveness and world market share that began in the mid-1980s or to compensate for deduction from GDP growth accounted for by a surge of imports in the 1990s. Although almost half of the exchange-rate appreciation between 1992 and 1995 was offset by the pricing policies of exporting firms, according to the OECD (1995b, pp. 22, 108), the remainder persisted and served to reduce competitiveness and increase imports. Thus, while both unit labor costs and effort continued to decline in domestic terms, both rose steeply relative to Japan's major trading partners. And the fact that relative unit labor costs rose more rapidly than relative export prices reveals the limited potential of a policy of wage restraint in promoting exports. Indeed, the effectiveness of an export-oriented wage policy is self-limiting as well as limited, for, to the extent that lower nominal wage increases have helped to maintain or increase exports in the face of currency appreciation, they tend to perpetuate external surpluses that are conducive to the persistence of appreciation. And continuing appreciation contributed heavily to three developments that further reduced the effectiveness of export-oriented wage policy in the first half of the 1990s. The first consisted in reduced willingness of Japanese investors to buy U.S. securities and thus help recycle the surplus on current account, due in part to the losses resulting from prior currency appreciation. The second (and more significant) development consisted in investing part of the current account surpluses in manufacturing facilities located abroad, especially in other Asian countries, where low labor costs increasingly attracted foreign direct investment as an alternative to domestic cost cutting in response to unappreciating exchange rate.

Finally, as long as the Japanese did succeed in maintaining their real exchange rate at competitive levels through wage restraint and increases in productivity, they furnished their international competitors with an incentive to become more cost-efficient themselves. Equally predictable were the political reactions abroad to Japanese trade surpluses. Foreigners (in the United States and Europe) sought to reduce Japanese efforts, whether by covert protectionism or complaints against "pricing to market" (a.k.a. "dumping"), and to increase imports into Japan, by the removal of barriers to entry in her own sheltered markets or by adoption by the Japanese of more expansionist fiscal-monetary policy.

For Nikkeiren, however, the remedy for the failure of wage restraint to prevent relative unit costs from rising through a deep recession appeared to be more of the same. The employers' federation called for a nominal wage freeze four years in a row. It mattered less to Nikkeiren that domestic unit labor costs had been reduced than that they stood a third higher than American unit labor costs at the end of 1995. Actually, the yen sharply reversed course in 1995 and depreciated against the dollar by 35 percent in six months; and exports rose strongly. But further growth in exports was necessary to permit overall growth of 3 percent, which is necessary to reduce unemployment from over 3 percent to the 2 percent level prevailing in the 1980s. To reach target levels of exports, it was essential (according to Nikkeiren) to restore domestic unit labor costs to competitive levels. It was recognized that, in order to prevent reappreciation of the currency at higher levels of exports, economic deregulation would be necessary in order to accompany the higher export levels with more imports—and it could also serve to raise real wages during a standstill in nominal wages (*Financial Times*, February 6, 1996, p. 6). But Nikkeiren's advocacy of the standstill was not conditioned on deregulation; and it maintained its historic emphasis on maintaining or improving the international competitiveness of Japanese industry in the face of low growth, (relatively) high unemployment, huge trade surpluses, and persistent currency appreciation followed by an uncertain recovery.

Nikkeiren had its own institutional axe to grind when it sought to minimize Shunto settlements. During the deep recession, the dispersion of individual settlements about the Shunto patterns increased as the average itself was progressively lowered. From the viewpoint of a central employers' federation, it was a race to the bottom—or, to apply Nikkeiren's own metaphor—an attempt to keep the slowest ships (the economically weakest firms) safely in the convoy by lowering the speed for all.

The unions rejected the standstill offer in 1996, as they had on all previous occasions. Their own advocacy of Shunto wage increases in excess of current movements in productivity, an advocacy that had been based on the presumed efficiency of Shunto wage increases in increasing consumer demand during the period of recession and stagnation, was defended on the need to avert a loss of consumer confidence, which a freeze would allegedly entail. The unions also claimed that their members deserved a share in their employers' profits, which had begun to recover after a four-year decline (*Financial Times*, January 19, 1996, p. 6).

While reportedly suffering divisions within its own ranks, Rengo acquired some strange bedfellows when some prominent industrialists broke ranks with Nikkeiren's spokesmen and advanced arguments for higher wages that were identical to those raised by the unions. They agreed that their profits had recovered sufficiently to support a more substantial wage increase and believed that failure to grant one would impair the morale of their employees—a position that reflected the efficiency-wage mentality of Japan's large-scale employers (discussed in Chapter 5) (*Financial Times*, January 27, 1996, p. 3). This proposal implied an increased dispersion in wage increases, but these employers announced their intention in paying out most of the increase as lump-sum bonus payments, and Nikkeiren had no objection to this practice.

On the other hand, some of the industrialists endorsed greater pay increases as a boost to consumer demand and, like the unions, feared that a Nikkeiren freeze would undermine consumer confidence and endanger a long-delayed economic recovery (*Financial Times*, January 27, 1996, p. 3). Unlike increases paid in order to prevent deterioration in employee morale and efficiency, a pay increase sufficient to raise consumer confidence would have to be an increase in the general level of pay; and it would also tend to raise relative unit labor costs in the open sector of the economy. However, large-scale firms had four reasons at this time to attach more importance to possible demand-raising effects of a general pay increase than to its cost-raising properties.

In the first place, a steep depreciation of the yen (which changed course in 1995) enabled these large-scale firms to maintain or improve their international competitiveness without exerting so much pressure on their wage costs. A second reason can be found in Japanese firms' foreign direct investment, which increased at an annual average rate of 6.5 percent between 1989 and 1994 while domestic investment fell (OECD, 1995b, p. 29). Investment in overseas capacity—whether undertaken primarily in response to lower labor costs (especially in Asia) and appreciation of the yen or to circumvent actual or potential barriers to exports—has been designed to enable firms to maintain their shares in foreign markets while reducing their dependence on exports and their demand for domestic labor. Smaller firms, however, have been less likely to locate facilities abroad.[5]

A third reason larger firms have assigned greater weight to potentially positive effects of contemplated wage increases on demand than to their negative effects on costs at the mid-decade can be found in the no-layoff guarantees that are activated when their demand for (domestic) labor is reduced below guaranteed levels of employment. Fixed labor costs were reduced by the payment to firms of Employment Adjustment Assistance for training workers retained in excess of requirements (OECD, 1995b, p. 17) and also by policies of relocation and attrition that have helped to reduce the proportion of regular employees in their establishments (Koshiro, 1995, Figure 4). Moreover, some firms voluntarily hoarded labor, especially younger workers, in anticipation of a future decline in the work force. Nevertheless, the official unemployment rate increased to over 3 percent in the mid-1990s from an average of about 2 percent in the previous decade, and the number of firms reporting excess workers exceeded the number reporting a shortage (OECD, 1995b, p. 17). And a decline in economic growth (of real GDP) from rates of 4 percent and higher in the 1980s to negative levels in 1993 and 1995 was reflected in a rate of youth unemployment reportedly as high as 17 percent (*Financial Times*, October 4, 1995b, p. 29). The industrialists, who, like the president of Toyota, supported higher Shunto settlements, feared that further increases in unemployment lay ahead (as indeed proved the case) despite an anticipated recovery and noted that when it reaches and exceeds "a threshold of 3 percent, . . . the ministry of labor comes to companies to ask them to employ more people" (ibid.).

Finally, these business leaders turned to wage increases as an instrument to bolster demand in the absence, as they saw it, of more efficient alternatives that the government and the bureaucratic authorities had failed to provide. Some went so far as to blame the government for having deliberately permitted the yen to rise in order to force the automobile and consumer electronics industries to reduce capacity and free resources for the development of new industries. When the government recoiled from the consequences, the Bank of Japan was obliged to reverse course and bring down the yen (*Financial Times,* October 4, 1995, p. 29). This charge was vigorously denied; but another one was more plausible and of greater import. If politicians, bureaucrats, and deeply entrenched private interests had not prevented the adoption of structural reforms in the economy (according to this argument), imports could have grown without squeezing exports; external surpluses could have shrunk without visiting the deflationary effects of massive currency appreciation on the economy; resources could have been freed from the least productive sectors of the economy for more productive uses; and economic growth could have been sustained at levels that permitted greater increases in real wages.

During the quarter-century of sharply reduced economic growth and higher unemployment (still extremely low by international standards) that followed the first oil shock in the 1970s, Shunto was able to function efficiently and cooperatively as an instrument of wage restraint, with patterns set by the major firms in the export sector at levels that could be promptly and closely followed (with some local variation) across the rest of the economy. And after the bursting of the "speculative bubble" of the late 1980s and a major appreciation of the currency drove economic growth to the vanishing point, raised unemployment by half, and depressed expectations concerning the long-term future of both variables, Shunto continued to restrain wages at least as efficiently as ever but, after a while, not so harmoniously. To the differences among big business, the bureaucracies in charge of monetary, fiscal, industrial, and employment policies, and the political party (Liberal Democrats) in charge of the government—who together have constituted a steering committee for the economy—were added differences within and among the ranks of the social partners inside Shunto proper. On the employer side, there was the divergence, noted above, between the larger firms, whose high growth rates in productivity and whose decisions to locate abroad and reduce their exposure to foreign competitors enabled them to pay higher wage increases to prevent loss of employee morale and productivity, and smaller firms, which allegedly were not in a position to follow the traditional pacesetters. And on the labor side, the industrial unions in the high-productivity export industries, led by IMF-JC, called for "self-determination" by the tan-sans in setting wage norms in their respective industries; and they joined forces with Nikkeiren in pushing for deregulation in order to raise productivity growth in low-productivity sectors, which would have permitted more generous Shunto patterns.

Moreover, support by private sector unions of deregulation and privatization in the public sector in order to avoid increases in social security and other taxes reopened their old conflict with unions in the public sector, which called for increased social welfare not only to solve the problem of an "aging society" but also as part of a program of public spending (the so-called living orientation) to reflate the post-bubble economy (Shinoda, 1995, pp. 6, 7).

The strategy of including some less dynamic industries in the pattern-setting group while excluding some more dynamic industries from the pattern-setting group failed as firms in the former category lagged behind the patterns, while firms in the latter category exceeded them. This contributed to an increased dispersion of Shunto settlements, which could not be reversed by further depressing wage settlements at the high end of the range without loss of worker morale, productivity, and consequently international competitiveness. Yet international competitiveness was already being eroded because a succession of reduced Shunto settlements failed to prevent hourly labor costs in Japan from exceeding levels prevailing in the United States, Europe (except Germany), and especially the emerging economies in East Asia. It required a sharp depreciation of the exchange rate to revive exports, but imports—notably from overseas branches of Japanese enterprises—continued to grow strongly.

Thus, as both the authorities and large-scale industry professed to lessen their reliance on (net) exports, and as the employers' association reacted to reduced rates of growth by calling for an end to across-the-board increases (via base-ups—i.e., raising basic wages—and seniority wages), the continued usefulness of Shunto as a centralized institution was called into question. Yet future abandonment of the long-standing policy objective of keeping the real exchange rate undervalued could make a productivity-based wage policy under Shunto effective once again in helping the economy to secure acceptably low rates of unemployment as well as inflation and acceptably high (if reduced) rates of growth.

Summary

After helping to boost wages for nearly two decades, as originally intended by its militant union founders in the early 1950s, Japan's Annual Spring Labor Offensive, or Shunto, underwent an abrupt conversion in the aftermath of the first oil crisis in 1973–1974 and has been helping to restrain wages ever since. Money wages, which before had risen more rapidly than the condition of labor markets and changes in consumer prices, terms of trade, and productivity growth might have led one to expect, rose less rapidly than predicted after the mid-1970s. In the 1970s, real wage growth declined much more abruptly—both in its own terms and relative to productivity—in Japan than in the United States and Europe; and while Japan resumed its leadership position in real wage growth in the following decade, the lag of real wages behind productivity continued to be more pronounced in that country than elsewhere.

After Shunto's change of course, it could be qualified as a neocorporatist or social contract institution in the European sense, although its characteristic features remained unchanged: widespread exchange of economic information among government agencies and union and management federations, key settlements in a few important sectors of the economy, and pattern following (with some variation) by the individual firms and enterprise unions with advice and coordination supplied by industry unions (tan-sans) and employer associations.

How could an instrument of wage enhancement be made to function as an instrument of restraint? And how could an instrument of wage restraint be made to operate efficiently in the absence of strongly centralized bargaining structures and/or governmental compulsion? In fact, certain features of the "soft" Japanese system have combined not only to make up for the absence of strong centralized authority (notably the absence of strong national unions and of formal industry-wide bargaining) but also to avoid the limitations encountered by rigid systems under stress. For example:

- "Information sharing" has been cited as a source of restraint because of its scale, intensity, and duration under the Shunto procedure—and because of the social coercion it inevitably generates. Yet information sharing alone could not induce goal sharing: the militant unionists who founded Sohyo refused to accept slower growth in the economy (after the early 1970s) as a reason for accepting wage restraint, and it was only after they were effectively displaced by a more moderate group of union leaders from the private sector that trilateral consensus could be achieved.

- The market power and prestige of the large corporations have constituted an effective alternative to formally centralized and authoritative labor market institutions. Their informal coordination within and across industry lines, their bargaining power at company level, and their market power over smaller firms (which serve as their suppliers or outlets) have contributed decisively to the effectiveness of the Shunto system of pattern setting and following. Employer power has been complemented by the pragmatic union leadership at federation levels (who generally accepted increases in productivity and in consumer prices as criteria for money wage increases) and by security-conscious workers and company-conscious enterprise unions. Employer bargaining power has also been associated with a stronger (if still informal) role played by governmental authorities in the Shunto process.

- The government helped to transform Shunto into an effective instrument of wage restraint in several ways. It helped to ensure more moderate pattern setting by moving vigorously to reduce the power of the militant and sheltered unions in the public sector. The latter were then excluded from the key group of pattern setters. Subsequently, the-cause of wage moderation was further served by retaining in the key group employers and unionists from some large but relatively declining industries in the open sector while excluding some of the newer and more dynamic industries.

- The government entered into extensive trilateral discussions of a range of non-wage matters during wage negotiations, after a "political exchange" involving a tax reduction and a Shunto wage norm had taken place (in 1976).

Government authorities sought to integrate Shunto wage setting into *macroeconomic policies* aimed separately at each of the two objectives of price stability and minimal unemployment. Due to the existence of no-layoff guarantees, excess supplies of labor could be converted in part into excess employment within firms rather than open unemployment. (In fact, authorities have intervened on an ad hoc basis to prevent layoffs, sometimes by granting subsidies to individual firms.) This would tend to lessen pressure on authorities to reflate demand and thus to minimize the rate of price inflation during recoveries. Fixed labor costs could put an extra squeeze on profits, but employers would then pressure their (unionized) employees to honor their own part of the implicit employment contracts by accepting smaller wage settlements. And, indeed, the willingness of employees to shoulder part of the cost of excess employment would be increased both by the lower rate of price inflation and by the knowledge that by doing so they would be securing their own future careers with their present employers. Finally, the pressure on both profits and wages would strengthen the incentive for bosses and workers to further reduce unit costs by raising productivity; and low unit labor costs would create a necessary condition for a noninflationary expansion in output and labor demand.

On the other hand, heavy reliance on downward flexibility in labor costs could result in further contraction in labor demand instead of recovery and expansion, but this risk would be lower the higher the underlying rate of growth in output and labor demand (and hence the shorter and shallower the recessions) and the more flexible labor costs improved international competitiveness, thereby generating export-led recoveries and expansions. In fact, wage behavior under Shunto helped the Japanese economy to record smaller increases in money wages and greater growth in productivity in the manufacturing sector than its major competitors and thus contributed to its external surpluses. This record reflected a tendency for wage increases to fall below predicted values, as noted above, and also to respond very sensitively to changes (including reductions) in the rate of increase in consumer prices and to respond to growth in general productivity rather than in the more dynamic export sectors alone.

Responsiveness of wages under Shunto to adverse movements in the terms of trade was exhibited at the end of the 1970s, when wage flexibility helped to relieve pressure on profits caused by the sharp rise in the price of oil. Real wages actually declined while unemployment barely increased. And in the 1980s, when external pressure originated on the demand side as Japanese exporters sought to absorb currency appreciations by nonaccommodative pricing, part of the cost was passed on to wage earners by restrained Shunto settlements.

However, while wage policy could help to restore a country's competitiveness in the short term—and while the short term could occupy a good chunk of historic time, as was the case with Japan in the 1980s—it could not be expected to protect a trade imbalance against corrective reactions (i.e., continued currency appreciation and increased competitiveness abroad) indefinitely. Its limitations became apparent during the deep and protracted "post-bubble" recession of the 1990s, which was characterized by a slowdown in the underlying rate of growth and by steep and persistent appreciation of the yen. The appreciation was once again countered by "pricing to market" and by very low Shunto settlements, but relative unit labor costs nevertheless rose strongly. Imports rose more strongly than exports; and recovery from the downsizing waited on the adoption of strongly reflationary policies by the authorities and a major depreciation of the yen. Meanwhile, unemployment rose steeply (from 2 to 3%); excess employment persisted (some firms were even requested to increase their hiring), and large-scale firms increasingly substituted production abroad for exports.

The failure of the combination of employment maintenance and wage flexibility to generate export-led expansion in the first half of the 1990s could not be blamed on Shunto, which certainly performed efficiently. But on this occasion the task appeared to exceed its capabilities. The employers' federation, pointing to the rise in comparative labor costs, demanded a halt to general wage increases (and to all across-the-board changes). The union federations impatiently proposed greater increases in order to increase purchasing power and domestic demand. And they were supported by some top corporate executives who feared that failure to grant greater wage increases would impair the morale and efficiency of their employees.

Thus, in the mid-1990s the consensus essential to Shunto's effectiveness was weakened more seriously than it had been since the early 1970s. In part, this could be traced to developments in the international economy, notably the competition offered by newly industrializing economies, which exerted a strongly decentralizing influence on systems of collective wage determination in the United States and Europe as well as Japan. But Shunto can still survive as a useful and viable institution in the maintenance of employment at comparatively high levels if the latter is retained as a major policy objective and also if the maintenance of net exports at unsustainable levels is well and truly abandoned as a policy objective and is replaced by policies of trade liberalization and of structural reform in domestic markets.

Shunto's task would then be to generate wage settlements that could help to increase domestic demand as well as to hold down cost and price inflation. The task would be difficult but not impossible: replacement of short-term movements in economywide productivity with sectoral trends as a wage norm might be helpful in this case. In any event, this mission should lie within the capability of a wage-setting institution that had helped to boost wages before it learned to restrain them and that, in its later period, had always accepted the concept that restraint in the interest of cost reduction could not always be exercised single-mindedly and without limits.

APPENDIX: ESTIMATION OF MONEY WAGE CHANGES
IN JAPAN, 1965–1993

Wage Equation Estimates

Our wage equations are based on the wage equation found in the Annex of the *OECD Economic Survey: Japan* (OECD, 1990). This wage equation is specified as a short-run Phillip's curve, with wage growth as the dependent variable.

Equation 6.1: $\text{WageG} = a_0 + a_1 \text{Jo/a} + a_2 P + a_3 \text{Prod} + a_4 \text{ToT}$

or, alternatively

Equation 6.2: $\text{WageG} = a_0 + a_1 \text{UR} + a_2 P + a_3 \text{Prod} + a_4 \text{ToT}$

where,

WageG = annual growth rate of nominal wages (all industries)
UR = the actual rate of unemployment
Jo/a = ratio of job openings to applications
P = annual rate of growth of consumer prices, average of the current and previous period
Prod = annual rate of productivity growth (GNP/Total Employment)
ToT = terms-of-trade indicator, defined as the CPI growth rate minus the GNP deflator growth rate

Ordinary least squares estimates over the period 1965:2 to 1993:2 yielded the following results.

	Period	Constant	UR	Jo/a	P	Prod	ToT	R^2
Equation 1	65:2–93:2	−1.02		1.69	1.04	0.36	−0.81	.855
		(−1.37)		(2.05)	(11.82)	(5.66)	(−3.88)	
Equation 2	65:2−93:2	5.46	−1.98		1.04	0.25	−0.93	.864
		(3.29)	(−3.33)		(12.13)	(3.36)	(−4.54)	

Note: t-statistics in parenthesis.

Residual Analysis

	Time Period	Sum of Residuals	Number of Positive Residuals	Number of Negative Residuals
Equation 1	65:2−75:1	36.889	29	11
	75:2−93:2	−36.889	24	49
Equation 2	65:2−75:1	20.367	25	15
	75:2−93:2	−20.367	29	44

Source: Bank of Japan (monthly, 1965–1996); International Monetary Fund (1996); Mitsubishi Economic Research Institute (monthly, 1965–1996).

NOTES

1. Originally, the only central federation of industrial unions involved in Shunto was Sohyo, its left-wing founder. Domei, a federation with right-wing socialist affiliations, which was formed by secession from Sohyo in the early 1950s, did not participate at first, but many of its affiliated industrial federations joined in as the economy gathered momentum and labor shortage developed. Two other smaller, independent central federations, Churitsu Roren and Shinsabetsu, joined Sohyo in the Shunto Joint Council, and all four central bodies cooperated in bargaining activities (Taira and Levine, 1985, pp. 284–288). Finally, after many attempts at unification, a single central council, Rengo, was formed in 1989 and has taken over the leadership role in Shunto. The existence of independent union councils in the industrial sector, which cut across political differences, should also be noted. In particular, the International Metalworkers, Japan Council, or IMF-JC, which originated in 1964, has come to acquire great influence in coordinating the bargaining of the national unions, or tan-sans, in steel, auto, electrical equipment, machinery, and shipbuilding.

2. One-shot bargaining in Japan was adopted in other sectors and ultimately became ritualized and softened, since announcement of a company's first and last offer is actually preceded by discussions between the parties. Still, the ritual can serve as a reminder of where the preponderance of bargaining power ultimately lies. It might be noted that this practice was found in the United States to be incompatible with the legal requirement that the employer bargain with the union in good faith.

3. We are indebted to Professor Mitsuo Ishida for the observation that after the first oil price shock, enterprise unions focused their bargaining on the welfare of their members over their entire employment careers with the firm. In this connection, they became concerned not only with employment security but also with such items as employee savings plans and housing subsidies and were willing to forgo some immediate increases in wages for concessions in all of these areas.

4. Recent examples include outsourcing assembly or other relatively unskilled operations abroad and even replacing conveyors with small groups of multiskilled functions, both of which would tend to increase the skill concentration of the domestic labor force and (in the latter case) increase the intensity of work (*Wall Street Journal,* October 24, 1994, pp. A1, A4; *The Economist,* October 29, 1994, pp. 83–84). Other forms of unit cost reduction include simplified product design (*Wall Street Journal,* October 26, 1994, p. A16). Toyota's increased profitability in the face of relatively stagnant domestic demand in 1994 has been attributed in part to cost reductions that helped it to increase exports in the face of a strong appreciation of the yen vis-à-vis the dollar. (Exports were also facilitated by strong domestic demand in the United States) (*Financial Times,* February 12, 19, 1995, p. 11.)

5. In 1994, manufacturing production overseas amounted to 8.2 percent of domestic manufacturing production, but production of multinational firms amounted to 20.9 percent of their domestic output. The differences in employment shares was even more striking—1.5 percent versus 10.8 percent (OECD, 1995b, Table 7, p. 29).

7

Conclusion

Our analysis of Japanese and U.S. employment and wage systems has identified the aspects of the Japanese system that have supported relatively high growth, low inflation, and an equitable distribution of income while maintaining high international competitiveness. However, Japan's superior performance in these areas has been accompanied by large social costs including strict gender roles, long working hours for men, limited time for family and vacation, and few opportunities for workers to improve their labor market position after early adulthood. In response to heightened international competition, especially from Japan, U.S. firms adopted several Japanese employment practices while tailoring adaptation of these policies to U.S. labor market institutions.

The comparison of Japan and the United States demonstrates that overall economic performance is not determined by either firm employment systems or national economic institutions. Firm practices, which affect a single company's competitiveness, can support or constrain a country's ability to achieve its economic goals, but the firms' practices cannot themselves determine a country's economic performance.

Within Japan, the economic slowdown of the 1990s called into question the durability of the Japanese security-based employment systems, and Japanese employers looked to U.S. companies for lessons in improving labor market mobility. However, we find that the business sector carried the burden of the recession, and the employment system in large and mid-sized Japanese companies along with the Shunto wage-setting process minimized the impact of the recession on income and unemployment. National economic policy, including a reluctance to increase demand, deregulate the economy, and resolve the banking crisis, was the primary constraint. Rather than hampering economic performance, the Japanese employment system was itself encumbered by national economic policy.

In this concluding chapter, we review the mechanisms underlying the successes of the Japanese system and consider the relationship between firms' employment practices and national economic institutions. We consider how the Japanese system changed in response to the 1990s recession and what lessons Japan can learn from the United States. We then discuss the U.S. response to the Japanese challenge, including the adoption and adaptation of Japanese employment practices in the United States.

The Successes of the Japanese System

The distinctive Japanese policies and practices reviewed in this study have helped the economy perform three conjuring feats:

1. Employment security within the firm has been converted into a source of employee efficiency and adaptability and into a source of national economic stability.
2. A strongly egalitarian distribution of earned income has been combined with comparatively high rates of economic growth.
3. Low unemployment has been combined with low inflation and high growth.

The systems of security, employee involvement, seniority-based wages, and training deserve a substantial amount of credit for this record of performance, as does the national system for determining annual wage changes (Shunto). Yet lifetime employment, age-based pay, and Shunto were not management innovations. Each was adopted in response to union pressure and labor unrest in the early postwar period, and they were not originally designed to increase efficiency or reduce costs. They were, however, soon made to serve these ends. The Japanese training system, a critical element in rationalizing lifetime employment and age-based pay, can be called a management innovation; yet it represents an adaptation to the introduction of the other features. Thus, Japan's corporate managers, unionists, and official policymakers found opportunities where others have feared obstacles to efficient performance. Moreover, they found complementarities rather than trade-offs among such desirable objectives as high employment and low inflation, or earnings equality and growth.

Efficiency through Security

While U.S. economists have argued that unemployment is necessary to moderate wage demands and prevent shirking on the job (Shapiro and Stiglitz, 1984), Japanese workers have been performing with unexcelled efficiency in firms that assure them uninterrupted employment for the duration of their "lifetime" tenure. The Japanese wage structures and management policies that form the subject of this study perform the task that U.S. theorists attribute to unemployment in raising productivity and restraining costs. In Japan, unemployment has been too low to play a significant policing role.

While the higher relative wages paid by large Japanese firms offer a disincentive to shirking, the firm's internal wage system offers a positive incentive to heightened levels of employee effort and proficiency. Although Japanese firms have attached increasing importance to supervisors' employee ratings as a determinant of an individual's pay, they do not usually employ piece-rate methods. Instead, they weight seniority heavily and limit opportunities and rewards for interfirm mobility as much as possible. In order to cash in on increased seniority, employees work under a virtual "lifetime" incentive to perform satisfactorily and to acquire the additional training required to upgrade continually their skills and capabilities. The steeper age–earnings profiles found in Japanese firms function more effectively as employee incentives than the flatter pay structures prevailing in U.S. firms, especially under collective bargaining. In large U.S. firms, a larger proportion of rewards is distributed in the form of general pay increases, and pay structures are often characterized by short job ladders and narrow job classifications.

In addition to enhancing employee desire for training, the seniority-based pay system rewards the Japanese employee for not quitting. Low quit rates in good times help firms to offset redundancy costs incurred during recessions, when no-layoff guarantees might oblige management to retain workers in excess of current requirements. In addition, the obligation to keep redundant workers on the payrolls implies that employer-provided training will have a very low cost, in terms of forgone production. This incentive to train does not exist in the United States, where redundant workers can be released more readily. The institution of lifetime employment in the firm raises the costs of quitting to employees, lowers the costs of training to employers, and increases the payout period on human capital investments. These factors help explain why Japanese firms provide more effective company-based training than their U.S. counterparts.

By retaining exclusive authority over assignments and transfers, Japanese management has avoided the squandering of training resources that occurs in the U.S. post-and-bid system when senior employees bid for new jobs with skill requirements that do not build on their own accumulated expertise. In the job change, valuable human capital is lost. In contrast, the Japanese system permits training to be delivered to the individual in small increments and mainly on the job—just in time for the employee to assume each new responsibility calling for additional skill. Since production workers in Japanese factories are trained for depth as well as breadth, management can assign them greater latitude in decision making on the shop floor and avoid the more rigid division of labor between supervisors and operators and among workers in operator and craft jobs still found in factories in the

United States. A versatile and deeply trained work force can produce the same output with fewer people than a work force of highly specialized workers, resulting in a lower fixed-cost liability to management under lifetime employment guarantees.

Japanese employers also attempt to maximize returns on their investments in lifetime training and to minimize the costs of employment security by shortening the work life while lengthening the work year. Mandatory retirement at early ages, relative to U.S. standards, not only permits employers to optimize the length of the amortization period of their investments in human capital. It also permits a higher inflow of better educated, more trainable, and lower-paid young "fresh-outs" from schools and universities. Long working hours, including overtime, increase the returns to training and enable employers to hire fewer workers under no-lay-off guarantees, thereby substituting variable for fixed employment costs and enhancing downward labor cost flexibility during recessions. In fact, the age of retirement has increased and hours of work have been reduced over time. But these developments have reflected pressure from a Ministry of Labor embarrassed by international comparisons and also from usually pliant enterprise unions. Employers have compensated by reducing the wages paid to older employees and also by transferring them to subsidiaries.

The system of performance evaluation used to assign, transfer, and train employees on the basis of skill and knowledge acquired provides managers ample opportunity to detect instances of shirking on the job at little or no extra cost. The conclusion of efficiency wage theory that unemployment is needed to deter shirking rests on the assumption that monitoring an employee's performance is difficult and costly. But if monitoring and evaluation are relatively easy, lesser deterrents than dismissal and unemployment can serve to maintain employee efficiency. For example, individual employee assessments help to determine the size of a worker's bonus and speed of promotion to a higher salary level. Evidence of the powerful incentive of these evaluations can be found in the fact that workers often forgo holidays and vacation time to which they are entitled for fear of downgrading their supervisor's assessment. Employees can be transferred to another firm for not achieving work targets, making a serious mistake, or not getting along with colleagues. Thus, the disciplinary deterrents and incentives held by an authoritarian management reinforce the pecuniary disincentives to shirking and quitting provided by the seniority wage system and the firm's relative wage structure.

Any account of Japanese effectiveness in combining employment security with productivity must stress a level of employee involvement that is remarkably high by U.S. standards. Japanese employee involvement is characterized by group activity and cooperative effort, such as work teams and quality circles, that emphasize continuous improvement and lowering costs. The premise is that highly trained production workers are capable of discovering ways to improve the production process. With the assistance of their supervisor, they are encouraged and expected to do so. More important, employee involvement produces a cooperative work force, secure in its employment within the firm, ready to accept change as indispensable to the viability of "their" company, and sympathetic to the objectives and plans of management.

The employees, the beneficiaries of employment security and career development, have been predisposed by custom and tradition to refrain from exploiting the opportunities presented by employment security for immediate gain. Moreover, they have been more willing to accept continual change as the price of security and economic advancement and to take personal satisfaction in the welfare of the work group and their company. At the same time, the maintenance of full employment within the Japanese firm has been underwritten by comparatively high levels and rates of growth of demand in the Japanese economy, which tend to minimize the cost to the firm of guaranteeing employment to its regular employees.

Equality and Growth

Income inequality has often been regarded as a key ingredient in the process of economic growth, on the grounds that it serves as both an incentive to individual effort and as a source of savings to finance investment. Yet it does not constitute a necessary or a sufficient condition of growth, as comparisons between the Japanese and U.S. economies indicate. In the United States, inequality in personal earnings is greater than in Japan and has increased rapidly in the 1980s, while economic growth has been very low and real wages have stagnated for nearly a generation. Japan, on the other hand, has been a leader in growth and in the equitable distribution of income, and it experienced only a modest increase in inequality in the 1980s.

One characteristic of Japanese society has generated inequality without making a positive contribution to economic growth: the unequal treatment of men and women in the labor market. Of course, this type of discrimination has also prevailed in the United States, where full-time female workers earned only three-fifths as much as their male counterparts for most of the postwar period up to the 1980s. In the 1980s, gender inequality began to decrease in the United States, as college-educated women increasingly entered and advanced in the professions and as the real wages of less-educated women rose while the pay of their male counterparts declined. In Japan, on the other hand, the relative pay of women rose from about 42 percent of male pay in the early 1960s to about 58 percent in the 1970s. This improvement coincided with a period of rapid economic growth. Since 1980, the female–male pay ratio has fallen to about 50 percent. Gender difference constitutes a more important source of income inequality in Japan than in the United States.

Japan and the United States have had similar levels of inequality in the structure of wage differences across manufacturing industries, but Japan has less wage inequality across broader economic sectors. In the United States, interindustry wage differences have been widening since the advent of an era of slower economic growth in the early 1970s, whereas in Japan they remained stable. Hence, Japan has been able to maintain superior growth rates with comparatively less inequality in the interindustry wage structure. More important, interindustry wage differentials are much smaller among large companies in Japan than in the United States. Japan's large companies managed to combine a comparatively high degree of distributional equality with comparatively high rates of growth.

Wage differentials by firm size, on the other hand, have been greater in Japan than in the United States. In Japan, this type of wage inequality has been conducive to employee efficiency and hence to growth. The wage premiums enjoyed and protected by large Japanese firms serve as incentives to their employees to work efficiently and to enhance their productivity via continual training. Economic growth has also affected firm-size differentials. During the period of very rapid economic growth and tight labor markets (1965–1973), firm-size wage differentials were reduced in Japan and then widened subsequently when growth slowed.

In the critical area of education, Japan has combined greater earnings equality with high levels of efficiency and growth. The difference between the value of lifetime earnings for university and high school graduates in Japan is smaller than in the United States. Whereas the gap increased in the United States in the 1980s, it remained constant in Japan and has narrowed over the longer term. Although the narrowing reflected a steep increase in the proportion of university to high school graduates, the more egalitarian income distribution also reflected the "white collarization of blue collar work" as well as the "blue collarization of white collar work" (Koike and Inoki, 1990). The narrow income differentials have not, however, prevented the supply of more highly educated labor from increasing readily in response to increased educational opportunity.

The low compensation of middle managers and chief executives relative to production workers in large Japanese firms, especially in comparison with their U.S. counterparts, constitutes a dramatic example of the coexistence of relative income equality with high economic growth. The practice of Japanese managers cutting their own pay—before imposing the pain and cost of restructuring on the rest of the employees—offers a stark contrast to practices in the United States and shows how relative equality can substitute for higher relative pay as a source of efficiency and growth. Relatively low executive pay has been criticized in Japan as "bad equality" and a disincentive to managers to adopt more draconian measures to improve the cost-efficiency of the enterprise when profits are low. But Japanese managers have never been accused of inefficiency by their competitors, nor have their own compensation policies fomented employee resentment or provoked union pay demands, as has happened in the United States. In short, Japanese management compensation policies demonstrate how relative income equality can be both a source of equity to employees and an incentive for growth.

Seniority-weighted pay, with its strong pecuniary incentive, can result in unequal pay for the same work and hence in wider dispersion of earnings within occupational groups. But it is not a source of inequality among workers in the same demographic cohort. Nor need it incur opposition from junior employees—as long as they are faced with the same prospects of advancement in the firm as seniors had enjoyed. Moreover, as deferred income to the career employee, seniority-weighted pay provides a source of savings within the firm and implicitly to the individual. It has thus contributed to the Japanese economy's high rates of savings and investment as well as of effort and skill, helping Japan to achieve relatively high levels of growth and high degrees of distributional equality at the same time.

Equality in the distribution of personal income need not result in lower rates of saving and hence investment when, as in the case of Japan, it is associated with a low share of wages in the functional distribution of income. Low labor shares have contributed to high savings rates in Japan, but not so emphatically as to disproportionately enrich individual recipients of property income. Instead, savings have been heavily retained and invested in the enterprise, where they can contribute directly to increased promotional opportunities to employees and hence can be regarded as "investment wages." Thus, these two distinguishing characteristics of Japanese income distribution—a comparatively equal distribution of personal income and a low labor share—complement and reinforce each other.

Price Stability from Full Employment

In Japan, the ability to combine employment security and efficiency in the firm has been matched by the ability to combine relative price stability and high levels of employment. In the United States, it has appeared that higher rates of unemployment are required to secure lower rates of inflation. In Japan, however, unemployment has not been accepted as a necessary cost of price stability.

The ability of the Japanese economy to achieve these ostensibly mutually exclusive goals results from several factors. Japanese employment systems engender labor cost flexibility in times of recession while restraining inflationary wage demands in times of labor scarcity. Moreover, the market power of large Japanese firms and the discretion of Japanese managers in assigning labor contributes to the maintenance of noninflationary labor shortages. Finally, the operation of the synchronized national system of wage determination (Shunto) further restrains inflationary wage pressures during periods of high growth while it has tended to equalize wages among employers.

As we have noted, the reinforcing policies of employment security, employee involvement, training, and compensation based on seniority and performance provide a source of continual productivity growth within the enterprise. This dynamic efficiency has permitted noninflationary wage growth at or below the rate of productivity increase. Workers have been able and willing to depend upon steady company growth to provide the promotions that reflect their tenure and skill development, and they have been willing to accept wage increases below productivity increases, which provides the company with the revenues to fuel the long-run growth. This implicit saving by workers, which at first enhances company profits, ultimately results in long-run wages growing faster than they would otherwise as the company feels obligated to use profits for growth. Furthermore, the lifetime employment guarantee furnishes regular employees with a strong incentive to accept reductions in the rate of wage increase during recessions. Workers thereby effectively share the cost of their employment assurance with employers, whose profits are reduced when they retain redundant labor on the payroll. Hence, employment rigidity within the firm has contributed to Japan's comparative ability to sustain moderate wage growth at full employment.

Lifetime employment and employee involvement in the enterprise have also contributed to the persistence of noninflationary labor shortages during periods of expansion and growth in the economy. When confronted with labor shortages, employers who are committed to lifetime employment have an incentive to minimize the size of the regular work force and to rely on overtime rather than new hires. Moreover, involved and security-conscious employees are reluctant to quit their jobs when quitting would mean a loss of accumulated seniority and of the prospects of future advancement in pay in a large, high-status firm.

By binding employees to the firm and largely insulating them from external market influences, Japanese policies strengthen the discretionary authority of management in allocating labor and rewarding employees within the enterprise. This authority is reinforced by the large firms' power over their smaller suppliers, which pay lower wages according to their rank in the hierarchy of firms. In addition to negotiating comparable union wages under Shunto, large competitors in the same industry have maintained informal agreements not to poach experienced workers from one another and have exchanged cost information in order to restrain wage increases and prevent "leapfrogging."

Shunto, the annual wage determination process, represents a significant economywide mechanism that has restrained inflationary wage pressures. Each year a pattern emerges from lead negotiations in a small group of major firms, which is then diffused through the remainder of the economy. The founders of the system originally intended to push wages up as rapidly as possible and to minimize wage differentials within and across industries. In reaction to the oil shocks of the 1970s and the subsequent reassertion of corporate power, however, Shunto was transformed from an instrument designed to boost wages to an instrument of relative wage moderation and restraint. The coordination of wage determination with fiscal and monetary policies, together with participation by government officials in tripartite discussions, qualify Shunto as a "social contract" or "neocorporatist" institution. But policymaking and implementation occur through a Japanese style of consensus building and information sharing rather than by reliance on strongly centralized bargaining structures.

A major source of restraint and compliance in the Shunto process is supplied by Japan's leading corporations. The conversion of Shunto into an instrument of wage moderation marked the reassertion of the influence and power of these corporations, who adopted productivity-determined pay increases and minimum international cost levels as the criteria for acceptable wage changes. The influence of big business is reflected in the changed composition of the pattern-setting groups in the post-OPEC order of slower growth and intensified international competition. Representatives from the more sheltered sectors of the economy have been excluded—not only public sector industries but also the rapidly growing wholesale and retail trade and business service sectors. The export sector took center stage as electronics took a leading place alongside autos, while steel and shipbuilding, which had become less dynamic and profitable, were retained. These omissions and retentions impart a conservative bias to pattern setting, as the lead industries include declining industries as well as high growth–high productivity industries, although some industries in the "tertiary" sector have tended to exceed the Shunto patterns. Moreover, the market power of the big firms in both labor and product markets, along with their coordination, substitutes for centralized bargaining structures and reinforces information sharing and consensus building in the pattern-following process.

The Evolution of the Japanese System

Japan Responds to Recession and Stagnation in the 1990s

The Japanese economy limped through the first half of the 1990s as the government relied upon the business sector to bear the brunt of the recession in lowered profits. Macroeconomic policy, including increasing aggregate demand with government spending and lowering interest rates on government securities, was used to only a minor extent until 1995. Although companies and the press engaged in public discussion about the possible challenges to the Japanese employment system during the long period of low growth, in the three major industries we studied the recession had surprisingly little impact on the basic elements of the system. Companies relied on their traditional tools of flexibility—reduced overtime hours, reduced employment of temporary and part-time workers, lower cost goals for suppliers, reduced profit margins, slower growth in wages and bonuses, and reductions in new hires. As the recession wore on, companies heightened their use of these options, including actual reductions in bonuses.

The adjustments affected workers and companies without undermining major relationships. The reduction in overtime hours mainly affected men's salaries, while reducing new hires and part-time and temporary workers reduced opportunities for women and new graduates. Variations in profitability across companies in the same industry increased during the recession, as did variation in Shunto wage settlements. Weaker companies were forced to reduce their labor costs and hours more than the stronger companies. Major firms increasingly located capacity abroad. But it was not necessary to abandon either the lifetime employment guarantee or age-based pay, the two key elements in the Japanese employment system. Shunto also functioned effectively in holding nominal wage increases below expected levels.

We began this book by noting that the Japanese system of employment and wage determination came in for a good share of criticism in the 1990s, when the country was mired in its worst recession since before World War II; and we asked how institutions that had received much credit for Japan's prior economic success could have suddenly turned sour. Our short answer is that these distinctive institutions—notably lifetime employment, seniority-based wages, and synchronous wage rounds—have performed effectively in maintaining employment and restraining labor costs during a sustained recessionary period.

Modifying the Japanese System in an Era of Slower Growth

Although Japan's labor market institutions held up well during the long recession, the 1990s ushered in a more constrained economic environment. Like the oil shock in the early 1970s, the collapse of the bubble economy of the late 1980s apparently marked a new era of lower economic growth and increased unemployment. To the extent that slower growth results in more excess labor being retained in large firms, the cost of employment security will rise. More unemployment would mean greater disparity between the guarantee of employment enjoyed by regular employees in the larger firms and the degree of security available on average to other members of the working population.

Other developments have also been altering the environment in which the Japanese employment systems operate or may do so in the future. These developments include the aging of the country's work force; increased leisure time; changes in the economic status of Japanese women; location overseas by Japanese firms; declining coverage of lifetime employment; greater reliance on domestic measures to increase or maintain aggregate demand; and deregulation and withdrawal of protection from sheltered markets. Each of these changes carries implications for one or more features of Japan's labor market system.

Aging labor force and reduced growth. The prospect and reality of an aging labor force has long preoccupied Japanese policymakers, managers, and unionists. Firms combining lifetime employment security with seniority-based wage structures must cope with increased wage costs as the average age of the work force increases. At the same time, regular male workers in those firms who might expect to attain the rank of supervisor or equivalent before retiring are confronted with potential slowdown in promotion rates. Some large firms have installed two-tier management systems to mitigate this problem, although this entails greater salary costs. Companies have also been pressing to substitute performance-based pay for seniority-based pay, although unions traditionally have been opposed and change has been slow. The unions have championed higher retirement ages under systems of seniority-based pay. Although this change would compensate for a reduced supply of workers, it would also increase both the average age of the firm's work force and its average wage. However, because a slower growth in demand is associated with reduced supplies of male labor, the aging process will make it easier for the economy to meet low-unemployment and low-inflation goals.

Increased leisure and the pace of reform. Japan's progress in achieving parity with the United States has been much more impressive in the realm of pay than in the domain of leisure and effort. Total hours of work remained significantly higher than U.S. levels at the end of the recession, despite governmental target setting and a considerable reduction in hours worked during the recession. It is significant that the unions have favored shorter hours, just as they favored later retirement. Further change will come through increases in paid vacation or holidays. Such change is likely to be slow because it is a basic characteristic—and, to a considerable degree, we believe, a strength—of the consensual Japanese system to proceed slowly in making major economic and social transformations. Long periods of discussion and preparation precede the changes; this process of consensus formation allows changes to proceed in a measured way with minimal disruption and dislocation.

A case for gradualism could be made here in terms of the cost and difficulty of a reduction in scheduled work hours in the Japanese system of employment security. In the 1980s, the case was made in reverse when employers sought to minimize regular employment by increasing overtime and employing more casual labor, which could be reduced during temporary recessions.

The place of women. The status of Japanese women in the labor force is another area with serious implications for the Japanese employment system. Equality of status would mean that women would have an equal chance of inclusion in jobs with career ladders and lifetime employment status. Increasing the total coverage of these systems would broaden the social base of the institution and could thus strengthen its popular support. Yet adding female workers to the existing regular labor force would increase the potential cost of the firm's employment guarantee. It would reduce the size of the buffer stock of labor that could be laid off during recessions, and it could require more wage restraint by all workers in the enterprise. And while the probability of inclusion under lifetime guarantees would rise for women, it could possibly decline for men.

Equal access to promotions and to higher-paying jobs for women could greatly weaken the basis of family-based pay, so that the earnings structure would no longer reflect life-cycle needs for men. This change would attenuate the incentives provided by the age-based wage structure. But many firms have expressed a preference for pay adjustments that reflect productivity and performance, which would give women a greater chance for success in achieving equality in the labor market.

In short, an equalization of status and opportunity for women in the labor market would yield great social gain in Japan, but it would not be without cost. If, however, the Japanese penchant for gradual reform is exercised in this area, the costs might be stretched out over time and offset in part by successively higher levels of productivity. Gradualism would minimize adverse impacts on the security and earnings of senior male employees and ease the adjustment of the institutional arrangements of lifetime earnings and age-based wages as well as gender roles in the family.

Overseas location of industry. The expansion of production capacity in overseas locations by large export firms poses potential difficulties for their systems of employment security. Lifetime employment guarantees have prevented firms from shutting down excess capacity at home as rapidly as they have expanded abroad. Although exporting potential or actual jobs instead of goods has provided firms with an alternative source of revenue earned overseas, it has also provided management with an additional source of pressure to increase productivity and reduce comparative costs in their domestic establishments. Hence, it could tend to reinforce management's control over workers in instigating desired changes, such as relying more on performance-based pay at the expense of seniority-based pay.

Demand management, wage policies, and deregulation. Given the continuance of economic and diplomatic pressures to reduce the trade surplus, policymakers will have to rely more heavily on increased domestic spending as opposed to increased exports to generate cyclical recoveries in output and employment. The maintenance of what by international standards would still be high levels of employment and low inflation would call for continued reliance on Shunto. But the consensus required for Shunto's effective operation became strained during the prolonged recession of the 1990s, under the twin pressures of currency appreciation and domestic price deflation. Better external balance and less-stringent demand management could allow Shunto to regain support as a valuable policy instrument.

The effectiveness of both demand management and wage policy could be enhanced by extensive deregulation of the protected and inefficient sectors of the Japanese economy as well as resolution of the banking crisis generated by the bubble economy in the 1980s. Structural reform could be expected to result in increased output potential and productivity, lower price levels, and higher real wages throughout the economy as a whole. The transitional costs of unemployment can be minimized if sufficient wage restraint permits redundant labor to be absorbed into more productive sectors. Unfortunately, serious political obstacles still remain in the way of structural and financial reforms. In this area of reform, gradualism has been carried to excess.

Challenges to employment and pay systems. The economic, demographic, and so-cial changes discussed above pose problems for lifetime employment and seniori-ty-based pay. But if employment security is weakened or career earnings profiles are flattened, the other elements of the system presumably would also be weakened. If Japanese companies dilute their security practices, their employment systems could be transformed by increased numbers of employees quitting for higher wages elsewhere, less employee commitment to the company's long-term goals and per-formance, and employee demands for input into job assignments and skill devel-opment as employees become more responsible for their own careers. If employ-ees become more autonomous, then managers would lose some of their power over the allocation of labor, including job assignment and skill development within the company.

If companies try to change the size of the regular work force in response to changes in product demand, unions may use short-run opportunities to raise wages for long-run gain, and they might even seek to bargain outside the compa-ny at the industry level directly through their industry federations. In short, Japan might find itself attempting to graft elements of a U.S.-type system, which relies on flexibility through mobility and on adversarial industrial relations for worker progress and enterprise competitiveness, onto a system that relies on continuity through stability and on consensus and goal sharing. This presents a strong case for approaching change gradually if it is to succeed at all.

Policy Lessons for Japan

For Japan, the challenge is to create more flexibility at minimum sacrifice to sta-bility. The United States furnishes an example of a mature economy that includes an active role of government in providing sufficient domestic demand and in sup-porting deregulation of the domestic economy and that allows women expanded labor market opportunities, workers more autonomy, and trade unions more in-dependence.

Although beset with severe budgetary constraints, the Japanese authorities should maintain demand at levels sufficient to facilitate the necessary deregulation and reform of its protected sectors, especially in the distribution systems that would allow lower-priced foreign goods access to Japanese consumer markets. Japan's trade surplus has been supported by protective domestic institutions that contribute to Japan's low propensity to import. The government's reliance upon a squeeze on profits and wages within the firm rather than upon domestic demand growth to weather the long period of slow growth in the 1990s upset the implicit understanding that firms would sacrifice only short-run profits in return for growth and market share. The maintenance of this implicit social contract provides the required national economic structure within which the Japanese system of em-ployment security and seniority wages functions. Meanwhile, slower growth and constrained profitability also strengthen incentives for management to minimize the fixed labor costs created by their employment guarantees. Thus, the national growth rate would have to be maintained at a level necessary to absorb graduates into the system and to maintain the steady promotion of experienced workers.

Innovation in Japan can improve with more autonomy and individual voice of professional and managerial workers, whose motivation and training support strong team work but constrain individual creativity. We have called this the blue collarization of white collar workers since professional and managerial workers in Japan face more rigid job ladders and less performance-based pay than in the United States and they are members of the enterprise union for the first ten to fifteen years of their work lives. Japanese enterprise unions could facilitate greater individual autonomy for union workers by playing a larger role in representing the grievances of individual workers. The Japanese could also look to the United States in learning how to provide less rigid gender roles with greater opportunities for women and more leisure time for men. These outcomes will require changes in a system that currently uses women as a buffer stock in the labor market and as the primary providers of family life and will require that families learn to spend more time together and more money on leisure-time activities.

These changes may well cause some deterioration in income equality, unemployment rates, and economic stability. But the strength of the Japanese institutions can be maintained while required changes proceed in orderly fashion, especially if Japan's national wage-determination process (Shunto) is retained, albeit with more variation in wage growth between companies and across industries, and if reciprocal joint commitment between the worker and the company is maintained as the rule rather than the exception.

The Evolution of the U.S. System

Adapting Firm Practices in the Untied States

Since the mid-1970s, U.S. companies have been forced to make major changes in their organization and strategy in response to Japanese competition for automobiles and electronic products in the U.S. market. Heightened international competition increased the punishment for failing to reduce costs and improve quality through adoption of best-practice systems. In response, U.S. firms began to experiment with elements of the Japanese production system, adapting them to the institutions of the U.S. labor market.

For U.S. production workers, Japanese employment security practices have been modified to be consistent with high individual mobility and with government programs that provide some income security. Employee involvement practices have been modified to be consistent with legal restraints on management's relationship to employee committees and with workers' desires for voluntary programs; and training has been modified to be consistent with workers' desire for mobility and for input into job assignment and with the relatively large supply of low-wage, less-skilled workers. Production and clerical (nonexempt) workers and professional and managerial (exempt) workers remain on separate tracks, consistent with their different legal status under the Fair Labor Standards Act.

The use of work teams and information technology has also brought U.S. practice closer to the Japanese model. The span of control across workers has increased in U.S. firms, especially for the first-line supervisor, and the levels of management have been reduced usually by one tier. Compensation systems in the United States emphasize equal pay for comparable job tasks rather than greater pay for more experience and better performance. Relative to Japanese wage structures, U.S. blue-collar workers' wages increase only marginally with seniority, on-the-job training, or performance, and their wages are more related to specific job titles or grades.

Recent trends in compensation include basing pay less on job classification and including some form of gain sharing. But these changes have been dominated by the reduction in the number of pay classifications and have resulted in a flattening of nonexempt wage profiles within a firm. For exempt workers, the emphasis on performance-based pay intensified, so that the variance across professionals and managers increased as the profiles steepened. In contrast to the situation in Japan, the low savings rate and high immigration rate in the United States have contributed to wage stagnation and rising inequality. Again, no implicit social contract exists in the United States that would constrain a dramatic rise in CEO salaries while production workers' wages stagnate or that would prevent downsizing while company revenues rise. Overall, the primary trend in U.S. wages has been toward increased inequality by education and stagnant average wages.

Changes in labor market institutions have been much more abrupt in the United States than in Japan, where it took a deep economic crisis before firms instituted cost-reducing practices. Even then, their adjustments have tended to be marginal and gradual compared to the changes undertaken by U.S. companies in the face of intense global competition.

In the United States, security systems weakened during the 1980s and 1990s. The unemployment insurance-based security system covered fewer unemployed workers, and most of the highly visible companies that had provided employment security, such as major (nonunion) electronics companies (IBM, Hewlett Packard, DEC), discarded these policies in the 1990s. A notable exception was Motorola, which kept its security commitment to employees with at least ten years' tenure, known as the President's Club. Enlisting worker involvement in decision making within the work group became less tied to employment security and more to job insecurity.

Policy Lessons for the United States

For the United States, the challenge for employers is to create more stability and continuity by making changes more gradually over a long period. Two broad areas in which U.S. managers and, in some cases, unions might profit from Japanese experience are improving consensus building and relying less on individual autonomy and adversarial relations and improving the effectiveness of training.

The Japanese have shown how to develop corporate values that emphasize long-run decision making and the welfare of employees as well as shareholders. In the United States, employment practices that provide flexible employment and allow mobility for workers hinder the ability of the economy to achieve low unemployment with moderate wage growth since flexibility reinforces the business cycle. Achievement of even better economic performance is constrained by firms' practices of short-term layoffs and long-term downsizing.

Japanese firms also set an example in developing consensus, cooperation, and a collective voice, which contrasts with the American emphasis on individualism and adversarial relations between union and management. Although "mature" union–management relationships have reduced confrontation, the relationship remains primarily adversarial rather than cooperative. Democratic union politics often oblige union leaders to be adversarial in their relationship with management.

A basic strength of the U.S. economy is the flexibility and adaptability of its work force and the opportunities available to women, minorities, and immigrants in the work place. The ability of managers to adjust the work force and the ability of employees to change jobs are jealously guarded, and any changes in the employment system must accommodate this flexibility and mobility. Also, worker autonomy and input into decisions concerning their jobs often make the U.S. worker creative and independent; these strengths and values should be supported.

Because of the emphasis placed on individual mobility, Japan's employment security system is not a viable option for the United States. One alternative, termed the high-wage, high-productivity economy, is for workers' security to reside in their skills, which are portable between employers. The highly skilled employee would be elevated to the status of a craft or professional worker, and labor's power would reside in knowledge and skills as opposed to the power to maintain a picket line (Marshall and Tucker, 1992).

Unfortunately, mobility in the United States, both within and between firms, often inhibits skill deepening and leads to a substantial waste of accumulated human capital. Since skill development on the job is, for the most part, not formally certified for the nonprofessional and noncraft workers, they are unable to transfer their accumulated knowledge from one employer to another. In addition, high interfirm mobility weakens the link between pay and skill depth and breadth. Moreover, the U.S. post-and-bid system of internal promotion often results in within-plant job transfers that are equivalent to a worker quitting in terms of the impact on skill retention and development. There is usually no wage penalty for a job transfer entailing a significant decline in the skills being used. On the other hand, situations in which workers' skills are upgraded but their job titles and pay remain the same are common. This lack of rationally constructed career paths inhibits productivity and wage growth within U.S. firms.

Businesses in the United States can look to Japan in learning how to form career ladders for all occupations in order to make effective development and use of knowledge, training, and skills. Effective career ladders are characterized by job assignments that are jointly determined by workers and supervisors but are constrained by the need to form rational career paths in which training builds on and deepens workers' skills. The development and recognition of structured on-the-job training and the long-run planning of skill acquisition, coupled with an integration of production and craft skills, can result in training that is more efficiently provided and more effectively used. Pay increases as the worker moves along the planned career path, since productivity and skills are also increasing. Here, pay reflects the ability to do various jobs as well as the level of skill in tasks such as troubleshooting and maintenance. Pay is not based on skill in the sense of paying for specific skill acquisition, however, since pay reflects one's accumulation of broader and deeper skills within one's job experience. The potential problem that results with skill-based pay—workers learning skills that they do not then use on their jobs—does not arise because skill acquisition is embedded in a job and so skills are learned as they are used.

For the United States to take advantage of the benefits of its flexibility—that is, for employers to adjust the work force and for employees to seek other jobs—firms must operate at high capacity, continually improve productivity, and have highly skilled workers. The development of a skill-based alternative must be supported by national economic policies that maintain adequate demand so that effective firm-based training is portable in a robust labor market.

In general, Japan has seemed better situated to maintain high wages and low unemployment than the United States because of its superior educational and training systems, its higher savings rate, its ability to achieve full employment without wage inflation, and its gradual, systematic approach to change. The U.S. strength lies in its labor market flexibility, its ability to generate large numbers of jobs, and its nurturing of innovation and creativity. Each country's success in learning from the other will depend on how well it can incorporate changes into its own distinctive employment and wage systems so as to improve its ability to reconcile the requirements of efficiency and security, distributional equity and economic growth, and low levels unemployment and inflation in a highly dynamic and ever more competitive global economy.

References

Abo, Tetsuo, ed. (1994). *Hybrid Factory: The Japanese Production System in the United States.* New York: Oxford University Press.

Abowd, John, and Michael Bognanno (1995). "International Differences in Executive and Managerial Compensation." Pp. 67–103 in Richard B. Freeman and Lawrence F. Katz, eds., *Differences and Changes in Wage Structure.* Chicago: University of Chicago Press.

Abraham, Katharine G., and Susan N. Houseman (1993a). "Job Security and Work Force Adjustment: How Different Are U.S. and Japanese Practices?" Pp. 180–199 in Christoph F. Buechtemann, ed., *Employment Security and Labor Market Behavior.* Ithaca, NY: ILR Press.

Abraham, Katharine G., and Susan N. Houseman (1993b). *Job Security in America: Lessons from Germany.* Washington, D.C.: Brookings Institution.

Akerlof, George, and Hajme Miyazaki (1980). "The Implicit Contract Theory of Unemployment Meets the Wage Bill Argument." *Review of Economic Studies* 47:321–338.

Altonji, Joseph G., and James R. Spletzer (1991). "Worker Characteristics, Job Characteristics, and the Receipt of On-the-Job Training." *Industrial and Labor Relations Review* 45, no. 1 (October): 58–79.

American Electronics Association (1994). *Setting the Standard: A Handbook on Skill Standards for the High-Tech Industry.* Santa Clara, Calif.: American Electronics Association, Workforce Skills Project.

Anderson, P. A., and B. D. Meyer (1994). "The Extent and Consequences of Job Turnover." Pp. 177–184 in *Brookings Papers on Economic Activity: Microeconomics.* Washington, D.C.: Brookings Institution.

Aoki, Masahiko (1984). *The Cooperative Theory of the Firm.* Oxford: Oxford University Press.

Aoki, Masahiko (1988). *Information, Incentives, and Bargaining in the Japanese Economy.* New York: Cambridge University Press.

Aoki, Masahiko (1990). "Towards an Economic Model of the Japanese Firm." *Journal of Economic Literature* 28, no. 1 (March): 1–27.

Appelbaum, Eileen, and Rosemary Batt (1994). *The New American Workplace.* Ithaca, N.Y.: ILR Press.

Asakura, Takashi (1993). "Working Women and Mental Stress." *Japan Labor Bulletin,* April 1, pp. 5–8.

Aukrust, Odd (1970). "PRIMI: A Model of the Price and Distribution Mechanism of an Open Economy." *Review of Income and Wealth Series* 16, no. 1 (March): 51–78.

Azariadis, Costas (1975). "Implicit Contracts and Underemployment Equilibria." *Journal of Political Economy* 83, no. 61:1183–1202.

Azariadis, Costas, and Joseph E. Stiglitz (1983). "Implicit Contracts and Fixed-Price Equilibria." *Quarterly Journal of Economics* 98 (Supplement): 1–22.

Bailey, Thomas (1992). "Discretionary Effort and the Organization of Work: Employee Participation and Work Reform since Hawthorne." Paper prepared for the Sloan Foundation.

Baily, Martin N. (1974). "Wages and Employment under Uncertain Demand." *Review of Economic Studies* 41:37–50.

Baker, Sandra E., and Lisa M. Lynch (1996). "Human-Capital Investment and Productivity." *American Economic Review* 86, no. 2 (May): 263–67.

Bank of Japan, Research and Statistics Department (monthly, 1965–1996). *Economic Statistics Monthly.* Tokyo: Bank of Japan.

Bank of Japan, Research and Statistics Department (1987). *Price Index Annual, 1986.* Tokyo: Bank of Japan.

Bank of Japan, Research and Statistics Department (1992). *Comparative Economic and Financial Statistics: Japan and Other Major Countries.* Vol. 29. Tokyo: Bank of Japan.

Bank of Japan, Research and Statistics Department (1994a). *Comparative Economic and Financial Statistics: Japan and Other Major Countries,* vol. 31. Tokyo: Bank of Japan.

Bank of Japan, Research and Statistics Department (1994b). *Price Index Annual, 1993.* Tokyo: Bank of Japan.

Bartel, Ann P. (1994). "Productivity Gains from the Implementation of Employee Training Programs." *Industrial Relations* 33:411–425.

Becker, Brian, and Craig Olson (1992). "Unions and Firm Profits." *Industrial Relations* 31, no. 3 (Fall): 395–415.

Becker, Gary S. (1964). *Human Capital: A Theoretical and Empirical Analysis, with Special Reference to Education.* Columbia University Press.

Bishop, John (1994). "Employer Training in the United States: A Review of the Literature." Background paper for the OECO. Paris: OECD.

Black, David, M. Berger, and James Barron (1993). *Job Training Approaches and Costs in Small and Large Firms.* Report no. PB93-192870, U.S. Department of Commerce. Washington, D.C.: Government Printing Office.

Blackburn, McKinley, and David Neumark (1992). "Unobserved Ability, Efficiency Wages, and Interindustry Wage Differentials." *Quarterly Journal of Economics* 107:1421–1436.

Blair, Margaret M. (1994). "CEO Pay: Why Such a Contentious Issue?" *Brookings Review* 12 (Winter): 23–27.

Blanchard, Olivier, and Lawrence Summers (1986). "Hysteresis and the European Unemployment Problem." Pp. 15–78 in *NBER Macroeconomics Annual, 1986.* Cambridge, Mass.: MIT Press.

Blau, Francine D., and Lawrence M. Kahn (1995). "The Gender Earnings Gap: Some International Evidence." Pp. 105–143 in Richard B. Freeman and Lawrence F. Katz, eds., *Differences and Changes in Wage Structures.* Chicago: University of Chicago Press.

Blau, Francine D., and Lawrence M. Kahn (1996). "International Differences in Male Wage Inequality: Institutions versus Market Forces." *Journal of Political Economy* 104, no. 4 (August): 791–837.

Blaustein, Saul J., with Wilbur J. Cohen and William Haber (1983). *Unemployment Insurance in the United States: The First Half Century.* Kalamazoo, Mich.: W. E. Upjohn Institute for Employment Research.

Blinder, A., and A. Krueger (1990). "International Differences in Labor Turnover: A Comparative Study with Emphasis on the U.S. and Japan." Princeton Working Paper, Economics Department, Princeton University.

Bowers, Brent (1994). "Businesses Fall in Love with Workplace Safety Teams." *Wall Street Journal,* March 16, p. B2.

Bowers, Norman (1993). "High Skills, Low Skills, No Skills: Workplace Training and Employment Security in the U.S., Japan, and Germany." Working paper prepared for the Joint Economic Committee, U.S. Congress, Washington, D.C.

Braconi, Joan Marie, and Alan Nicholas Kopke (1994). *California Workers Rights: A Manual of Job Rights, Protections, and Remedies.* Berkeley, Calif.: Center for Labor Research and Education, Institute of Industrial Relations, University of California.

Brinton, Mary C. (1993). *Women and the Economic Miracle: Gender and Work in Postwar Japan.* Berkeley: University of California Press.

Brinton, Mary C., and Hang-Yue Ngo (1993). "Age and Sex in the Occupational Structure: A U.S.-Japan Comparison." *Sociological Forum* 8, no. 1 (March): 93–111.

Brown, Charles (1990). "Empirical Evidence on Private Training." Pp. 97–113 in Ronald Ehrenberg, ed., *Research in Labor Economics.* Greenwich, Conn.: JAI Press.

Brown, Charles, and James L. Medoff (1989). "The Employer Size-Wage Effect." *Journal of Political Economy* 97:1027–1059.

Brown, Clair, and Michael Reich (1989). "When Does Union-Management Cooperation Work? A Look at NUMMI and GM-Van Nuys." *California Management Review* 31, no. 4 (Summer): 26–44.

Brown, Clair, Michael Reich, and David Stern (1993). "Becoming a High-Performance Work Organization: The Role of Security, Employee Involvement, and Training." *International Journal of Human Resource Management* 4, no. 2 (May): 247–275.

Bureau of National Affairs (1978). *Employment Promotion and Transfer Policies,* PPF Survey series 120. Washington, D.C.: Bureau of National Affairs.

Calmfors, Lars (1993). *Centralization of Wage Bargaining and Macroeconomic Performance: A Survey.* Economics Department Working Paper no. 131. Paris: OECD.

Calmfors, Lars, and J. Driffil (1988). "Bargaining Structure, Corporatism, and Macroeconomic Performance." *Economic Policy* 6:14–61.

Campbell, John Creighton (1992). *How Policies Change: The Japanese Government and the Aging Society.* Princeton: Princeton University Press.

Carnevale, Anthony, and Leila J. Gainer (1989). *The Learning Enterprise.* Washington, D.C.: American Society for Training and Development.

Chan-Lee, James H., David T. Coe, and Menahim Prywes (1989). "Microeconomic Changes and Macroeconomic Wage Disinflation in the 1980s." *OECD Economic Studies,* no. 8 (Spring): 121–157.

Clark, Robert L., and Naohira Ogawa (1992). "Employment, Tenure and Earnings Profiles in Japan and the United States: Comment." *American Economic Review* 82, 1: 336–45.

Coe, David T. (1985). "Nominal Wages, the NAIRU, and Wage Flexibility." *OECD Economic Studies,* no. 5 (Autumn): 83–125.

Cohen, Stephen S., and John Zysman (1987). *Manufacturing Matters: The Myth of the Post-Industrial Economy.* New York: Basic Books.

Cole, Robert E. (1989). *Strategies for Learning: Small-Group Activities in American, Japanese, and Swedish Industry.* Berkeley: University of California Press.

Cole, Robert E., ed. (1995). *The Death and Life of the American Quality Movement.* New York: Oxford University Press.

Cole, Robert E., Paul Bacdayan, and Joseph White (1993). "Quality, Participation and Competitiveness." *California Management Review* 35, no. 3 (Spring): 68–81.

Commission on the Skills of the American Workforce (1990). *America's Choice—High Skills or Low Wages!: The Report of the Commission on the Skills of the American Workforce.* Rochester, N.Y.: National Center on Education and the Economy.

Cooke, William N. (1990). *Labor-Management Cooperation: New Partnerships or Going in Circles?* Kalamazoo, Mich.: W. E. Upjohn Institute for Employment Research.

Cooke, William N. (1994). "Employee Participation, Group-based Pay Incentives, and Company Performance: A Union-Nonunion Comparison." *Industrial and Labor Relations Review* 47:594–609.

Crystal, Graef S. (1991). *In Search of Excess: Overcompensation of American Executives.* New York: W. W. Norton.

Davidson, Carlos, and Michael Reich (1988). "Income Inequality: An Interindustry View." *Industrial Relations* 27, no. 3 (Fall): 263–286.

Davis, Steven J. (1992). "Cross-Country Patterns of Change in Relative Wages." Pp. 239–292 in Olivier Blanchard and Stanley S. Fischer, eds., *NBER Macroeconomics Annual 1992.* Cambridge, Mass.: MIT Press.

Dertouzos, Michael L., Richard K. Lester, Robert M. Solow, and MIT Commission on Industrial Productivity (1989). *Made in America: Regaining the Productive Edge.* Cambridge, Mass.: MIT Press.

Dickens, William T., and Lawrence F. Katz (1987). "Inter-Industry Wage Differences and Industry Characteristics." Pp. 48–89 in Kevin Lang and Jonathan Leonard, eds., *Unemployment and the Structure of Labor Markets.* Oxford: Blackwell.

Dickens, William T., and Kevin Lang (1992). *Labor Market Segmentation Theory: Reconsidering the Evidence.* Working Paper no. 4087. Cambridge, Mass.: National Bureau of Economic Research.

Diebold, F., D. Neumark, and D. Polsky (1994). *Job Stability in the United States.* Working Paper no. 4859. Cambridge, Mass.: National Bureau of Economic Research.

Doeringer, Peter B., and Michael J. Piore (1971). *Internal Labor Markets and Manpower Analysis.* Lexington, Mass.: Heath.

Dore, Ronald (1973). *British Factory/Japanese Factory.* Berkeley: University of California Press.

Dore, Ronald (1986). *Flexible Rigidities: Industrial Policy and Structural Adjustment in the Japanese Economy, 1970–1980.* Palo Alto: Stanford University Press.

Dore, Ronald P., and Mario Sako (1989). *How the Japanese Learn to Work.* London: Routledge.

Drago, Robert (1988). "Quality Circle Survival: an Exploratory Analysis." *Industrial Relations* 27, no. 3 (Fall): 336–351.

Duesenberry, James S. (1958). *Business Cycles and Economic Growth.* New York: McGraw-Hill.

Dunlop, John T. (1994). *Commission on the Future of Worker-Management Relations.* Fact-Finding Report. Washington, D.C.: Bureau of National Affairs.

Eaton, Adrienne E., and Paula B. Voos (1994). "Productivity-Enhancing Innovations in Work Organization, Compensation, and Employee Participation in the Union versus Nonunion Sectors." Pp. 37–62 in David Lewin and Donna Sockell, eds., *Advances in Industrial and Labor Relations.* Westport, Conn.: JAI Press.

Eaton, Susan C. (1992). *Women Workers, Unions, and Industrial Sectors in North America.* Geneva: International Labour Office. Englewood Cliffs, N.J.: Prentice Hall.

Eaton, Susan C., and Paula B. Voos (1992). "Unions and Contemporary Innovations in Work Organization, Compensation, and Employee Participation." Pp. 212–249 in Lawrence Mishel and Paula B. Voos, eds., *Unions and Ecoomic Competitiveness.* Armonk, N.Y.: M. E. Sharpe.

Eck, Alan (1993). "Job-Related Education and Training: Their Impact on Earnings." *Monthly Labor Review* 116, no. 10 (October): 21–38.

Edgren, Gosta, Karl-Olof Faxén, and Klas-Erik Odhner (1973). *Wage Formation and the Economy.* London: Allen & Unwin.

Ehrenberg, Ronald G., and Robert S. Smith (1994). *Modern Labor Economics.* 5th ed. New York: HarperCollins.

Elmeskov, Jørgen, and Karl Pichelman, (1993). "Unemployment and Labour Force Participation: Trends and Cycles." OECD Economics Department Working Papers No. 130. Paris: OECD.

Endo, Koshi (1994). "Satei (Personal Assessment) and Interworker Competition in Japanese Firms." *Industrial Relations* 33, no. 1 (January): 70–105.

Farber, Henry S. (1993). "The Incidence and Costs of Job Loss: 1982–91." *Brookings Papers on Economic Activity: Microeconomics.* 1:73–132.

Farber, Henry S. (1995). *Are Lifetime Jobs Disappearing: Job Duration in the United States, 1973–93.* Working Paper no. 341. Princeton: Industrial Relations Section, Princeton University.

Farber, Henry S. (1996). *The Changing Face of Job Loss in the United States, 1981–1993.* Working Paper no. 360. Princeton: Industrial Relations Section, Princeton University.

Ferman, Louis A., Michele Hoyman, Joel Cutcher-Gershenfeld, and Ernst J. Savoie, eds.

(1991). *Joint Training Programs: A Union-Management Approach to Preparing Workers for the Future.* Ithaca, N.Y.: ILR Press.

Flanagan, Robert, David Soskice, and Lloyd Ulman (1983). *Unionism, Economic Stabilization, and Incomes Policies.* Washington, D.C.: Brookings Institution.

Foulkes, Fred K., ed. (1989). *Human Resources Management: Readings.* Englewood Cliffs, N.J.: Prentice Hall.

Frazis, Harley J., Diane E. Herz, and Michael W. Horrigan (1995). "Employer Provided Training: Results from a New Survey." *Monthly Labor Review* 118, no. 5 (May): 3–17.

Freeman, Richard Bard, and Martin L. Weitzman (1987). "Bonuses and Employment in Japan." *Journal of the Japanese and International Economies* 1:168–194.

Freeman, Richard Bard, ed. (1994). *Small Differences That Matter.* New York: Russell Sage.

Friedman, S., and L. Fisher (1989). "Collective Bargaining and Employment Security." Pp. 418–429 in John F. Burton, Jr., ed., *Industrial Relations Research Association Series: Proceedings of the Forty-First Annual Meeting.* Madison, Wis.: Industrial Relations Research Association.

Fucini, Joseph J., and Suzy Fucini (1990). *Working for the Japanese: Inside Mazda's American Auto Plant.* New York: Free Press.

Galenson, Walter, and Konosuke Odaka (1976). "The Japanese Labor Market." Pp. 587–673 in Hugh Patrick and Henry Rosovsky, eds., *Asia's New Giant.* Washington, D.C.: Brookings Institution.

Gardner, Jennifer M. (1995). "Worker Displacement: A Decade of Change." *Monthly Labor Review* 118, no. 4 (April): 45–57.

Genda, Yuji (1994). "Japan." Toshiaki Tachibanaki, ed., *A Study of International Comparisons of Wage Structure.* Tokyo: Labor Research Center. (In Japanese.)

Ghilarducci, Teresa (1992). *Labor's Capital: The Economics and Politics of Private Pension.* Cambridge, Mass.: MIT Press.

Gibbons, Robert, and Lawrence F. Katz (1992). "Does Unmeasured Ability Explain Inter-Industry Wage Differentials?" *Review of Economic Studies* 59:515–535.

Gordon, Andrew (1985). *The Evolution of Labor Relations in Japan: Heavy Industry, 1853–1955.* Cambridge, Mass.: Harvard University Press.

Gordon, Andrew (1993). *Postwar Japan as History.* Berkeley: University of California Press.

Gordon, David M., Richard Edwards, and Michael Reich (1982). *Segmented Work, Divided Workers.* New York: Cambridge University Press.

Gould, William B. (1984). *Japan's Reshaping of American Labor Law.* Cambridge, Mass.: MIT Press.

Green, Gordon, J. Coder, and Paul Ryscavage (1992). "International Comparisons of Earning Inequality for Men in the 1980s." *Review of Income and Wealth* 38:1–15.

Hanami, Tadashi (1991). *Managing Japanese Workers.* Tokyo: Japan Institute of Labor.

Hashimoto, Masahito (1990). *The Japanese Labor Market in a Comparative Perspective with the United States.* Kalamazoo, Mich.: Upjohn Institute for Employment Research.

Hashimoto, Masanori, and John Raisan (1985). "Employment Tenure and Earnings Profiles in Japan and the United States." *American Economic Review* 75:721–735.

Hashimoto, Masanori, and John Raisan (1988). "The Structure and Short-run Adaptability of Labor Markets in Japan and the U.S." Pp. 314–340 in Robert A. Hart, ed., *Employment, Unemployment, and Labor Utilization.* Boston, Mass.: Unwin Hyman.

Hashimoto, Masanori, and John Raisian (1992). "Employment Tenure and Earnings Profiles in Japan and the United States: Reply." *American Economic Review* 82, no. 1 (March): 346–354.

Heckman, James J. (1994). "Is Job Training Oversold?" *Public Interest* 115 (Spring): 91–115.

Higuchi, Yoshio (1987). "A Comparative Study of Japanese Plants Operating in the U.S. and American Plants: Recruitment, Job Training, Wage Structure, and Job Separation." Typescript, Department of Economics, Columbia University.

Higuchi, Yoshio (1994). "Effects of Job Training and Productivity Growth on Retention of Male and Female Workers in Japan." Pp. 155–182 in Toshiaki Tachibanaki, ed., *Labour Market and Economic Performance.* New York: St. Martin's Press.

Holzer, Harry J. (1990). "The Determinants of Employee Productivity and Earnings." *Industrial Relations,* 29, no. 3 (Fall): 403–422.

Houseman, Susan N. (1995). "Part-time Employment in Europe and Japan." *Journal of Labor Research* 16, no. 3 (Summer): 249–258.

Houseman, Susan N., and Machiko Osawa (1995). "Part-time and Temporary Employment in Japan." *Monthly Labor Review* 118, no. 10 (October): 10–18.

Ichniowski, Casey, Thomas A. Kochan, David Levine, Craig Olsen, and Goerge Strauss (1996). "What Works at Work?: Overview and Assessment." *Industrial Relations* 35, no. 3 (July): 299–333.

Inagami, Takeshi (1988). "Japanese Workplace Industrial Relations." *Japanese Industrial Relations Series,* no. 14. Tokyo: Japan Institute of Labor.

International Monetary Fund (1996). *International Financial Statistics* (CD-ROM). Washington, D.C.: International Monetary Fund.

Ishida, Mitsuo (1990). *The Social Foundation of Wage Systems.* Tokyo: Chuo Keizai Sha. (In Japanese.)

Ishikawa, Tsuneo, and Takahisa Dejima (1993). "Measuring the Extent of Duality in the Japanese Labor Market." Discussion Paper Series, no. 93-F-10. Faculty of Economics, University of Tokyo.

Jacobs, Ronald L., Michael J. Jones, and Sue Neil (1992). "A Case Study in Forecasting and Financial Benefits of Unstructured and Structured On-the-Job Training." *Human Resource Development Quarterly* 3, no. 2:113–139.

Jacoby, Sanford (1985). *Employing Bureaucracy: Managers, Unions, and the Transformation of Work in American Industry, 1900–1945.* New York: Columbia University Press.

Japan Institute of Labor (1992). *Japanese Working Life Profile: Labor Statistics, 1993–1994.* Tokyo: Japan Institute of Labor.

Japan Economic Planning Agency (1990). *Economic Survey of Japan (Economic White Paper).* Tokyo: Government of Japan.

Japan Institute of Labor (1993). *White Paper on Labour.* Tokyo: Japan Institute of Labor, 1993.

Japan Institute of Labor (1994a). *Japanese Employment Practices and the Law.* Tokyo: Japan Institute of Labor.

Japan Institute of Labor (1994b). *Management Flexibility in an Era of Change.* JIL Report no. 3. Tokyo: Japan Institute of Labor.

Japan Management and Coordination Agency (1951–1996). *Japan Statistical Yearbook.* Tokyo: Japan Management and Coordination Agency.

Japan Management and Coordination Agency (1987). *Employment Status Survey.* Tokyo: Nihon Tokei Kyokai.

Japan Management and Coordination Agency (1992). *Employment Status Survey.* Tokyo: Nihon Tokei Kyokai.

Japan Management and Coordination Agency (1994). *Employment Structure of Japan: Summary Results and Analyses of 1992 Employment Status Survey.* Tokyo: Soumu-cho Tokeikyoku.

Japan Ministry of Labor (1969–1993). *Basic Survey of Wage Structure.* Tokyo: Ministry of Labor. (In Japanese.)

Japan Ministry of Labor (1989a). *The Reality of Working Hours and Labor Costs.* Tokyo: Rodo Horei Kyokai.

Japan Ministry of Labor (1989b). *Surey on Employment Trends, 1988.* Tokyo: Japan Ministry of Labor.

Japan Ministry of Labor (1991). *Survey of Vocational Training in Private Enterprises, 1990.* Tokyo: Japan Ministry of Labor.

Japan Ministry of Labor (1992a). *Survey on Employment Trends, 1991.* Tokyo: Japan Ministry of Labor.

Japan Ministry of Labor (1992b). "White Paper on Labor." Excerpted in *Japan Labor Bulletin,* September 1, pp. 9–14.

Japan Ministry of Labor (1993a). *Manuals for Benefit Procedures of Employment Insurance.* Tokyo: Japan Ministry of Labor.

Japan Ministry of Labor (1993b). *Monthly Labor Statistics and Research Bulletin* 45, no. 1: 25–27.

Japan Ministry of Labor (1993c). *Survey on Employment Trends, 1992.* Tokyo: Japan Ministry of Labor.

Japan Ministry of Labor (1993d). *The Survey on Retirement Allowance Systems and Retirement Allowance Payment, 1993.* Tokyo: Japan Ministry of Labor.

Japan Ministry of Labor (1993e). *Yearbook of Labor Statistics 1992.* Tokyo: Minister's Secretariat.

Japan Ministry of Labor (1994a). *Annual Report on Employment Insurance Activity.* Tokyo: Japan Ministry of Labor.

Japan Ministry of Labor (1994b). *Survey on Employment Trends, 1993.* Tokyo: Japan Ministry of Labor.

Japan Ministry of Labor (1995). *Annual Report on Employment Insurance Activity.* Tokyo: Japan Ministry of Labor.

Jenkins, G. Douglas, Jr., Gerald E. Ledford, Jr., Nina Gupta, and Harold Doty (1992). *Skill-Based Pay: Practices, Payoffs, Pitfalls, and Prescriptions.* Scottsdale, Ariz.: American Compensation Association.

JTUC Rengo (1992). *The Spring Struggle for a Better Living: 1992.* Tokyo: JTUC Rengo.

Kalleberg, Arne L., and James R. Lincoln (1988). "The Structure of Earnings Inequality in the United States and Japan." *American Journal of Sociology* 94 (Supplement): S121–S153.

Katz, Lawrence F., Gary W. Loveman, and David G. Blanchiflower (1995). "A Comparison of Changes in the Structure of Wages in Four OECD Countries." Pp. 25–65 in Richard B. Freeman and Lawrence F. Katz, eds., *Differences and Changes in Wage Structures.* Chicago: University of Chicago Press.

Katz, Lawrence F., and Ana L. Ravenga (1989). "Changes in the Structure of Wages: The United States versus Japan." *Journal of the Japanese and International Economies* 3:522–553.

Kawahita, Takashi (1992). "Is the Japanese Labor Market Dual-Structured?" *Japan Labor Bulletin*, August 1, pp. 5–8.

Kawanishi, Hirosuke (1992). *Enterprise Unionism in Japan*. London: Kegan Paul.

Kelley, Mary-Ellen R. (1989). "Unionization and Job Design under Programmable Automation." *Industiral Relations*, 28, no. 2 (Spring): 174–187.

Kletzer, Lori G. (1989). "Returns to Seniority after Permanent Job Loss." *American Economic Review* 79 (1989): 536–543.

Kochan, Thomas, and Paul Osterman (1990). "Employment Security and Employment Policy: An Assessment of the Issues." Pp. 155–180 in Katharine G. Abraham and Robert B. McKersie, eds., *New Developments in the Labor Market*. Cambridge, Mass.: MIT Press.

Kochan, Thomas A., and Michael Useem, eds. (1992). *Transforming Organizations*. New York: Oxford University Press.

Koike, Kazuo (1983). "Internal Labor Markets: Workers in Large Firms." Pp. 29–62 in Taishiro Shirai, ed., *Contemporary Industrial Relations in Japan*. Madison: University of Wisconsin Press.

Koike, Kazuo (1987). "Japanese Redundancy: The Impact of Key Labor Market Institutions on the Economic Flexibility of the Japanese Economy." Pp. 79–101 in Peter T. Chinloy and Ernst W. Stromsdorfer, eds., *Labor Market Adjustments in the Pacific Basin*. Boston, Mass.: Kluwer-Nijhoff.

Koike, Kazuo (1988). *Understanding Industrial Relations in Modern Japan*. New York: St. Martin's Press.

Koike, Kazuo (1994). "Learning and Incentive Systems in Japanese Industry." Pp. 41–65 in M. Aoki and R. Dore, eds., *The Japanese Firm: The Sources of Competitive Strength*. New York: Oxford University Press.

Koike, Kazuo, and T. Inoki (1990). *Skill Formation in Japan and Southeast Asia*. Tokyo: University of Tokyo Press.

Komiya, Ryutaro (1987). "Japanese Firms, Chinese Firms: Problems for Economic Reforms in China, Part I." *Journal of the Japanese and International Economies* 1, no. 1 (March): 31–61.

Koshiro, Kazutoshi (1976). "Anti-Inflationary Wage Determination under Free Collective Bargaining in Japan from 1974 to 1976 (II)." *Japan Labor Bulletin*, June 1, pp. 5–8.

Koshiro, K. (1977). "The 1977 Spring Labor Offensive: Symbolizing a Shift in Theories of the Japanese Labor Movement." *Japan Labor Bulletin*, July 1, pp. 5–8.

Koshiro, K. (1983a). "The Development of Collective Bargaining in Postwar Japan." Pp. 205–258 in Taishiro Shirai, ed., *Contemporary Industrial Relations in Japan*. Madison: University of Wisconsin Press.

Koshiro, K. (1983b). "Labor Relations in Public Enterprises." Pp. 259–294 in Taishiro Shirai, ed., *Contemporary Industrial Relations in Japan*. Madison: University of Wisconsin Press.

Koshiro, K. (1983c). "The Quality of Working Life in Japanese Factories." Pp. 63–89 in Taishiro Shirai, ed., *Contemporary Industrial Relations in Japan*. Madison: University of Wisconsin Press.

Koshiro, K. (1984). "Lifetime Employment in Japan: Three Models of the Concept." *Monthly Labor Review,* 107, no. 8 (August): 34–35.

Koshiro, K. (1986). "Labor Market Flexibility in Japan—with Special Reference to Wage Flexibility." Typescript, Economics Department, Yokohama National University.

Koshiro, K. (1994). "The Link between Labor-Management Relations and Job Security." Typescript, Economics Department, Yokohama National University.

Koshiro, Kazutoshi (1995). "Company-Based Collective Wage Determination in Japan: Its Viability Revisited amid Global Competition." Pp. 1–8 in *Japan-Australia International Seminar on Industrial Relations.* Melbourne, Australia.

Krueger, Alan B. (1993). "How Computers Have Changed the Wage Structure: Evidence from Microdata, 1984–89." *Quarterly Journal of Economics* 108:33–60.

Krueger, Alan B., and Lawrence H. Summers (1988). "Efficiency Wages and the Inter-industry Wage Structure." *Econometrica* 56:259–293.

Kruse, Douglas (1992). "Supervision, Working Conditions and the Employer Size-Wage Effect." *Industrial Relations* 31:229–249.

Kruse, Douglas (1993). *Profit-Sharing and Productivity: A Survey.* Working Paper no. 4542. Cambridge, Mass.: National Bureau of Economic Research.

Kuwahara, Yasuo (1990). "Are Workers Really in Short Supply?" *Japan Labor Bulletin,* March 1, pp. 4–8.

Lawler, Edward E., Susan A. Mohrman, and Gerald E. Ledford Jr. (1992). *Employee Involvement and Total Quality Management: Practices and Results in Fortune 1000 Companies.* San Francisco: Jossey-Bass.

Lawler, Edward E., Susan A. Mohrman, and Gerald E. Ledford, Jr. (1995). *Creating High Performance Organizations: Practices and Results of Employee Involvement and Total Quality Management in Fortune 1000 Companies.* San Francisco: Jossey-Bass.

Lazear, Edward (1979). "Why Is There Mandatory Retirement?" *Journal of Political Economy* 87:1261–1284.

Lazear, Edward (1989). "Pay Equality and Industrial Politics." *Journal of Political Economy* 97:561–580.

Lazear, Edward (1990). "Job Security Provisions and Employment." *Quarterly Journal of Economics* 105, no. 3: 699–726.

Leadbeater, Charles (1993). "This Crisis Is Different." *Financial Times Survey,* July 30, p. 1.

Leontieff, Wassily (1946). "The Pure Theory of the Guaranteed Annual Wage Contract." *Journal of Political Economy* 54:76–79.

Levine, David I. (1994). *Reinventing the Workplace.* Washington, D.C.: Brookings Institution.

Levine, David I., and Douglas Kruse (1991). "Employee Involvement: Incidence, Correlates, and Effects." Working paper, Haas School of Business, University of California, Berkeley.

Levine, David, and Laura Tyson (1990). "Participation, Productivity, and the Firm's Environment." Pp. 183–243 in Alan S. Blinder, ed., *Paying for Productivity.* Washington, D.C.: Brookings Institution.

Levine, Solomon B. (1958). *Industrial Relations in Postwar Japan.* Urbana: University of Illinois Press.

Levine, Solomon B. (1984). "Employers Associations in Japan." Pp. 318–354 in John P.

Windmuller and Alan Gladstone, eds., *Employers Associations and Industrial Relations: A Comparative Study.* Oxford: Clarendon Press.

Levy, Frank, and Richard J. Murnane (1992). "U.S. Earnings Levels and Earnings Inequalities: A Review of Recent Trends and Proposed Explanations." *Journal of Economic Literature* 30:1333–1381.

Lewin, David, and Daniel J. B. Mitchell (1992). "Systems of Employee Voice: Theoretical and Empirical Perspectives." *California Management Review* 34, no. 3 (Spring): 95–111.

Lillard, Lee A., and Hong W. Tan (1992). "Private Sector Training: Who Gets It and What Are Its Effects?" *Research in Labor Economics,* 13:1–62

Lindbeck, Assar, and Dennis J. Snower (1988). *The Insider-Outsider Theory of Employment and Unemployment.* Cambridge, Mass.: MIT Press.

Loewenstein, Mark A., and James R. Spletzer (1994). *Informal Training: A Review of Existing Data and Some New Evidence.* NLS Discussion Paper 94–20. Washington, D.C.: Bureau of Labor Statistics.

Louis, Arthur M. (1993). "Pay Disparity Threatens U.S." *San Francisco Chronicle,* May 24, p. C1.

Lynch, Lisa M. (1991). "The Role of Off-the-Job vs. On-the-Job Training for the Mobility of Women Workers." *American Economic Review* 81, no. 2 (May): 151–156.

Lynch, Lisa M. (1992). "Private-Sector Training and the Earnings of Young Workers." *American Economic Review* 82:299–312.

Lynch, Lisa M. (1994). "Introduction." Pp. 1–24 in L. Lynch, ed., *Training and the Private Sector: International Comparisons.* Chicago: University of Chicago Press.

Lynch, Lisa M., and Sandra E. Black (1995). *Beyond the Incidence of Training.* Working Paper no. 5231. Cambridge, Mass.: National Bureau of Economic Research.

MacDuffie, John Paul, and Thomas Kochan (1995). "Do U.S. Firms Invest Less in Human Resources?: Training in the World Auto Industry." *Industrial Relations,* 34, no. 2 (April): 147–168.

Marshall, Alfred (1892). *Elements of the Economics of Industry.* London: Macmillan.

Marshall, Ray, and Marc Tucker (1992). *Thinking for a Living: Education and the Wealth of Nations.* New York: Basic Books.

Masumara, Wilfred, and Paul Ryscavage (1994). *Dynamics of Economic Well-Being: Labor Force and Income, 1990 to 1992.* Washington, D.C.: Bureau of the Census.

Matsuzaki, Tadashi (1993). *Wage Negotiation in the Japanese Steel Industry: Key Bargaining in the Shunto.* Pacific Economic Papers no. 106. Melbourne: Australia-Japan Research Centre.

McNabb, Robert, and Keith Whitfield (1995). "Financial Participation, Employee Involvement, and Financial Performance at the Workplace." Working paper, Economics Section, Cardiff Business School.

Milgrom, Paul, and John Roberts (1992). *Economics, Organization, and Management.* Englewood Cliffs, N.J.: Prentice Hall.

Milkman, Ruth (1991). *Japan's California Factories.* Monograph and Research Series no. 55. Los Angeles: Institute of Industrial Relations, UCLA.

Mills, D. Quinn (1984). "Seniority versus Ability in Promotion Decisions." *Industrial and Labor Relations Review* 38:421–425.

Mincer, Jacob, and Yuchio Higuchi (1988). "Wage Structures and Labor Turnover in the United States and Japan." *Journal of the Japanese and International Economies* 2:97–133.

Mishel, Lawrence, and Jared Bernstein (1994). *The State of Working America, 1994–95*. Armonk, N.Y.: M. E. Sharpe.

Mishel, Lawrence, and Paula B. Voos, eds. (1992). *Unions and Economic Competitiveness*. Armonk, N.Y.: M. E. Sharpe.

Mitchell, Daniel J. B. (1994). "A Decade of Concession Bargaining." Pp. 435–474 in Clark Kerr and Paul D. Staudohar, eds., *Labor Economics and Industrial Relations*. Cambridge, Mass.: Harvard University Press.

Mitsubishi Economic Research Institute (monthly, 1965–1993). *MERI's Monthly Circular*. Tokyo: Kokusai Bunken Insatsusha.

Mizuno, A. (1987–1988). "Wage Flexibility and Employment Changes." *Japanese Economic Studies* 16:38–73.

Mosk, Carl (1995). *Competition and Cooperation in Japanese Labour Markets*. New York: St. Martin's Press.

Mosk, Carl, and Yoshifumi Nakata (1985). "The Age–Wage Profile and Structural Change in the Japanese Labor Market for Males, 1964–82." *Journal of Human Resources* 20:100–116.

Murphy, K., and F. Welch (1992). "The Structure of Wages." *Quarterly Journal of Economics* 107, no. 1 (February): 285–327.

Nakamura, Keisuke (1991). "Types and Functions of Industry-wide Labor Organizations in Japan," *Japan Labor Bulletin*, January 1, pp. 5–8.

Nakata, Yoshifumi (1987). "An Analysis of Age-Seniority Wage Profiles: a Case Study of the Japanese Nenko Wage System." Ph.D. dissertation, University of California, Berkeley.

Nakata, Yoshifumi (1990). "An Analysis of Employment Stability in U.S. and Japan." *Hyouron Syakaikagaku* (Doshisha University), no. 40: 35–81.

Nakata, Yoshifumi (1991a). "An Analysis of Japanese Occupational Wages: Examination of the Survey of Wage Structure." Pp. 31–56 in Labor Research Center, ed., *Basic Research on Changing Human Resource Management and Wage Structure*. (In Japanese.)

Nakata, Yoshifumi (1991b). "Occupation and Wage Determination." Pp. 137–179 in Toshiaki Tachibanaki, ed., *Promotion, Appraisal, and Wage Determination*. Tokyo: Touyoukeizai Shinpousa. (In Japanese.)

Nakata, Yoshifumi, and Carl Mosk (1987). "The Demand for College Education in Postwar Japan." *Journal of Human Resources* 22:377–404.

Neal, Derek (1995). "Industry-Specific Capital: Evidence from Displaced Workers." *Journal of Labor Economics* 13:653–677.

Ng, Igace, and Dennis Maki (1994). "Trade Union Influence on Human Resource Management Practices," *Industrial Relations* 33:121–135.

Nitta, Michio (1988). "Birth of Rengo and Reformation of Union Organization." *Japan Labor Bulletin*, February 1, pp. 5–8.

Nitta, Michio (1990). "Where Will Shunto Go?" *Japan Labor Bulletin*, December 1, pp. 4–8.

Noda, Nobou (1988). *Nihon Kindai Keieishi: Sono Shiteki Bunseki* (Modern Japanese business history: Historical analysis). Tokyo: Sangyou Nouritu Daigaku Syuppanbu.

OECD (1973). *OECD Economic Surveys, 1972–1973: Japan.* Paris: OECD.

OECD (1975). *OECD Economic Surveys, 1974–1975: Japan.* Paris: OECD.

OECD (1980). *OECD Economic Surveys, 1979–1980: Japan.* Paris: OECD.

OECD (1981). *OECD Economic Surveys, 1980–1981: Japan.* Paris: OECD.

OECD (1982). *OECD Economic Surveys, 1981–1982: Japan.* Paris: OECD.

OECD (1983). *OECD Economic Surveys, 1982–1983: Japan.* Paris: OECD.

OECD (1986a). *Flexibility in the Labour Market: The Current Debate.* Paris: OECD.

OECD (1986b) *OECD Economic Surveys, 1985–1986: Japan.* Paris: OECD.

OECD (1989a). *Economies in Transition: Structural Adjustment in OECD Countries.* Paris: OECD.

OECD (1989b). *OECD Economic Surveys, 1988–1989: Japan.* Paris: OECD.

OECD (1990). *OECD Economic Surveys, 1989–1990: Japan.* Paris: OECD.

OECD (1991). *OECD Economic Surveys, 1990–1991: Japan.* Paris: OECD.

OECD (1992a). *Historical Statistics, 1960–1990.* Paris: OECD.

OECD (1992b). *OECD Economic Surveys, 1991–1992: Japan.* Paris: OECD.

OECD (1993a). *Employment Outlook.* Paris: OECD.

OECD (1993b). *OECD Economic Surveys, 1992–1993: Japan.* Paris: OECD.

OECD (1994a). *National Accounts.* Paris: OECD.

OECD (1994b). *OECD Economic Surveys, 1993–1994: Japan.* Paris: OECD.

OECD (1995a). *Historical Statistics, 1960–1993.* Paris: OECD.

OCED (1995b). *OECD Economic Surveys, 1994–1995: Japan.* Paris: OECD.

OECD (1996). *Employment Outlook.* Paris: OECD.

Ono, Akira (1987). "Two Competing Hypotheses for the Nenko Wage System." *Hitotsubashi Journal of Economics* 28:1–25.

Ono, Tsuneo (1974). "The 1974 Spring Labor Offensive: A Summary and Some Further Comments." *Japan Labor Bulletin,* August 1, pp. 4–8.

Ono, Tsuneo (1976). "The Extent of Union Influence in Japanese Wage Negotiations (Shunto Formula): Recent Trends and Historical Review." *Japan Labor Bulletin,* August 1, pp. 5–8.

Osterman, Paul (1987). "Turnover, Employment Security, and the Performance of the Firm." Pp. 275–318 in M. Kleiner et al., (eds.), *Human Resources and the Performance of the Firm.* Madison, Wis.: Industrial Relations Research Association.

Osterman, Paul (1988). *Employment Futures: Reorganization, Dislocation, and Public Policy.* New York: Oxford University Press.

Osterman, Paul (1994). "How Common Is Workplace Transformation and Who Adopts It?" *Industrial and Labor Relations Review* 47:173–188.

Osterman, Paul (1995). "Skill, Training and Work Organization in American Establishments." *Industrial Relations* 34, no. 2 (April): 125–146.

Parker, Mike, and Jane Slaughter (1988). *Choosing Sides: Unions and the Team Concept.* Boston: South End Press.

Pearlstein, Steven (1994). "Employers Reluctant to Share Profits." *San Francisco Chronicle,* September 5, p. D1.

Persson, Torsten, and Guido Tabellini (1994). "Is Inequality Harmful for Growth?" *American Economic Review* 84:600–621.

Pollert, Anna, ed. (1991). *Farewell to Flexibility?*. Oxford, U.K.: B. Blackwell.

Price Waterhouse (1994). *U.S. Business Views on Workforce Training.* Washington, D.C.: American Society for Training and Development.

Rebick, Marcus E. (1993). "The Persistence of Firm-Size Earnings Differentials and Labor Market Segmentation in Japan." *Journal of the Japanese and International Economies* 7, no. 2 (June): 132–156.

Reder, Melvin and Lloyd Ulman (1993). "Unionism and Unification." Pp. 13–44 in Lloyd Ulman, Barry Eichengreen, and William T. Dickens, eds., *Labor and an Integrated Europe.* Washington, D.C.: Brookings Institution.

Rogers, Joel, and Wolfgang Streeck (1995). *Works Councils.* Chicago: University of Chicago Press.

Rothwell, William J., and H. C. Kazanis (1994). *Improving On-the-Job Training.* San Francisco: Jossey-Bass.

Ruhm, Christopher J. (1987). "The Economic Consequences of Labor Mobility." *Industrial and Labor Relations Review* 41:30–42.

Ruhm, Christopher J. (1991). "Are Workers Permanently Scarred by Job Displacement?" *American Economic Review* 81:319–325.

Sakakibara, Eisuke (1993). *Beyond Capitalism.* Lanham, Md.: Economic Strategy Institute.

Sakamoto, Authur, and Meichu D. Chen (1993). "Earnings Inequality and Segmentation by Firm Size in Japan and the United States." *Research in Social Stratification and Mobility* 12:185–211.

Sakurabayashi, Makoto (1982). *Wages in Japan Today.* Bocum, Germany: Studienverlag Brockmeyer.

Schmitter, Philippe, and Gerhard Lehmbruch (1979). *Trends toward Corporatist Intermediation.* Beverly Hills: Sage Publications.

Seike, Atushi (1995). "Taisyokukin, Kigyou Nenkin no Keizai Kouka" (Economic effect of retirement allowance and pension). Pp. 229–255 in Takenori Inoki and Yoshio Higuchi, eds., *Nihon no Koyousisutemu to Roudoushijyou* (The employment system and the labor market in japan). Tokyo: Nohon Keizai Shinbun Sha. 229–255.

Shaiken, Harley, Stephen Lopez, and Isaac Mankita (1996). "Experienced Workers and New Ways of Organizing Work: A Case Study of Saturn and Chrysler Jefferson North." New Working Paper no. 7. Berkeley: National Center for the Workplace.

Shapiro, C., and J. E. Stiglitz (1984). "Equilibrium Unemployment as a Worker Discipline Device." *American Economic Review,* 74 no. 3 (June): 433–444.

Shimada, Haruo (1983). "Wage Determination and Information Sharing: An Alternative Approach to Incomes Policy?" *Journal of Industrial Relations* 25, no. 2 (June): 177–200.

Shimada, Haruo (1987). "Analysis of the 1987 Spring Wage Negotiations." *Japan Labor Bulletin,* August 1, p. 5.

Shimada, Haruo (1988). "Analysis of the 1988 Spring Labor Offensive." *Japan Labor Bulletin,* August 1, pp. 4–8.

Shimada, Haruo (1990). "The Labor Crisis: A Strategic Response to Structural Changes." *Japan Labor Bulletin,* November 1, pp. 5–8.

Shimada, Haruo (1992). "The Globalization of Business and the New World of Work." *Japan Labor Bulletin,* April 1, pp. 4–8.

Shinoda, Toru (1995). "The Tale of Cain and Abel?: A Study of the Contemporary Japanese Labor Politics." *Japan Labor Bulletin* 34 (November): 4–8.

Shirai, Taishiro (1983). "A Theory of Enterprise Unionism." Pp. 117–144 in Taishiro Shirai, ed., *Contemporary Industrial Relations in Japan.* Madison: University of Wisconsin Press.

Slichter, Sumner H. (1941). *Union Policies and Industrial Management.* Washington, D.C.: Brookings Institution.

Sloman, M. (1989). "On-the-Job Training: A Costly Poor Relation." *Personnel Management* 21, no. 2:38–41.

Soskice, David (1990). "Reinterpreting Corporatism and Explaining Unemployment: Coordinated and Noncoordinated Market Economies." Pp. 170–211 in Renato Brunetta and Carlo Dell'Aringa, eds., *Labour Relations and Economic Performance.* New York: New York University Press.

Stern, David (1992). "Institutions and Incentives for Developing Work-Related Knowledge and Skill." Pp. 149–186 in Paul Adler, ed., *Technology and the Future of Work.* New York: Oxford University Press.

Stern, David, and J. M. Ritzen, eds. (1991). *Market Failure in Training?* Berlin: Springer-Verlag.

Stieber, Jack (1959). *The Steel Industry Wage Structure.* Cambridge, Mass.: Harvard University Press.

Sweezy, Paul M. (1939). "Demand under Conditions of Oligopoly." *Journal of Political Economy* 47:568–573.

Swinnerton, K., and H. Wial (1995). "Is Job Stability Declining in the U.S. Economy?" *Industrial and Labor Relations Review* 48:293–304.

Tabb, William K. (1995). *The Postwar Japanese System: Cultural Economy and Economic Transformation.* New York: Oxford University Press.

Tachibanaki, Toshiaki (1987). "Labour Market Flexibility in Japanin Comparison with Europe and the U.S." *European Economic Review* 31:447–684.

Tachibanaki, Toshiaki (1993). *The Employer Size Effect on Wage Differentials in Japan Revived. Discussion Paper Series,* no. 377. Kyoto: Kyoto Institute of Economic Research, University of Kyoto.

Tachibanaki, Toshiaki, ed. (1994). *Labor Market and Economic Performance.* New York: St. Martin's Press.

Tachibanaki, Toshiaki (1996). *Wage Determination and Distribution in Japan.* New York: Oxford University Press.

Tachibanaki, Toshiaki and T. Noda (1992). "Wages, Working Conditions, and Labor Unions." Pp. 182–189 in Toshiaki Tachibanaki and Rengo Research Institute, eds., *Economics of Labor Unions.* Tokyo: Toyoshinpo Keizaisha. (In Japanese.)

Tachibanaki, Toshiaki, and Souichi Ohta (1994). "Wage Differentials by Industry and the Size of Firm, and Labor Market in Japan." Pp. 56–92 in Toshiaki Tachibanaki, ed. *Labor Market and Economic Performance: Europe, Japan and the USA.* New York: St. Martin's Press.

Tadashi, Hanami (1991). *Managing Japanese Workers: Personnel Management Law and Practice in Japan.* Tokyo: Japan Institute of Labor.

Taira, Koji, and Solomon B. Levine (1985). "Japan's Industrial Relations: A Social Compact Emerges." Pp. 247–300 in Industrial Relations Research Association, ed., *Industrial Relations in a Decade of Economic Change.* Madison: University of Wisconsin Press.

Takanashi, Akira (1992). "Changing the Concept of Employment Policy." *Japan Labor Bulletin,* June 1, pp. 5–8.

Takanashi, Akira, et al. (1989). *Shunto Wage Offensive.* Japanese Industrial Relations Series no. 15. Tokyo: Japan Institute of Labor.

Takayama, Noriyuki (1992). *The Greying of Japan: An Economic Perspective on Public Pensions.* New York: Oxford University Press.

Taylor, John (1989). "Differences in Economic Fluctuations in Japan and the U.S.: The Role of Nominal Rigidities." *Journal of the Japanese and the International Economies* 3:127–144.

Tokunaga, Shigeyoshi (1983). "A Marxist Interpretation of Japanese Industrial Relations, with Special Reference to Large Private Enterprises." Pp. 313–330 in Taishiro Shirai, ed., *Contemporary Industrial Relations in Japan.* Madison: University of Wisconsin Press.

Tomita, Y. (1992). "Separation Rates and the Voice Effect of Labor Unions." Pp. 182–188 in Toshiaki Tachibanaki and Rengo Research Institute, eds., *Economics of Labor Unions.* Tokyo: Toyoshinpo Keizasha. (In Japanese.)

Topel, R., and B. Ward (1992). "Job Mobility and the Careers of Young Men." *Quarterly Journal of Economics* 107:439–480.

Tsuru, Tsuyoshi (1992). *The Spring Offensive: The Spillover Effect and the Wage-Setting Institution in Japan.* Discussion Paper Series no. 247. Institute of Economic Research, Tokyo: Hitotsubashi University.

Tsuru, Tsuyoshi (1993). *Shunto: The Spillover Effect and the Wage-Setting Institution in Japan.* Discussion Papers. Geneva: International Institute for Labour Studies.

Tsuru, Tsuyoshi, and James Rebitzer (1995). "The Limits of Enterprise Unionism: Prospects for Continuing Union Decline in Japan." *British Journal of Industrial Relations* 33, no. 3:459–492.

Ulman, Lloyd (1955). *The Rise of the National Trade Union.* Cambridge, Mass.: Harvard University Press.

Ulman, Lloyd (1990). "Labor Market Analysis and Concerted Behavior." *Industrial Relations* 29, no. 2 (Spring): 281–299.

Ulman, Lloyd, and Yoshifumi Nakata (1994). "Enterprise Bargaining and Social Contract in Japan." Pp. 339–348 in Paula B. Voos, ed., *Industrial Relations Research Association Series: Proceedings of the Forty-Sixth Annual Meeting.* Madison, Wis.: Industrial Relations Research Association.

Upham, Frank K. (1987). *Law and Social Change in Postwar Japan.* Cambridge, Mass.: Harvard University Press.

Ureta, M. (1992). "The Importance of Lifetime Jobs in the U.S. Economy Revisited." *American Economic Review* 82, no. 1 (March): 322–335.

U.S. Bureau of the Census (1977). *Money Income in 1975 of Families and Persons in the*

United States. Current Population Reports Series P-60, no. 105. Washington, D.C.: Government Printing Office.

U.S. Bureau of the Census (1981). *Money Income of Households, Families, and Persons in the United States, 1979*. Current Population Reports Series P-60, no. 129. Washington, D.C.: U.S. Government Printing Office.

U.S. Bureau of the Census (1993a). *1980 Census of the Population*. Washington, D.C.: Government Printing Office.

U.S. Bureau of the Census (1983b). *Money Income of Households, Families, and Persons in the United States, 1981*. Current Population Reports Series P-60, no. 138. Washington, D.C.: U.S. Government Printing Office.

U.S. Bureau of the Census (1991a). *Money Income of Households, Families, and Persons in the United States, 1988 and 1989*. Current Population Reports Series P-60, no. 172. Wahsington, D.C.: U.S. Government Printing Office.

U.S. Bureau of the Census (1991b). *Money Income of Households, Families, and Persons in the United States, 1990*. Current Population Reports Series P-60, no. 174. Washington, D.C.: U.S. Government Printint Office.

U.S. Bureau of the Census (1993). *Money Income of Households, Families, and Persons in the United States, 1992*. Current Population Reports Series P-60, no. 184. Washington, D.C.: U.S. Government Printing Office.

U.S. Bureau of the Census (1994). *Statistical Abstract of the United States, 1994*. Washington, D.C.: Government Printing Office.

U.S. Department of Labor, Bureau of Labor Statistics (monthly, various years). *Employment and Earnings*. Washington, D.C.: U.S. Government Printing Office.

U.S. Department of Labor, Bureau of Labor Statistics (1992). *How Workers Get Their Training: 1991 Update*. Bulletin 2407. Washington, D.C.: U.S. Government Printing Office.

U.S. Department of Labor (1993). *Comparison of State Unemployment Insurance Laws*. Washington, D.C.: U.S. Government Printing Office.

U.S. Department of Labor, Bureau of Labor Statistics (1994). *Employer-Provided Formal Training*. Washington, D.C.: Bureau of Labor Statistics.

U.S. Department of Labor, Bureau of Labor Statistics (1995a). *Contingent and Alternative Employment Arrangements*. Report 900. Washington, D.C.: Government Printing Office.

U.S. Department of Labor, Bureau of Labor Statistics (1995b). *International Comparisons of Hourly Compensation Costs for Production Workers in Manufacturing, 1994*. Report 893. Washington, D.C.: Bureau of Labor Statistics.

U.S. Department of Labor, Bureau of Labor Statistics (1995c). *International Comparisons of Manufacturing Productivity and Unit Labor Cost Trends*. USDL 96-294. Washington, D.C.: Bureau of Labor Statistics.

U.S. Department of Labor, Bureau of Labor Statistics (1996). *Work and Family: Learning to Do the Job*. Report 903. Washington, D.C.: U.S. Government Printing Office.

U.S. Office of Technology Assessment (1990). *Worker Training: Competing in the New International Economy*. Washington, D.C.: U.S. Government Printing Office.

U.S. President (1994). *Economic Report of the President 1994*. Washington, D.C.: U.S. Government Printing Office.

U.S. President (1995). *Economic Report of the President 1995*. Washington, D.C.: U.S. Government Printing Office.

Veum, Jonathan R. (1993). "Training among Young Adults: Who, What Kind, and for How Long?" *Monthly Labor Review* 116, no. 8 (August): 27–32.

Vickery, C. (1979). "Unemployment Insurance: A Positive Reappraisal." *Industrial Relations* 18:1–17.

Walton, Richard E., with Christopher Allen and Michael Gaffney (1987). *Innovating to Compete: Lessons for Diffusing and Managing Change in the Workplace*. San Francisco: Jossey-Bass.

Weil, David N. (1991). "Enforcing OSHA: The Role of Labor Unions." *Industiral Relations* 30, no. 1 (Winter): 20–36.

Weisskopf, Thomas E. (1987). "The Effect of Unemployment on Labor Productivity: An International Comparative Analysis." *International Review of Applied Economics* 1, no. 2: 127–151.

Williams, Michael (1994). "Nissan Cuts U.S. Price of Maxima 10%, Fueling Debate on Charges of Dumping." *Wall Street Journal*, May 20, pp. A2, A5.

Womack, James, Daniel T. Jones, and Daniel Roos (1991). *The Machine That Changed the World*. New York: HarperCollins.

Work in America Institute, Inc., and Japan Institute of Labor (1995). *Employment Security: Changing Characteristics in U.S. and Japan*. Scarsdale, N.Y.: Work in America Institute.

Yamaguchi, Koichiro (1983). "The Public Sector: Civil Servants." Pp. 295–312 in Taishiro Shirai, ed., *Contemporary Industrial Relations in Japan*. Madison: University of Wisconsin Press.

Yamazaki, Kiyoshi (1988). *Nihon no Taishokukin Seido* (The Japanese retirement allowance system). Tokyo: Nihon Roudou Kyoukai. (In Japanese.)

Index